T0300273

Transforming Agricultural Technology by Artificial Intelligence and Robotics

This book discusses major issues in the field of agriculture: crop diseases, lack of storage management, pesticide control, weed management, lack of irrigation and water management and their effective resolution via automation, including IoT, wireless communications, machine learning, artificial intelligence, and deep learning. It further discusses the sterile insect technique, which is a replacement of conventional pesticide and fertilizer techniques. Hydroponics and vertical farming, two of the top-ranked agricultural engineering accomplishments of the past century, are also discussed.

Features:

- Offers in-depth insights regarding the fundamentals of technologies associated with the agriculture sector.
- Synthesizes earlier works of researchers and inventors in this field.
- Sheds light on the challenges and problems of supply and demand worldwide.
- Encourages the reader to innovate and ideate upon those issues.
- Analyses the wide array of services provided by companies worldwide and discusses recent breakthrough in agriculture automation.

This book is aimed at the work of many researchers to obtain a concise overview of the current implementation of automation in agriculture and derive important insight into its upcoming challenges.

Transforming Agricultural Technology by Artificial Intelligence and Robotics

Manan Shah, Aalap Doshi, Kanish Shah and
Ameya Kshirsagar

CRC Press
Taylor & Francis Group
Boca Raton London New York

CRC Press is an imprint of the
Taylor & Francis Group, an **informa** business

Designed cover image: © Shutterstock

First published 2024
by CRC Press/Balkema
4 Park Square, Milton Park, Abingdon, Oxon, OX14 4RN

and by CRC Press/Balkema
2385 NW Executive Center Drive, Suite 320, Boca Raton FL 33431

CRC Press/Balkema is an imprint of the Taylor & Francis Group, an informa business

© 2024 Manan Shah, Aalap Doshi, Kanish Shah and Ameya Kshirsagar

British Library Cataloguing-in-Publication Data
A catalogue record for this book is available from the British Library

ISBN: 9781032072425 (hbk)
ISBN: 9781032100807 (pbk)
ISBN: 9781003213550 (ebk)

DOI: 10.1201/9781003213550

Typeset in Times
by Newgen Publishing UK

Contents

Preface

It was our last semester of undergraduate studies and one of our team members came up with the idea of introducing a Machine Learning model for image recognition of leaves and flowers. Owing to the idea, we began a literature survey on the topic of Machine Learning and Artificial Intelligence in Agriculture. Though numerous researches had been already done in the field, the information is scattered on the Internet as well as in the books available on the market. We perused more than a hundred research papers and various journals that were closely related to Agtech.

The main aim of our paper at that time was to include Embedded Systems, Hardware, Software, Robotics, Machine Learning, and most important Artificial Intelligence involved in Agriculture. Thus, when the opportunity came to sum up all the knowledge from every technological field and bind it in a book, we are more than delighted to accept it. This book will be a one-stop-shop for anyone who is looking for advancements in the Farming Sector. The authors of this book come from multi-disciplinary fields such as Embedded Electronics, Control Systems, Geothermal, and Machine Learning, which gives this book a wide array of informative knowledge, and in one place.

This book is a guide for anyone who seeks to gain insights about technological innovations in Agriculture. There is a systematic approach to each invention of machinery that revolutionized the face of agriculture and these are in chronological order. Several notable contributions by various scientists are acknowledged. The importance of farming and its impact on the global economy is discussed. Although, Artificial Intelligence is pervasive in almost all sectors of the economy due to its robustness, there are areas of farming where it has not yet made a considerable impact. Common challenges faced by the farmer are crop disease infestation, lack of storage management, pesticide management, weed management, lack of irrigation facilities, and so forth. This book brings together successful research carried on in these areas and provides an in-depth analysis of the methods used.

This book is a ready reference for anyone who is passionate to engage in the professional field of smart farming. The terminologies used in this literature are lucid and clear, and the information contained in this book spans from 1784 to 2020. Furthermore, the roles of scientists, engineers, data analysts, entrepreneurs, investors, and so forth are explained. There is no room for question whether any of the techniques involved in farming are left to be bridged by technology in this book. Specific sections have been devoted to explaining Artificial Intelligence, Machine Learning, Robotics and Embedded Systems.

All the chapters are written in an analogous way and facts are peer-reviewed. We believe this book will act as a steppingstone for professionals passionate enough to direct themselves toward Agricultural Automation.

Upon completion of the book, we assure that you will bolster our saying: Food served with Intelligence.

About the Authors

Manan Shah is a BE in Chemical Engineering from the LD College of Engineering, Gujarat Technological University, and M. Tech. in Petroleum Engineering from the School of Petroleum Technology, PDPU, Gandhinagar, Gujarat. He has completed his PhD in the area of exploration and exploitation of Geothermal Energy in the state of Gujarat. He is currently an assistant professor in the Department of Chemical Engineering, School of Energy Technology (SOT), PDEU and a Research Scientist in the Centre of Excellence for Geothermal Energy (CEGE). His area of research includes power generation from low enthalpy geothermal reservoirs using Organic Rankine Cycle. He was also involved in designing of Geothermal Space Heating and Cooling system at Dholera, Gujarat, and doing research on hybrid setups in the renewable energy sector. Dr. Shah has received the Young Scientist Award from India's Science and Engineering Research Board (SERB). He has published several articles in reputed international journals in the area of the renewable energy sector, petroleum engineering, water quality, and chemical engineering. He serves as an active reviewer for several international journals as well.

Aalap Doshi holds a Master's degree in Electrical Engineering with a specialization in Control Systems from the Ira A. Fulton Schools of Engineering at Arizona State University (ASU). Prior to this, he completed his B.Tech in Electronics and Communication from L.D College of Engineering, Gujarat Technological University. Aalap currently serves as an Automation Engineer at CertainTeed Saint-Gobain. During his academic pursuits, Aalap gained a comprehensive understanding of classical control theory through specialized courses such as Feedback Control Systems, Design Multivariable Control Systems, and Linear Systems Theory, among others. His academic journey was enriched by his involvement with the "BIRTH Lab" at ASU, where he contributed as an electronics engineer, focusing on the electronics and feedback control aspects of the Lizard Inspired Tube Inspection Robot (LTI) research project. Aalap's professional portfolio boasts an array of projects in the domains of electronics and automation. He is passionate about solving challenges that have the potential to impact the future of humanity, with specific interests lying in Robotics and Control Systems, as well as Electronics and Electrical Engineering. Aalap aspires to channel his expertise and passion into the domain of Agriculture Automation. Furthermore, Aalap has made notable contributions to the academic sphere, being the author of two research papers in the agriculture automation domain. His dedication and impact in this field were acknowledged with the Best Paper Award, recognizing the paper with the highest number of citations in a single year. Aalap is an active reviewer for esteemed international journals where he further contributes to the advancement of scientific knowledge and research in his areas of expertise.

Kanish Shah has done his Master's in Computer Science from the University of Southern California, Los Angeles and B.Tech in Computer Engineering from Indus University. In the past he worked as a Machine Learning Developer at LogicRays

Technologies and is currently working as a Software Engineer III at Walmart in Sunnyvale, California. His area of interest includes machine learning and its applications along with software development. He has worked in various software companies as an Intern, one of them being at Indian Space Research Organization and Software Intern at Walmart. He has been greatly involved in the research work during his Engineering days. He has published several research papers in renowned scopus journals and also is a reviewer in many journals.

Ameya Kshirsagar is BTech in Information Technology from Symbiosis Institute of Technology, Pune, Maharashtra. He has published several articles in reputed international journals in the area of computer science, data science, machine earning, finance and so forth. He has also served as a reviewer for a reputable international journal.

1 History of Agriculture

1.1 WORLD BEFORE AGRICULTURE

Looking back to roughly around 15,000 to 20,000 years ago, archaeologists have no evidence whether agriculture existed or not among our ancestors. According to the archaeologists instead of agriculture our ancestors depended strictly on hunting and foraging for food and are termed as leading nomadic hunter-gatherer lifestyles. There were times when they had abundant food after killing a big animal, so they knew what to do with it and how to eat it. This is because there was no certainty as to when they next would have abundant food or even whether they would have food at all. So, in order to avoid starvation, they would eat it very carefully. Moreover, in search of food they had to walk for miles. So, the majority of their energy went into just getting more energy, that is food required for running the body for growing.

According to some historians, the world population before 10,000 years ago was around six to ten million. An average group of hunter-foragers would have needed to be the only population on 100 to 500 square kilometres to survive in places rich with resources, such as that of tropical rain forests. So, there were no humans living in only one particular area, since there was so much food to be found and killed and, therefore, they had to keep searching for food from one place to another. As agriculture didn't exist at that time, and hunting and foraging were the only means of gathering food, it was estimated that the Earth could only support around 10 million people.

1.1.1 NEOLITHIC REVOLUTION

It is believed that agriculture began during the Neolithic Era, around 9000 BCE, when the last Ice Age ended. However, scholars are still not sure about the emergence of agriculture. The Neolithic Revolution, also termed as the Agriculture Revolution, began around 12,000 years ago, coinciding with that last Ice Age. It started in the Fertile Crescent of the Middle East, where the humans first started farming. This revolution completely changed the way humans lived, ate and survived, making the way for modern civilization. The previous topic mentioned how hunter-gatherers roamed around different places in search of food. Now in the Neolithic period these hunters-gatherers turned into farmers, which was a dramatic shift, as their lives changed from being nomadic to a more settled one.

DOI: 10.1201/9781003213550-1   1

This civilization was characterized by permanent settlements and a reliable food supply rather than the hunter-gatherer's style of collecting food. As the civilizations grew, the population also increased because the crops and animals such as cows, sheep, buffaloes, and many others were farmed to meet the demand of people. According to the *National Geographic* reports the population was at least five million at the time Neolithic period started and due to the Agriculture Revolution, it touches seven billion today. It is believed that this revolution was not due to a single factor in the entire world. Instead, there were many factors that caused people to take up farming in different parts of the world. For instance, in the Near East, it is believed that a climate change at the end of last Ice Age favoured annual plants such as cereals.

1.1.2 CAUSES OF THE NEOLITHIC REVOLUTION

As mentioned above, the Neolithic Revolution occurred due to different factors and varied from one region to another. Some scientists believe that the Agriculture Revolution occurred because the Earth entered into a warming trend at the culmination of the last Ice Age, so agriculture is the result of climate change. Most people during those times lived in the boomerang-shaped region of the Middle East, known as the Fertile Crescent or the Cradle of Civilization. The latter name was given to the Fertile Crescent because this was where number of technological innovations took place, which included the use of irrigation, writing and, most important, was the wheel which was the major improvement in the transportation of goods.

There are many other sources that shed light on what caused the Neolithic Revolution. One theory was given by Harland who gave three different causes of the Neolithic Revolution. First, one reasons can be the rise in population. Many animals died at the end of last Ice Age, and the human population was increasing so fast that there was food crisis. This is when people started doing agriculture. Another reason can be due to the rise of religions. As time passed, people these beliefs increased. The last reason according to Harland was that the hunter gatherers cared for their young, they came to know about the edibility of plants and how much help they are in curing some of the illness. It was also being found that hunter-gatherer societies had more gender equality than did agricultural societies [1, 2]. They also domesticated animals, which then travelled with the humans.

The Fertile Crescent mainly covered almost all the Middle East, including present-day Turkey, Iraq, Iran, Lebanon, Egypt, Israel, Palestine, and Jordan. It ranges from the Nile in the South to the North in part of Turkey. On the West it is bounded by the Mediterranean Sea and by the Persian Gulf on the East. It generally consists of fertile soil, brackish wetlands and fresh water. With these kind of resources available the humans therefore experimented with the cultivation of cereals and grains around 10,000 BCE as they moved from hunter-gatherers to more settled communities.

The Neolithic period began when the first people gave up their hunter-gatherer life in order to begin farming. However, it must have taken hundreds to thousands of years for this evolution, as they completely shifted from being dependent on hunting animals and foraging plants for food to maintaining large crop fields. Neolithic farmers hunted animals such as gazelles, wild cattle, and roe deer [3, 4, 5]. It is believed that humans started gathering plants and seeds around 23,000 years ago and started farming cereal grains around 11,000 years ago. After cereals they shifted to protein-rich foods, such as peas and lentils. These practices would have brought stability in food production and at the same time required the storing of these crops, which require a more settled form of life. With the advent of the Neolithic Period two very important events took place: Plant Domestication and Animal Domestication.

1.1.3   ORIGIN OF DOMESTICATION DURING THE NEOLITHIC PERIOD

The domestication of plants and animals began during the Mesolithic Period. The first plant domestication indicated the onset of Neolithic Period, around 9500 BCE. Prior to that, the social activity that occurred during this period consisted of primitive agriculture. Dogs were the first animal to be domesticated before 15,000 years ago by small groups of hunters and gatherers. Goats and cattle were also domesticated during the Neolithic times. Many plants and animals were developed and selected during that period. For instance sugar beet existed as a major sugar-yielding plant in the nineteenth century ,while mint was used in agricultural production in the twentieth century. Animals such as the rabbit were domesticated during the middle Neolithic period.

1.1.3.1   Plant Domestication

It is believed that the crops such as barley, wheat and peas originated in the Middle East region, whereas cereals were grown in Syria around 9,000 years ago. There were many other places where different crops were grown, for instance fig trees were planted around 11,000 years ago in the Jordan Valley. Origins of rice were discovered in Eastern China as the world's oldest rice fields were found there. Also, millet farming was practiced in the China around 6000 BCE. Squash was also cultivated in Mexico around 10,000 years ago and maize-like plants from teosinte were cultivated there around 9,000 years ago. Sunflower was farmed in North America around 5,000 years ago. Neolithic villages were found with grinding stones in the houses, which showed transition from nomadic to settled organizations. Fishing nets were made from the strong fibres of some domesticated plants. Hemp, which has its origin in India, is used for many purposes, such as to obtain oil from its seeds, narcotic hash from its flowers, and fibres from its stalks. The tobacco plant was the main source for the production of narcotics and was also used in smoking and narcotic drinks by the Indo-American tribes. Apart from that the plants for tea and coffee were also discovered and cultivated. This showed the humans were gradually achieving a sufficiently high level of culture.

1.1.3.2   Animal Domestication

As the experiments with farming started, they also started domesticating animals in parallel. Cattle, sheep, goats, and pigs were herded in parts of Anatolia, which is modern-day Turkey, Iraq, and southwestern Iran around 10,000 to 13,000 years ago. Some of these animals were used for labor, which helped in intensive farming and in providing milk and meat for the growing population. Dogs helped in hunting wild animals, guarding and warning human settlements about possible danger. However, their main importance was that they were also eaten by humans. In a similar manner, during the initial stages of domestication sheep and goats were also eaten, but in the later stages their importance in producing commodities such as milk and wool changed the people's perspective. Moreover, horses were also used for meat and skin in the initial period of domestication. During the later stages, around the second millennium BCE, they were used to pull chariots in waging war.

Animals such as donkeys and camels were used as modes of transportation as they were not preferred for food. In the later stages the animals were also used in various sports. Roosters were used in cockfighting. The cocks also had religious significance as it was associated with the protection of good against evil. In Greece, the cocks were also sacrificed to gods. High production of eggs and meat from hens came into the later stages of domestication. Bees were then domesticated when the Neolithic Period was at the verge of termination because honey played a vital role in human nutrition. Apart from that, bees also had medicinal value as they provided wax and bee venom which was used in curing diseases. Around 3000 BCE the silkworm was domesticated in China for obtaining silk. The humans took longer time in domestication when they transitioned from the old world to the new world. They entered into a new world during the end of Pleistocene Epoch period, which lasted from 2.58 million to 11,700 years ago.

1.2 CONVENTIONAL METHODS USED IN FARMING

1.2.1 WHAT IS CONVENTIONAL FARMING?

The modern era has various names for conventional agriculture, such as industrial farming or modern agriculture. These names were given because of the tremendous growth and output generated in food production. With the increase in population the demand for food is ever increasing and the production of food has risen in the past 50 years worldwide. According to the reports this significant increase in food production is due to the conventional agriculture and not due to the greater amount of land being allocated for high cultivation of crops.

This meeting of food demands for billions of people due to the rise of productivity in the crops happened due to unnatural practices carried out by humans. So, if there has been any plant or crop that has used synthetic chemicals then it can be categorized to have grown under conventional farming. Farming practices with the use of Nitrogen not only enhance availability of crops, but can also alter soil and carbon dynamics [6]. Using these chemicals has resulted in the highest-ever yield of crops. These practices alter the natural environment, affect biodiversity, and the soil quality is deteriorated. This was a method that was introduced for making farming more efficient, but the productivity has increased at the cost of the environment. The increase in crop production is achieved through the use of chemicals, cross pollination methods, and using industrial products. Due to that, ecological health gets compromised along with the soil fertility. Once the conventional methods gets incorporated then the farms require constant maintenance but produce maximal yields.

The conventional means of farming often gets criticized due to the unnatural methods used by humans, and many people have agreed that organic farming practices are more environmentally beneficial than conventional [7, 8]. This form of agricultural systems tends to affect the system negatively [7, 9, 10, 11]. However according to a survey done by some researchers, they have made some crucial findings in support of conventional farms. The first finding stated that even if a particular farm gets polluted more as compared to some other farm, but yields more crops then that particular farm, it is better than the other. Another finding stated that a small parcel of land that does more intensive agriculture produces less pollutants, loses less water and harms the soil less. Finally, the last finding states that those farms that produce fewer crops (kind of organic farming) tend to harm the environment more compared to those where conventional methods have been used. The conventional methods of food production during the second half of previous century increased food production greatly, which increased food access [7, 12, 13].

Conventional farming differs from country to country and even farm to farm. It mainly depends on characteristics such as the technological innovations of a particular country, capital investments in the technology and equipment used, and the capacity and kind of pesticides and fertilizers used in farming. Conventional means have changed the way particular crops grow. For instance, previously the orange tree was designed to grow in special soils with more leaves, a particular ratio of fruit to leaves, fixed size of fruit and many other characteristics. With the advent of conventional methods, these characteristics can be modified, and now the orange tree can be grown that has fewer leaves, more fruit, fewer seeds and much more.

1.2.2 EVOLUTION OF AGRICULTURAL TECHNOLOGIES AND THE KIND OF MACHINERY USED IN CONVENTIONAL FARMING

The evolution in agricultural technology began around 10,000 years ago. It all began with simple hand tools that provided relief to the people doing the farming in those times, tools that are now common equipment today. We have come a long way to when horses were the main power house to carry the objects and some other farming practices. But as time evolved tractors successfully replaced animals such as oxen, horses and cows used in farming activities. Although manpower also decreased with the evolution, however, people were required to take care of those operations. Agricultural technology gradually shifted from low-tech to high-tech in the modern twenty-first century. The way these machines now operate have made tasks much more flexible and easier. The use of sensors (IOT) and Artificial Intelligence has played a major role in shaping this revolution. Most of the agricultural equipment now a days is a blend of sensors or mechanics along with the software-based Artificial Intelligence termed as robotics. This high-tech mechanization aims to support human functionalities and capabilities such as decision making and sensing. Recent progresses in agricultural equipment is due to the improvements in sensor technology, computer vision and artificial intelligence.

These technological advancements have introduced much equipment such as autonomous tractors, robotic harvesters, seeding robots, drones, and automated watering equipment, which greatly shaped the way farmers do farming. These advancements make farm activities automated, which is termed as farm automation or smart farming. These make the farms more efficient and automate the crop production cycle. Many agritech-based companies are focusing on building autonomous equipment and are quickly adopting farm automation. Robotics and Artificial Intelligence have greatly shaped modern agriculture. These high-tech mechanization tools greatly help in solving the real-world problems, such as shortage of food with rising global population, labour shortages and the environmental footprint of farming. The agritech industry has so much evolved that there are hundreds of different equipment types and machines available today to carry out the farming activities, and it is not possible to mention every piece of machinery in this book. Therefore, we have mentioned a few of them, which are commonly used. Below is the list of equipment that are most commonly used in agriculture.

1. Tractor: This is the most common form of machinery one will encounter in farming. Tractors are used by both commercial as well as subsistence farmers. It is irony that tractors don't do any kind of farming activities but instead there are different kinds of equipment that get attached to them and which carry out farming activities. It is one of the important farm vehicles and it can power the mechanized equipment. It is available in different sizes and can be used for ploughing, tilling, planting, harrowing, and many other kinds of farming activities.

2. Field Cultivator: Based on the title, it can be easily inferred that the main task of this machinery is to make the soil softer as well as for preparing the soil for cultivation. Once the crops start to germinate it is used to make the soil softer and help to get rid of weeds. It makes the soil aerated. For easy penetration of nutrients and water these field cultivators (see Figure 1.1) are used to make hard soil softer.

3. Harrows: This tool is used for cultivating the surface of the soil. It is generally carried out after plowing. Ploughing is used for deeper cultivation. So, after the ploughing process is over the land gets somewhat rough, and harrowing smoothens the rough patches. It works by breaking up the lumps of soil and provides a smoother finish. It is also used to cover the seeds after sowing. Spike harrows, dish harrows and drag harrows are the main type of harrows (see Figure 1.2).

4. Conveyor belt: This system belongs to conveyor belt structure and consists of two or more pulleys with a never-ending moving medium and the belt that rotates it. The material moves forward on the belt as both the pulleys are powered. These powered pulleys are known as the drive pulleys and the unpowered pulleys are known as the idler pulleys.

5. Harvesting machines: These are also one of the most common machines to be found in farms. There are different kinds of harvesting machines – for instance grains are harvested using grain harvesting machines, and root crops such as sugarcane are harvested with the help of root crop harvesting machines which

FIGURE 1.1   Field cultivators.

FIGURE 1.2   Harrows.

in previous times was done by diggers (see Figure 1.3). A similar case is with the vegetables as they get harvested with vegetable harvesting machines.

6. Irrigation equipment: Irrigation is generally used for assisting crops to grow and is mainly used in dry places, where there is shortage of water or rainfall. Different kinds of irrigation tools are available, such as centrifugal pumps, sprinklers, drip irrigation, submersible pumps, and so forth, depending on the kind of usage and capacity of farmers.

FIGURE 1.3   Harvesters.

1.2.3   Ecological Concerns of Conventional Farming

Conventional farming as discussed earlier has been beneficial in fulfilling the demands of billions of people due to the high productivity, with the help of several chemicals and fertilizers. However, this creates a negative impact on the soil productivity. This can be due to several factors such as soil compaction, loss of water-holding capacity, loss of soil organic matter, and salinization of soils. Some parts of Africa have a malpractice of converting the agriculture land to desert, which is mainly caused by overgrazing by livestock. These kinds of agricultural practices have been found to contribute to non-point source water pollutants, which include fertilizers, pesticides, and herbicides. Pesticides are the most common chemical class found in places where conventional farming is practiced. Many lakes, rivers, and oceans become affected by eutrophication, which occurs due to the practices adopted by farmers in conventional farming. Due to this, the water quality becomes deteriorated and that affects crop production, fishery production, and also the drinking water supply. Water scarcity is also a major issue because water usage is increased to a great extent for irrigation, and water stability is damaged.

Crops are also subjected to diseases like mite pests, illness caused due to different kinds of insects, hundreds of fungal pathogens and to those who have become resistant to one or more pesticides. This conversion of wildlands into agricultural fields has caused habitat loss and affected entire ecosystems. For farming purposes, destruction of tropical rainforests happens, and other native vegetation is affected. The level of carbon dioxide and other related greenhouse gases is elevated if the agricultural practices are not followed properly.

Moreover, excessive use of pesticides and herbicides while practicing conventional farming may degrade the soil quality and at the same time can have negative impact on the amount of entomopathogens. Many studies have shown that excessive use of herbicides reduce the germination and development of them. Instead of killing pathogens pesticides sometimes affect the soil in a negative manner. Insecticides can also be harmful to the entomopathogenic fungi (EPF) when the hosts are removed from the agro system. Hence, these were some of the ecological impacts that generally come into effect during conventional farming.

1.2.4 IMPACT OF CONVENTIONAL FARMING ON ENVIRONMENT AND HUMAN HEALTH

In the previous sections we saw how conventional farming has helped and is helping in solving the food demands of global population. However, everything has a positive and a negative side. Therefore, in this section we will discuss how these practices are causing a negative impact on Mother Nature as well as well as to human health. Some of these negative impacts are listed below.

1. Effect on climate: Due to the excessive usage of synthetic fertilizers there is serious concern about the greenhouse gas emissions. For instance conventional farming relies on nitrogen fertilizers produced by mixing sufficient amounts of ammonia and methane. So, these nitrogen fertilizers release some amount of nitrous oxide, which is an extremely dangerous greenhouse gas with a much higher warming capacity per unit released by the carbon.
2. Transfer of viruses from animals to humans: This can occur due to intensive livestock farming as these practices can serve as a bridge for pathogens that can pass from wild animals to farm animals and from them to humans. As this livestock farming can produce genetic similarities within flocks and herds, it makes them more susceptible to pathogens, so viruses can spread from one animal to another because they are kept closed together in the farms.
3. Impact of microorganisms on humans: Generally antimicrobials help to accelerate livestock growth. Due to this microorganisms develop resistance making antimicrobials less effective in medicines. According to World Health Organization reports, this development of resistance is causing harm to modern medicines as they are gradually becoming ineffective, and about 700,000 people die annually due to resistant infections.
4. Impact of pesticides on human health: Use of excessive fertilizers and pesticides causes humans to be exposed to these harmful pesticides through the food they consume, resulting in adverse health effects. Due to this various effects such as abnormal growth patterns, changes in immune system, endocrine disruptors, incidences of breast cancer and many more are seen as the side effects.
5. Contamination of water and soil: In the previous point we saw how these fertilizers and pesticides are causing negative impacts on human health. At the same time they are also affecting the environment. These harmful practices cause water and soil pollution. Soil loses its fertility making its more susceptible to erosion; and the release chemicals in to the water harms the aquatic life which in turn affects the humans indirectly when they consume sea food.
6. Epidemics of chronic disease: The commodity crops are used in a variety of inexpensive and calorie-dense foods. Rice, maize and wheat account for

60 percent of all dietary energy. This calorie-based approach fails to meet nutritional recommendations. Moreover, the demand of processed and packaged foods has increased in this generation due to which obesity has increased among the people. Due to this, people all over the globe are suffering from diseases such as heart attacks, diabetes, stroke and even cancers.

1.3   ANDREW MEIKLE AND HIS THRESHING MACHINE

1.3.1   BACKGROUND AND THE THRESHING MACHINE

Andrew Meikle, a Scottish inventor was born in 1719 at Saltoun, Haddingtonshire, which is now known as East Lothian. At the age of 16, just like his father he worked as a country millwright and followed father's trade in Houston mill, East Linton. Like his father he was also a country millwright and an engineer in the field of power transmission and generation when power was generated by wind, water and animals. In 1768 he patented a machine, along with Robert Mackell, that could dress the grains. In 1772 Andrew invented windmill that allowed sails to be better controlled.

In 1778 he constructed the first threshing machine. The design of threshing machines depended somewhat on one patented in 1734 by Michael Menzies. However that design was a complete failure. Menzies's second design, based on a Northumberland model, also failed. Meikle analyzed these threshers and constructed a drum with fixed beaters that can beat rather than rub the grains. In 1786, when Andrew Meikle was 67 years old, he designed and built the first threshing machine. The threshing machine could separate the grain from stalks and husks, which greatly helped in reducing the labour as well as time because before that the grains were separated manually by hand, which was very time consuming and laborious. Hours of work was completed within minutes and that, with just one operator. Later in 1788 he patented his drum threshing machine and began manufacturing it a year later (see Figure 1.4). The threshing machine used fluted rollers to feed sheaves of corn against the concave, or curved, casing. By 1789 these threshing machines were offered for sale so other inventors made some modification because, in its early stage, the machine was quite primitive so they improved the effectiveness of it and made it for general use by 1800.

1.4   ELI WHITNEY AND HIS COTTON GIN: DISCUSSION OF FIRST MACHINE IN AGRICULTURE SECTOR

1.4.1   BACKGROUND

Eli Whitney was an American manufacturer as well as inventor. He was born at Westboro, Massachusetts in 1765 and grew up in a farming family. So, he had considerable knowledge and experience in farming and its related activities. He was a mechanical engineer and became famous for the cotton gin invention and for introducing the concept of mass production of interchangeable parts. Whitney learned many different concepts of science during that period. In 1792 Whitney left New

FIGURE 1.4 Andrew Meikle's threshing machine.

England and headed to the South. He went to Georgia, where he got the job of private tutor on a plantation. Moreover, America at that time was witnessing a decline in slavery because the land owners found that their crops such as cotton and tobacco were producing less profits due to which they had to release the black slaves they had employed. During that time there was very heavy demand for cotton in the English mills and very little of it was exported to them from the South. The fibre from this seed got separated once it passed into the rollers. However, the problem came when it was a sticky green seed and short staple variety. The fiber adhered to the seed and was very difficult to separate and time-consuming to pick out the white cotton balls. The South's planters desperately needed to make the growth of cotton profitable. Whitney thought that a machine for the green-seed cotton could make the South rich and prosperous. Apart from that motive, he also hoped to make a profit because he also had debts.

1.4.2 ELI WHITNEY'S COTTON GIN

It took months to make the cotton gin and he had to put aside his plans of studying law in favor of continuously working on the cotton gin. Whitney's first crude model consisted of four major parts. A hopper to feed cotton in to the gin. Next was the revolving cylinder with hundreds of short wire hooks. The third was a stationary mesh or grid that prevented the seeds to pass through, allowing the large cotton fibres to pass, and the last one was a cylinder with bristles moving in opposite directions to each other. For the rights to this model, he was offered huge sum of money, but Whitney turned down the offer. Instead of selling it he worked on optimizing the model. The final version was known as the cotton gin. Whitney claimed that his cotton gin could efficiently separate the fibers from the cotton plants much better than the traditional methods.

In 1794, Eli Whitney went on to patent the cotton gin. But patenting and making profit from it were two completely different things. Along with his business partner Phineas Miller, he decided to make and sell these gins throughout Georgia and the South. They were also charging farmers for doing ginning for them and their charge was two-fifths of the actual profit, which was paid in the form of cotton itself. The troubles for Whitney started cultivating. Farmers resented buying Whitney's cotton gins as they had to pay exorbitant taxes. Instead they started making their own versions of cotton gin and claimed their new inventions. Phineas Miller brought costly suits on those who invented the pirated version of cotton gin but because of a flaw in the law they were unable to win any suits. They started suffering as they were not able to make profits. Moreover, their resources were also wasted in legal battles so they decided to sell the cotton gins at a reasonable price. Slavery was almost abolished from the North and, for South, the landowners required more slaves for increasing the cotton output. The work for the slave labour became never ending and as the large plantations spread in the South the large investment in slaves inhibited the growth of cities as well as industries. In the meantime the number of slaves in the South drastically increased, which would cause the United States to split in two with the Civil War of 1861–1865. Whitney died in 1825 and did not witness the social and economic effects his invention was largely responsible for. When the war ended the basic technology of the cotton gin continued to be used and modified. Today's generation of cotton gins are capable of processing huge amounts of cotton bales automatically (Figure 1.5).

1.5 CYRUS MCCORMICK AND HIS MECHANICAL REAPER

1.5.1 BACKGROUND

Cyrus Hall McCormick was born in 1809 at his family's 532-acre Virginia farm. As a youth he was quite skilled in both agriculture and in inventing things. In 1824 when Cyrus was 15, he invented a lightweight cradle, which was used for carting harvested grain. Cyrus's education in local schools was limited. He was reserved, determined and serious-minded and helped in his father's blacksmith shop. The father was also a farmer and inventor. Like many inventors, he created several farm implements and also tried to build mechanical reaper but failed to do it. In 1831 his father gave up the idea of producing a working model, and Cyrus took up the challenge.

During that period grain was harvested manually similar to the dawn of agriculture. In the nineteenth century it was very difficult for the farmers to do harvesting as it required a lot of labourers. Farmers had to face crop loss if the farm had insufficient number of enslaved workers. When McCormick's reaper was tested it promised to reduce the amount of labours.

FIGURE 1.5 Eli Whitney's cotton gin.

1.5.2 McCormick's Reaper

Reapers are machines that help in harvesting of grain. Cyrus McCormick was the first person who successfully built the mechanical reaper. After the unsuccessful attempt by his father he designed the model that would automatically cut, thresh and bundle those grains. McCormick's reaper was horse drawn, which sharply reduced the amount of manual labour required to harvest grain. It had a straight blade which was linked to the drive wheel and moved in a back and forth motion to cut the stalks of grain. These cut grains were then collected on a platform and taken out by a worker. This reaper greatly increased production from two to three acres to almost ten acres a day.

McCormick built this reaper within six weeks. In this duration of time he had built, tested on farms, modified the model and gave a demonstration to the public. The mechanical reaper suddenly increased the potential of farms to great extent. However, the farmers didn't show much interest in the reaper and as a result the sales of the were virtually zero for nine years. In 1834, McCormick patented his reaper after doing modifications for ten years. Due to some novel business practices adopted by McCormick in 1841, the sales of his reaper finally started rising and as a result he had to shift his mechanical reaper production from his father's blacksmith shop to a factory in Chicago in 1847.

Due to rising sales, in 1847 McCormick opened a small factory in the lakeside town of Chicago in a partnership with the mayor, William Ogden. In the initial year he

FIGURE 1.6   McCormick's reaper.

was able to sell 800 reapers, and the number increased as the years gradually passed. By 1851, McCormick was known all over the world for his invention. He also won the Gold Medal at the London Crystal Palace exhibition. He went on to become an industrialist helped the growth of Chicago, as in the next five years his business became the largest farm implement factory in the world. By 1856 McCormick was selling around 4,000 machines every year. The press named him "Thor of the Industry." After he died in 1884, the business continued to grow and, by 1902, McCormick Harvesting Machine joined with other companies, which together came to be known as the International Harvester company (see Figure 1.6).

1.6 TIMELINE OF INVENTIONS IN AGRICULTURE

Farm machinery and technologies came a long way from the Neolithic period, but the largest number of inventions took place between 1700 to late 1900s, which drastically changed the agricultural industry. So, in this topic we are going to provide the readers a very comprehensive and concise version of all the agricultural inventions that took place all over the world in the past, and our focus is to cover all the countries where these inventions occurred, paving the way for modern agritech.

1500 BC – Trench silos used in an Egyptian town for the storage of grain used to produce bread and beer. Wooden plows pulled by domesticated animals became the tool for ground planting.

475 BC – Iron plow developed in China, which suddenly saw their agriculture flourish.

16th century – In the American Southwest regions Spanish cattle were introduced.

1698 – Thomas Savery, an English inventor introduced a steam-powered device/ engine which led to the development of the steam engine.

1702 – Jethro Tull, from Berkshire, England, perfected a horse-draw seed drill that sowed the seeds in neat rows and was one of the person responsible for the Agriculture Revolution.

1784 – In this year two inventions took place. Scottish inventor Andrew Meikle invented a threshing machine which was not successful commercially. Then US President Thomas Jefferson, developed a plow tool that helped in reducing soil resistance during plowing.

1785 – James Small from England developed a plow that featured a cast iron moldboard.

1793 – Scythe and cradle was introduced in the same period. In the same year Eli Whitney introduced the cotton gin which contributed to the success of producing bulk amounts of cotton bales.

1794 – The first long distance road of about 62 miles was paved in the United States, commonly known as the Philadelphia and Lancaster Turnpike, and was the first successful toll road. And later that year Jefferson's moldboard of least resistance was tested.

1797 – A blacksmith from New Jersey named Charles Newbold patented his cast-iron plow. However, it was not successful commercially as the farmers somewhat refrained from buying it because they thought that iron might poison the soil and in turn affect the crops.

1801 – The first icebox refrigerator was invented by Thomas Moore.

1805 – Cotton gradually began to replace tobacco as the chief cash crop.

1815–1830 – Cotton finally emerged as the most important cash crop in the South.

1819 – Jethro Woods, a blacksmith from New York, patented a cast iron plow that was previously patented by Charles Newbold (which had been quite unsuccessful commercially) by performing some modifications and changing some parts in it.

1819–1825 – The first food canning industry was established in the United States.

1822 – A horse-drawn machine with revolving wheel consisting of six knives was patented for cutting hay and other related materials by Jeremiah Bailey.

1825 – In this year the machine for a dumping hay rake was developed. K\It was known as whoa-back hay rake where the operator had to stop the rake and dump the hay by backing up the horse.

1830 – Around 250–300 labour hours was required to produce five acres of wheat with brush harrow, sickle and flail.

1833 – Obed Hussey, an American inventor developed the first reaper for smaller grains.

1834 – Here two events took place. John Lane from Northwestern Illinois made the first steel plow with steel saw blades four years prior to John Deere who made it in 1837. Cyrus McCormick also patented a mechanical reaper in 1834. Joab Center from New York patented a machine for turning and spreading hay.

1836 – Machines for mowing, winnowing and threshing grains were developed in this year.

1837 – Leonard Andrus and John Deere began manufacturing a steel plow. A practical threshing machine was also patented this year.

1840 – Commercial farming was highly encouraged due to factory-made agriculture machineries and, because of that, cash flow also increased in the market and for farmers, too.

1841 – Practical drain grill was patented in this year by Moses and Samuel Pennock.

1842–1850 – In New York in 1842 the first grain elevator was introduced. In 1843 scientist Sir John Lawes created a commercial fertilizer by developing a procedure for manufacturing superphosphate. In the very next year a practical mowing machine was invented. In 1849, mixed chemical fertilizers started selling in the market commercially. Lately in 1850, around 90 labour hours were required to produce 2.5 acres of corn harrow and walking plow. A corn picker was also developed in this year by Edmund Quincy. The first commercial successful hay press was introduced.

1853 – Walter Abbott Wood, an American politician, introduced a spring tooth dump rake especially for farmers who worked with mowers.

1856 – Tiles were first laid for draining wet fields by John Johnston from New York. A two-horse straddle row cultivator was also patented.

1858 – A hay mowing machine was patented by Lewis Miller from Ohio. In addition, mason jars which are generally used for home canning were invented in this year.

1862 – Thomas Aveling commonly known as iron founder and agricultural engineer, developed a self-moving steam engine along with Thomas Porter which later was named as Aveling & Porter.

1864 – John Deere received his first patent for a mold used in casting steel plows.

1865 – People gradually started using gang plows and sulky plows.

1869 – The first steam powered engine was produced by J.I. Case Co. that replaced animals in farming operations. In this year spring tooth harrows for seedbed preparations appeared.

1872 – The first knotter used for binding bundles of grain was designed by Charles Withington.

1873 – Fred Hetch along with his father Lewis Hetch erected the first tower silo on their farm.

1876 – The first mechanical corn planter was patented by George Lambert.

1880 – Hexelbank Ensilage Cutter was developed by Louis Lucas and Silberzahn and was the predecessor to the modern forage harvester.

1882–1890 – Cyrus McCormick built the first daisy mechanical reaper in 1882. In 1884, George Berry from California developed the first self-propelled combine. In the next year William Deering and company developed binder twine, which was used on their harvesters. The next three years were dedicated to Charter Gasoline Engine, which created a gasoline-fueled engine, and their first production run was for six traction engines.

1891 – The first mechanical manure spreader was developed by Henry Synck and Joseph Oppenheim in Ohio.

1893 – First corn silage harvester was patented by Iowan Charles C. Fenno in 1892. The first diesel engine by Rudolph Diesel was patented in this year.

1897 – The first machine that eventually came to be known as a tractor was built by Charles Hart and Charles Parr.

1902 – The first soil pulverizer was developed by Brillion Iron Works to produce smooth seedbeds for planting

1904 – Crawler tractors equipped with tracks were first introduced by Benjamin Holt. These tracks prevent heavy tractors from sinking into the soil.

1905 – The first friction drive tractor was introduced by International Harvester.

1907 – Henry Ford started developing an experimental gasoline-powered tractor, which was known as an automobile plow during that time.

1912 – The first powered rotary tiller was produced by Arthur Clifford.

1915–1920 – Horse drawn running harvester was patented by Minnesota farmers in 1915 and, by 1918, they start manufacturing this harvester. By 1919, International Harvester developed the first commercially available power take-off system.

1921–1930 – Gleaner combine was developed by the Baldwin brothers in 1923. In the same year International Harvester introduced Farmall Tractor. In 1927, International Harvester became the first company to offer swathers for sale. In 1929, the Ann Harbour Bale became the world's first pickup baler.

1931–1950 – The first commercially successful pickup forage harvester was developed by Erwin Saiberlich in 1932. The year 1933 brought a revolution for tractors by introducing air-filled rubber tires for them. In 1937, Noble cultivator, which reduced soil erosion and water loss was patented by Charles Noble from Alberta, Canada. In 1940, automatic pickup and straw balers were developed by New Holland Machine Co. In the year 1941 Massey Ferguson developed first successful self-propelled combined machine. In 1945 the first posthole tractor driven digger was developed. Moreover, in the year 1946 the first tractor mounted rotary cutter was developed by Woods Brother Equipment Company. In the next year first chain drive front tile tiller was designed by Clayton Merry. In 1949, tomato harvesters were developed by the University of California Davis by Jack Hanna and Coby Lorenzen.

1951–1970 – In 1954, Valmount Industries developed the first successful irrigation system and in the next year the first self-propelled swather was developed by Hesston Manufacturing Company. In 1957, Cyril and Louis Keller designed the first skid steel loader and, in the very next year, the first drive-in loader was designed and introduced by Maskiner. In 1960, International Harvester launches the first lawn and garden tractors. In 1962, turbo-charged diesel engines were developed by Allis Chalmers in order to increase the capacity of engines. After four years, in 1966, Chalmers introduced the first no-till planter. In 1967, International Harvester developed the first hydrostatic drive combine machines. The first grain wagon was introduced by Kinze manufacturing from Iowa. In 1970, a quick attach system was introduced known as Bob-Tach implement system.

1.7 TECHNOLOGICAL DEVELOPMENTS IN FORESTRY AND FARMING

Just like the technological advancements happening in the agricultural field, those advancements are also being applied to the forestry. Conservationists are bringing in the latest technologies to make a difference for forests and oceans. The solution to the challenges faced in the forests originate close to the forest or within it. There were lot of forests and large-scale plantation began in the 1960s [14, 15]. Often people criticize these technologies due to their negative impacts on society. Technological developments might have positive and negative impacts on forest areas and conditions [16]. However, these technological developments on the other hand benefit the forests. There are many instances of the kind of support these technologies provide, such as:

(a) Land productivity and yields have significantly increased due to different techniques being introduced in plantations and tree breeding.
(b) Impact logging being reduced.
(c) Remote sensing techniques to improve the reliability on inventory.
(d) Use of computer software's for management simulation.
(e) Land being reverted to forests due to the technological developments in the agricultural sectors but just limited to developed countries for now.

Let's dive into some of the technological advancements that really helped forestry industry.

1. Deforestation detection: Artificial Intelligence has found its way in almost every aspect of the field, and it can be useful in monitoring the trees in the forest. Governments are shifting to artificial programs that use real-time rainfall data to predict how green a given forest is going to be. This prediction is then matched with the images of forest taken from the monitoring satellite rotating around the Earth.
2. Drones: Drones play an important role in agriculture. In forestry, too, conservationists have found their use. Drones are used to monitor wildlife and habitats in places where it is somewhat difficult for humans to reach. They have also been useful for assessing coral reefs at the Caribbean Sea.
3. Super farming: Efficient land pressure-reducing activities such as robotic agriculture and vertical forests have brought evolvement in forestry. Highly efficient farming methods tend to take pressure off the forests by providing higher crop yields and giving less wastage, and the expenditure of land is also less.
4. Common transparent system: Governments of different countries should come together and decide on a common system that could keep track of illegal forest-related activities such as illegal logging and so forth. The system should be such that it can be accessed by anyone from anywhere, commonly termed as open-sourced as well as decentralized.
5. Wildfire issues: Many countries, such as the United States of America, Australia and so forth, face the issue of forest fires that cause damage to thousands of acres of valuable land and destroys the habitat, too. Therefore, there is a need for highly efficient wildfire prevention as well as mitigation techniques should be introduced for reducing the wildfires. Currently,

governments are also working on techniques that could detect the forest fire at a very early stage, that is, before its origination.

6. Use of camera traps: Conservationists often use this technique to keep a track of some animals by deploying camera traps at some places. Camera traps have become so inexpensive and easily accessible that they are commonly used by people in tracking foxes and raccoons. Generally, conservationists utilize them to monitor the presence of rare birds and even nocturnal animals. These camera traps are also used by wildlife photographers to capture some unique images but that can take years of dedication.

7. Bioacoustics: It is quite difficult to assess the biodiversity of forest that is somewhat remote and those with robust habitats. Acoustic monitoring can record each and every sound erupting from the forests such as birds chirping, insects buzzing, and different animals. The acoustic monitoring equipment also records the sound of rainforest and records them. The healthier the complex soundscape is, then so is the ecosystem and more diverse is the biodiversity.

8. Tracking of wildlife: Biologists still believe that even today major part of the Earth's water bodies are unexplored. For decades biologists had the practice of attaching a radio collar to an animal in order to keep track of it in forests. However those devices were somewhat bulky and not reliable. But the current generations of trackers are very efficient and can gather more data as well track a wide range of creatures. Those trackers are known as micro tags, which are very lightweight and even allow very tiny creatures to be tracked.

9. Laser technology for mapping forests: For reducing the impacts of logging, a new technique has been introduced where an airplane flies over a region of forest and beams down pulses of light to measure the amount of time it takes for those pulses to bounce from the vegetation and return back to the airplane. The costs involved in this process makes it expensive, but if the costs can be reduced in the near future then it can prove itself be very useful.

10. Plastic woods: This kind of synthetic wood can be made from plastic, which can be used as a sustainable alternative replacement of wood which possesses the same quality and strength with that of natural wood.

11. Regeneration of forests: This is the need of hour as the forest cover is getting reduced day by day. Therefore, there should be some of the cost-effective methods that can help bring back or restore the forest cover as well as establish new ones too. For those different modern technologies can be used such as robotics, drones and by taking care of the forests at regular intervals of time.

12. Carbon storage: Carbon released in to the atmosphere can be used for storage which can help reduce the burden on climate change, mitigating the effects of carbon in atmosphere as well as reduce the depletion of the ozone layer.

So, these are some of the latest technologies on which research is still going, and some have already started getting implemented. Technological advancements will continue to have an impact on the forests and the ecosystem both in a positive as well as negative manner. Talking about these developments, it comprises just not of the software but also hardware [17]. These technologies will only create a positive impact if and only if relevant policies are being decided by the government and followed by people.

1.8   DISCUSSION OF ROBOTICS TECHNIQUE IN AGRICULTURE

The agricultural industry has constantly evolved due to the advancement in technologies and to farmer trying out different ways to increase the yield of their lands. Along with that they have to deal with the rising cost of inputs such as different kinds of fertilizers, pesticides, adaptation of new technological equipment on their farms. According to the survey the investment and innovation in robotics is anticipated to increase to more than $17B by 2021 and there is no stopping in the future.

Many of the robotic techniques have emerged in the past recent years due to the advancement in technology, and these agricultural robots are efficient in doing almost every possible task in a much efficient and faster way and are useful in tasks such as avoiding hazards, harvesting crops, identifying diseases, collecting fruits and vegetables from farms and many more. Cameras play a very important role in these robots in various activities such as monitoring of crops and their behavior, finding out the anomalies in them, pulling of weeds, sorting and packing. This is possible due to involvement of machine vision technology in robots. In addition to that another important terminology which plays a major role in robots is machine learning. For instance, autonomous vehicles deployed to carry out farm activities use this technology to identify and avoid any unwanted objects in their path.

So, following are various kinds of robots being commonly used in agriculture.

1. Self-driving robots: Here, the role of both machine vision and sensors come into play in order to avoid obstacles while navigating the field. So, these robots create a 3D model view of the surface using high resolution single or multiple cameras with which they are able to navigate quite easily. These robots are integrated with self-driving technology, a GPS system, a satellite corrected technology and much more. These technologies help identify the correct path to traverse and, by integrating computer vision with machine learning, these robots can easily identify obstacles in their path (see Figure 1.7).
2. Unmanned autonomous vehicle: Drones are used as seeders for wide spreading of seeds in the fields. There are some areas in some of the gigantic farms which are quite difficult to reach so these drones can be used in those places, and drone seeders can sow seeds there without endangering workers. These drones are capable of planting thousands of trees a day with just one or two operators running a few drones. Some of the new-technology drones use a combination of robotics along with Geographic Information Systems to generate a map of the field and generate various information about the soil properties such as its quality and soil density. For instance Agribotix drone is a low cost tool for farmers that collects crop data in real time and helps in monitoring large areas of crops.

FIGURE 1.7 Image of a self-driving robot.

3. Robots employed in the weeding process: One of the most important struggles for farmers is to make sure crops grow in a proper way by combatting weeds. This machine vision technology employed in robots helps in removing weeds one by one without the use of chemicals. These kinds of robots can help feed great numbers of people by removing weeds from the crops.

4. Picking: One of the most intensive farming activities is the harvesting. If a farmer doesn't harvest the crops on time then they will get damaged. Harvesting of crops requires a lot of labour and time. This process is very intense and farmers experiences a shortage of workers due to the backbreaking nature of doing the harvesting. In some fruits Machine Learning technology helps robots identify whether a particular fruit is ripe or not. If it's ripe then the robot will pluck it. These robots make sure that they make no contact with the fruits and are cut perfectly just above the plant's calyx. For instance the Energid Citrus Picking systems are fast and efficient as they have the capability to pick a fruit every 2–3 seconds and it is also very cheap to build.

5. Greenhouses robots: Indoor growing is the booming practice which is continuously growing in the past few years. Many companies are shifting to the fully automated systems. This kind of agriculture is termed as automated indoor agriculture. Sensors are used in one of the robots which analyses and picks the plants while the other robot lifts and transports the trays across the room. The productivity is the same as conventional farmland. The main benefit of

indoor farming is that it uses 90 percent less water compared to conventional farming, and all these plants are grown using specialized LED lights.

6. Sprayer robots: These robots uses high-resolution cameras to identify weeds in the plants using computer vision technology. They scan individual plants and identify any anomalies in them. After that they activate the nozzles according to the requirement for spreading herbicides for removing the weeds. These robots, unlike manual spraying, ensure that there is less wastage of herbicides, that herbicide resistance is reduced and the crops receive a proper amount of herbicide. For instance, Ecorobotix robot is a fully autonomous drone with solar power and GPS installed in it. This uses a camera system to target and spray weeds (see Figure 1.8).

1.9   ECOLOGY AND AGRICULTURE – A HARMONY

Whenever someone talks about anything related to agriculture, they most of the time forget to take ecology into consideration. Ecology simply describes the process influencing the distribution and quantity of organisms and how they interact with each other. The Earth has been more developed because there is more farming happening and the forest land is decreasing day by day. Due to exposure of more land for farming activities the lifecycle of pests was many times broken. The growth of insects and weeds were suppressed due to the growth of multiple crops on the same land.

Most people who talk about the Green Revolution say how it reshaped the agricultural industry with the introduction of modern machinery, synthetic fertilizers and chemicals. This was all because of the human insecurity towards food and in order to meet the growing demands for food. Apart from environmental changes caused by industries, these agricultural systems created by humans are also largely responsible for threatening food production. And this is the chief reason behind the disturbance of the linkage between ecology and farming. A large amount of disturbance is caused due to which the nature has to suffer and because of that there has been damage to soil due to soil erosion, fresh water supplies is being affected, loss of marine life, forests being devastated, groundwater being depleted and much more. The indiscriminate use of pesticides has had a negative impact on crops as the pests are gradually becoming resistant to it. In addition to that these fertilizers are affecting water bodies and depleting ozone layers. So, these modern systems are becoming a major threat to food production. Pesticides are also responsible for harming the environment. Around 90 percent of pesticides don't target the pests that they are meant to and instead harm the environment by contaminating the air, soil and water.

Synthetic pesticides affect crops even more than the organic ones. They enter the residual of the crops and remain there even after harvesting. Due to that they get transferred to the other crops. Due to soil contamination the roots tend to take more chemicals in them which, in turn, affect their health and affect their different parts. They can also enter the food chain and can disturb it, too, eventually affecting human health, which can cause serious health issues such a cancer, infection of the intestines and many more. Instead synthetic fertilizers should be used in such a way that they

FIGURE 1.8   Sprayers.

neither affect the plants nor the soil. The soil, water and air pollution can easily be brought under control by using the synthetic fertilizers in a proper way and efficiently spraying them on the crops.

This current evolution is benefitting neither the farmers nor the environment. Although it is able to provide adequate food to the people but, on the other hand the soil and plant quality is becoming poor gradually. So, in order to stop that, appropriate technology should be adopted. In addition to that farmers should focus on small-scale, production of food that is local and use appropriate technology that is the need of the hour. This will surely help in maintaining a harmony between ecology and agriculture.

REFERENCES

[1] P.G. Fredriksson, S.K. Gupta (2018). "The neolithic revolution and contemporary sex ratios." *Economics Letters* vol. 173. https://doi.org/10.1016/j.econlet.2018.09.014

[2] T. Iversen (2011). *Institution for Social and Policy St: Women, Work and Politics: The Political Economy of Gender Inequality.* Yale University Press, 2010.

[3] C.G. Scanes (2018). "Chapter 6 – The Neolithic Revolution, animal domestication, and early forms of animal agriculture." In *Animals and Human Society*, 103–131. https://doi.org/10.1016/B978-0-12-805247-1.00006-X

[4] O. Bar-Yosef (1998). "The Natufian culture in the Levant, threshold to the origins of agriculture." *Evolutionary Anthropology.* https://doi.org/10.1002/(SICI)1520-6505(1998)6:5<159::AID-EVAN4>3.0.CO;2-7

[5] A.M. Rosen (2012). "Climate change, adaptive cycles, and the persistence of foraging economies during the late Pleistocene/Holocene transition in the Levant." *PNAS* vol. 109, no. 10, 3640–3645. https://doi.org/10.1073/pnas.1113931109

[6] T.N. Bwana, N.A. Amuri, E. Semu, L. Elsgaard, K. ButterbachBahl, D.E. Pelster, J.E. Olesen (2021). "Soil N2O emission from organic and conventional cotton farming in Northern Tanzania." *Science of the Total Environment* vol. 785. https://doi.org/10.1016/j.scitotenv.2021.147301

[7] J. Stubenrauch, F. Ekardt, K. Heyl, B. Garske, V.L. Schott, S. Ober. (2021). "How to legally overcome the distinction between organic and conventional farming – Governance approaches for sustainable farming on 100% of the land." *Sustainable Production and Consumption* vol. 28, 716–725. https://doi.org/10.1016/j.spc.2021.06.006

[8] K. Lorenz and R. Lal (2016). "Chapter Three – Environmental Impact of Organic Agriculture." *Advances in Agronomy* vol. 139. https://doi.org/10.1016/bs.agron.2016.05.003

[9] M. Agovino, M. Casaccia, M. Ciommi, M. Ferrara, K. Marchesano (2021). "Agriculture, climate change and sustainability: The case of EU-28." *Ecological Indicators* vol. 105. https://doi.org/10.1016/j.ecolind.2018.04.064

[10] M.A. Clark, N.G.G Domingo, K. Colgan, S.K. Thakrar, D. Tilman, J. Lynch, I.L. Azevedo, J.D. Hill (2020). "Global food system emissions could preclude achieving the 1.5° and 2°C climate change targets." *Science* vol. 370, no. 6517. www.science.org/doi/10.1126/science.aba7357

[11] F. Hedenus, S. Wirsenius, D.J.A. Johansson (2014). "The importance of reduced meat and dairy consumption for meeting stringent climate change targets." *Climatic Change* vol. 124, 74–91. https://link.springer.com/article/10.1007/s10584-014-1104-5

[12] R.E. Evenson, D. Gollin (2003). "Assessing the impact of the Green Revolution, 1960 to 2000." *Science* vol. 300, no. 5620. www.science.org/doi/10.1126/science.1078710

[13] P.L. Pingali, et. al (2012). "Green Revolution: Impacts, limits, and the path ahead." *PNAS* July 31. https://doi.org/10.1073/pnas.0912953109

[14] A. McEwan, E. Marchi, R. Spinelli, M. Brink (2019). "Past, present and future of industrial plantation forestry and implication on future timber harvesting technology." *Journal of Forestry Research* vol. 26, no. 31, 339–351. https://doi.org/10.1007/s11676-019-01019-3

[15] Szulecka, J., Pretzsch, J., Secco, L. (2014). "Paradigms in tropical forest plantations: a critical reflection on historical shifts in plantation approaches." *International Forestry Review* vol. 16, 128–143. https://doi.org/10.1505/146554814811724829

[16] M.H. El-Lakany and J. Ball (2001). "Technology and the forest landscape: rapid changes and their real impacts." *International Forestry Review* vol. 3, no. 3, 184–187. www.jstor.org/stable/42609383?seq=1

[17] M. Holopainen, J. Hyypa, L. Vaario, G. Mery (2010). "Implications of technological development to forestry." www.researchgate.net/publication/233397959_Implications_of_Technological_Development_to_Forestry

2 Types of Farming and How AI and Robotics Can Help

2.1 ARABLE FARMING

2.1.1 Introduction

2.1.1.1 What Is Arable Farming?

Arable farming is termed as the process of growing crops in fields that are usually ploughed before planting. It means that these crops are grown on land or a field that is then sold by the farmers according to their needs. This kind of farming generally needs a bit of sloping land, soil with balanced moisture, fertile ground, and a number of human resources. In the United Kingdom these kinds of farms are found mostly in Southern and Eastern parts. Some of the crops that are grown using arable farming are wheat, maize (corn), barley, oats, and peas. These crops are made into food for humans and animals. Arable farming is generally characterized by larger farm sizes, and annual crops there are more susceptible to weather changes compared to permanent crops, which are more resilient due to their deeper roots [1].

During the initial phase of arable farming in New Zealand, ploughing was the first tedious task as the ground needed to be prepared for planting. Bushes had to be cut and burned with the stumps removed. By doing this, the soil was broken up in order to make the ground ready for planting and cultivation. But the land became very hard when it was first ploughed. In modern times tractors are there to do all the ploughing work, but previously horses or bullocks used to pull the ploughs. Correct allocation of arable land for the cultivation of crops makes the transition easier and also will comply with the nutritional intake [2].

After ploughing. seeds are planted in the soil mostly in autumn or the spring, using machines with drillers. Fertilizers are then added, which is helpful for the plants to grow. Water is needed for the crops that are grown in dry regions. Pests are generally controlled by spraying chemicals, while some plants are grown in such a way that they are resistant to diseases. After doing these procedures it's time for harvesting. Crops in New Zealand are usually harvested during summer. The work force required for harvesting crops is quite high for farmers and vendors. At the end the grain is loaded and taken to warehouses to be stored or processed.

2.1.1.2   History Behind Arable Farming

It is believed that in New Zealand arable farming was first started in the mid 1800s by the early missionaries when they grew wheat and oats for the first time. Wellington, Whanganui, and Nelson were the New Zealand settlements that focused mainly on arable farming and its production rather than animal farming. During the nineteenth century buying and selling practices were carried out by the Maori communities that grew wheat, which was exported to Australia to be sold to the settlers. Similarly, these companies also did export on a limited basis, and the focus was mainly on animal products such as wool and dairy.

Doing arable farming on new land was a very tedious task during previous times. In the North Island County, the forests were burned and the logs were removed before the beginning of ploughing. Similarly in the South Island grasslands the shrubs and tussock were cleared while the vegetation was burnt before ploughing. The wool prices declined in the year 1870, due to which the pastoralists turned to large-scale arable farming as their source of income.

2.1.1.3   Arable Farming Processes

There are certain fixed steps as to how these plants are grown – the planting, adding fertilizers, cultivation, doing irrigation, protecting crops from diseases and pests, harvesting and at last selling them in markets. In the initial period, when the traditional arable practices were carried out, the land was left as it is until the existing vegetation had died. Ploughing removed approximately 15 centimetres of the soil. Clod breaking played a vital role in traditional arable farming ,where tools like grubber were mostly used. This kind of tool reduced the clod size and flattened the soil surface to reduce the loss of moisture.

In modern arable farming practices power harrows consisting of spikes were attached to tractors and were driven by this type of power, which greatly reduced the time difference between planting crops. The tractors used were quite powerful, requiring only one or two passes to complete a single seedbed. Drilling played a major role here once the seedbeds were ready. Drillers were used to sow the seeds at a certain depth and sometimes fertilizers were also applied by the drill. After this task rollers were used for compacting the earth for good contact with the seeds as well as to prevent moisture loss. For irrigation the water is supplied in the right amount, as too much can be wasted if it leaches off nutrients, while insufficient water can reduce the water quality. Similarly soil moisture not only affects crop yields but also quality. The majority of GHG emissions in this system are in the form of N2O, mostly from fertilizers and emissions of N2O [3]. Crops such as wheat may not grow properly if there is a lack of water in the plants while the grain is forming. And if there is an excess of water then the protein content of crops may be reduced.

However, by the end of 20th century farmers gradually stopped ploughing and shifted to direct drilling. Existing vegetation gets sprayed with herbicides, and once that vegetation has died the seed is drilled directly into the soil. Due to this, the soil can retain moisture within it. Talking about the costs, this method saves cultivation costs compared to the previous drilling methods. Overall costs were divided in to the steps mentioned in the initial part of this topic. Cultivation and drilling cost

20 percent of the total production of arable crops. Sowing seed account for about 15 percent of the total cost.

2.1.1.3.1 Technologies Used in Arable Farming

Precision agriculture plays a very important role by which crops are provided with the exact amount of nutrients and treatments required for a higher yield. Using various technologies prevents over-application of chemicals responsible for either higher yield or removal of pests and diseases which not only saves money but also reduces polluting the environment. Therefore, let us delve into the different kinds of technologies used in arable farming.

1. Synchronisation of Machines: This is a kind of team work where two machines work in synchronization and carry out the farming activities. For instance combined harvesters help in reaping, winnowing, and threshing activities. It is useful for crops such as wheat, oats, maize, barley, soya beans and oilseeds. These harvesters separate the straw, which is less nutritional, from the grains. The straws can be left as a residue or used to feed livestock. Modern machines avoid the duplication of activity while spraying, fertilizing and sowing of seeds.

2. Assistance of Robots: Following the same route while harvesting crops is very important, as the robots should not drive over the crop or affect the compacting of soil. Therefore, the modern generation tractors are equipped with satellite-based positioning systems to determine their positions within a couple of centimeters so that they can reproduce the same route for purposes such as sowing, fertilizing and harvesting. New generation robots have auto-steering, which can make simple turns without much control from the driver, but the driver still needs to keep an eye on it. The applications of robots in agriculture is still in progress as there is a lot of scope in this field.

3. Monitoring and mapping: Yield map generation is a crucial part where the yield monitoring sensors captures the composition of harvested grains and displays them through the yield maps. These sensors can be fitted to machines like combined harvesters where these sensors are connected to the Global Positioning system or the Global Navigation Satellite System that can identify the low and high performing areas of the field. With these maps farmers are able to identify the amount of agrochemicals that need to be applied to the crops.

4. Soil and Plant Sensing: Sensors that are attached to the moving robots can measure different kinds of soil parameters such as composition, moisture content and density. Even these sensors can help vehicles identify the exact location of plants. Due to these sensors vehicles can easily determine how much water and fertilizers needs to be added so that the yield is maximum and the damage to the crops is as low as possible. Soil sensing helps in monitoring the conditions on the field without compacting or mixing the soil. At time of harvesting the crop can also be determined with sensing. This is possible

through a technology, Near Infrared Reflectance, which measures the reflectance of different wavelengths for monitoring the composition of grains.

5. Advanced Modelling: Machine Learning encompasses different properties of weather, soil and plants for determining the yield of crops. The main idea behind its wide usage is that this technology learns from itself, due to which it can over time adapt different functionalities with by even providing appropriate suggestions to the farmers. Machine Learning is being used in various tasks, such as
   (a) Irrigation
   (b) Diagnosis of diseases
   (c) Weather forecasting
   (d) Water management, and
   (e) How to make use of land in an optimal way.

2.1.1.3.2 Machinery Used in Arable Farming

1. Semi Mounted Ploughs: The name of the device is VariTitan, which has different versions ranging from nine to twelve furrows and widths up to 660 cm with maximum acres of land performance. The width adjustment is made very easy to operate, which is very helpful in arable farming and at the same time is environment friendly. VariTitan has turning and lifting functions that are managed by the electric controls that make the plough more steerable as well as faster. The back side of this machine can be moved upwards, laterally and downwards. In tough conditions VariTitan can be operated with front ploughs without need for much adjustment.

2. Self-propelled Sprayers: Model 5430i Series sprayers are capable of doing the task for bigger arable farms. These models are useful for farm contractors, who demand high productivity. Their outstanding spray accuracy as well as versatility to spray any type of crops, whether tall or short or higher value crops. They provide the operator much more comfort and reliability that will help do the job faster and without much effort. This series of models have fully integrated command systems, which increase the maximum spraying accuracy. They have a multi-mode four steering wheel that can travel at a speed of 40kmph. They also have a 4,000L solution tank capacity.

3. Model K Series Tractors: This device is known as as Agrotron, and it has four different series, ranging from 65 to 130. Agrotron meets high demands of arable and grass farms with its flexibility, versatility, and compactness, and it has equipment that can meet some special requirements and is detachable.

4. Seed Drillers: Amazone is used for large area seed drilling. Seed drilling and sowing is usually a tedious task where high work rates are required with cost-effective sowing. With this machine it is possible to achieve very high precision of sowing seeds in areas where yield per acre is often high as well as in areas where the yield is medium or somewhat less. The Cirrus series is a perfectly crafted seed drill that can do a work in an area of around 5ha/h. This machine is loaded with RoTeC Control Coulter system. There is a control 25-depth guidance that has a contact surface of 25mm.

5. Granules Applicator: TechNeat is the name of the aranular applicator developed specifically for arable farming and very useful in blackgrass control and wild oats. Generally a hydraulic fan or high-capacity electric fans are used. It has a 200L Hopper with a narrow width of around 550 mm. Electronic GPS system is attached to it. which helps in metering granules in a more accurate way. It is more suitable for drill and roll application. It has low-level filling height and can also be applied to seeds such as Rape and Mustard.

6. Cultivator: With the working widths of 3.0, 3.5 and 4.0 this is the perfect machine for the fast medium-deep to deep cultivation of soil and the intensive incorporation of straw residue. Catros+ is a program that provides a high output and robustness. It has a coupling frame between 9 and 12 meters. Land Rollers with a working width of 6 to 15 meters can do very smooth soil recompaction.

7. Inter-Row Hoeing Systems: The hoeing systems used in arable farming is Cameleon. This system is designed to farm without pesticides by providing more flexibility. It works as a seeder by drilling the crops in exact spacing, which allows for perfect inter-row hoeing. This system can also provide inter-row fertilization. This is far better than traditional technology as it provides more precision, reduces machine costs and has a much higher return. The seeding is also done very accurately and with less horsepower. It is being designed with several carriers with bout blades being mounted, which provides much more stability in maintaining the precision for hoeing.

8. Combination Drillers: The machine used here is AD-P Special 750 pneumatic seed driller. It has a quite compact design with a working width of around 4 meters. This driller was developed for medium-sized farms with a size of around 200 to 500 hectares as well as for agricultural contractors. It has a hopping capacity of 750I and can be increased up to 1000I. Seed drillers have passive soil tillage whenever there is a need of cost effective sowing with high work rates. With the help of the Cirrus machine mentioned above it is possible to achieve very precise sowing with higher output in medium to high yielding areas. The Green Drill seeder, which is Amazone's new solution, can be used in reseeding the grasses as well as sowing of cash crops.

2.2 MIXED FARMING

2.2.1 INTRODUCTION

2.2.1.1 What is Mixed Farming?

Mixed farming, as the name suggests, is a form of agriculture that involves both crops and livestock. The major benefit a farmer gets is crop rotation because with mixed farming there are several external and internal factors involved – external factors such as market prices, development of technologies over time, weather, and so forth. Internal factors relate to the means of the farmer and his family, soil characteristics, and so forth. Accounting for these factors, farmers can opt to do different farming combinations, according to which they can save resources. In this form of farming, farmers can do interchanging of crops development: for instance they can grow one crop at a particular place and after harvesting they can sow its seeds in some other place and grow another crop in the original place. With the increase in agricultural production there is a gradual disappearance of fallowing, which is a traditional mixed farming system [4]. This process of sowing permits the farmer better and wider crop rotations and greatly reduces dependence on chemicals as this technique allows more diversification which, in turn, is better for risk management.

This kind of practice has been common worldwide. It is found in places such as the northern parts of North America, the pampas of Argentina, and in New Zealand, Australia, South Africa and many other places. Mixed Farming is generally found in areas that are densely populated, industrialized and urban, societies dependent on high incomes from the sale of products. As it is found majorly in industrialized societies, it has higher agricultural returns due to some of the factors involved, such as excellent transport facilities, urban markets being closer to the farms, and efficient methods of farming. The cool moist summers and mild winters, not only enable the growth of hay crops, but also the pastures remain green every year and large flocks of sheep are grazed there. In some countries, such as Bangladesh, the farming systems are mixed where rice, livestock and pond aquaculture are being integrated on the same farm [5].

Grass occupies 20 percent of the cultivated land as it is an important crop of the mixed farming system. In the maritime regions, grass occupy up to 75 percent of the total cropped area. The main feature of mixed farming is that the farms produce both crops and livestock. Perennial pastures play an important role in supplying feed for livestock and restoring soil fertility and helps in combatting soil-borne diseases [6]. Wheat and maize are the dominating crops in Europe and the United States, respectively. In Europe the second most grown crops are potatoes, turnips and sugar beets. Most of a country's agriculture is highly dependent on mixed crop-livestock farming system [7]. While there is a high yield involved in mixed farming, there are lots of resources involved, such as high expenditures on farming, excessive use of fertilizers and manure and, more important, skilled farmers who have the correct knowledge to get the best from these resources.

2.2.1.2 History of Mixed Farming

According to a recent invention of the agricultural industrial complex, the term monocultural agriculture, which means planting single crops in enormous fields, was done. However, it doesn't match with the archaeological evidence as it is believed that most of the agricultural fields involved some kind of mixed farming even in the distant past. The primary reason for mixed farming during ancient times could be accounted for by the needs of the farming family. Even if the residues of plant crops are discovered in ancient fields it is very difficult to know that they have been the result of rotation cropping.

The standard instance for mixed farming can be that of the American three sisters: namely cucurbits, maize and beans. These three sisters combined to form one of the chief Native American cuisines. These three crops were given their names because they were interconnected as they grew. The planting method involved planting all three seeds in a same hole. As they grow the maize provides a stalk to the beans to climb, the beans contains more nutrients so they offset to those taken out by the maize and squash combats weed growth as it grows low to the ground and helps in preventing water evaporation from the soil.

2.2.1.3 Forms of Mixed Farming

Classification of mixed farming can be done in different ways based on the land size, geographical distribution, different types of crops and animals, orientation of market and so forth. Therefore, there are three main categories with four different modes of farming. These modes depend on availability of land and labor as well as inputs. It is quite important to understand the meaning of each of these forms of mixed farming and just by seeing these names it is somewhat difficult to understand, so let's consider the different types of mixed farming: A. Integrated vs diversified systems; B: Between farms versus on farm mixing; C: Mixing within crops and/or animal systems.

A. Integrated versus diversified system

Integrated systems are being carried out to recycle the resources efficiently. These kinds of systems are generally found in mixed ecological farms of temperate countries as well as in southwestern and southern parts of Australia, where there is relatively low input land. These systems are also found in tropical countries consisting of Low External Input Agricultural (LEIA) design farms where the by-product of one component serves as a resource for another. However, these systems tend to become more vulnerable to disturbance because the system often becomes become more complex due to mixing of resources.

On the other hand diversified systems contain components such as crops and livestock that co-exist independently from each other. The farmers who own High External Input Agricultural (HEIA) farms can have crops, pigs and dairy as independent units. Here unlike that of integrated systems, mixing of crops and livestock minimizes risk and the need to recycle resources.

B. Between farm vs on farm mixing

Between farms mixing refers to exchange of resources between two farms whereas on farm mixing refers to mixing the resources on the same farm. The between farm mixing most commonly occurs in High External Input Agriculture farm designs in countries such as Netherlands where this system is used to curb the waste coming from specialized farming. On the other hand on farm mixing occurs precisely in Low External Input Agricultural farm designs. The main motive of farmers here is to recycle the resources that come from their own farms. Between farms mixing occurs at a regional level in the storage cattle systems of the United States and United Kingdom. Here, animals are raised in one area and fed in other area where plenty of food (here grain) is available.

Exchanging crops and livestock between nearby farms has the same advantages as on farm mixing. It was believed that the pastoralists in West Africa and those from the Indian subcontinent also exchanged cattle and crop products with crop farmers. However, there are still some differences between transaction costs and social organization.

C. Mixing within crops and/or animal systems
    This kind of system refers to the conditions where multiple cropping is practiced over time as well as different types of animals are kept together on the farm itself. Mixing within crops and/or animal systems occurs more frequently but is not apparent. Within the crop mixing takes place where crop rotations have been practiced over years. For instance a farmer can do a rotation of potato-beet-grain in order to avoid disease in potatoes, so from this one can infer that this system requires really good skills and knowledge in order to perform crop rotations and trying out various combinations to maintain minimum damage to the crops. Apart from disease spreading, plant rotation also helps in taking maximum advantage of light and moisture in order to suppress weeds or prevent leaching of nutrients.

2.2.2 MODERN TECHNOLOGIES AND MACHINERIES USED

Mixed farming has this vast range of modern technologies which need to be distinguished. Some of them are:

1. Defusing versus accelerating technologies
2. Management and input based technologies
3. Technology for farmers and society
4. Regenerative and exploitative technologies
5. Exogenous and indigenous technologies

Let us look deeper into these modern technologies in order to differentiate them.

1. Defusing versus Accelerating Technologies: The difference between these two technologies is somewhat difficult. However it is related to exploitative and regenerative technologies. To understand accelerating technologies let us understand with examples. For instance, if a cow is given medicine that forces it to become pregnant even if the body is too weak to give birth. By forcing it to conceive again the cow will collapse and more inputs will be required to bring the cow back to shape. Cassava of the soils can be considered a good example of this technology. Cassava is the tuber crop for human consumption, and it grows well in poor soil which, in turn, exhausts an already poor soil even more.

    On the other hand defusing technologies is completely opposite to accelerating technology and considers the problem to a greater depth. It goes for the root causes and observes how the basic process can be stalled. Defusing technologies are often relevant in Natural Capital Accounting (NCA), and they tend to use fallow land. They require less usage of chemicals and instead rotation of crops, which enhances the fertility to combat weeds and reduce erosion.

2. Management and input based technologies: Input based technologies, also termed mechanization oriented technology, helps to increase the output

of a particular farm or animal by providing more inputs such as fertilizers, manure and pesticides, also by using machines (for instance robots) to save on labor, and even sometimes by digging wells if there is a shortage of water. On the other side, in management based technologies the primary focus is on understanding the combination of soils in farm, underground water reservoirs, people, plants, animals, and so forth. Proper management helps in avoiding loss whenever possible, for instance while building the sheds the housing can be unnecessarily built letting the sunshine enter the house or sun enters the time when it is actually needed. Another instance can be where the cow stands up in the morning and takes its time to stretch and to defecate so the farmer has to wait for some time before bringing the cow out so that he can collect urine and dung inside the shed itself.

3. Technology for farmers and society: In order to supply inputs, work on saving and credit as well as working on a watershed program, cooperatives are useful for farmer organizations in order to do more development. Sometimes not all technologies are useful for cooperative actions. For instance, vaccination campaigns require organization of groups. Also, many a time the birth of a child depends on the individual interests. The investment decision of farmers as well as cropping and livestock growing strategies are completely dependent on farmers along with their family members, whereas the farmers study groups is a total collective action and not an individual one.

4. Regenerative and exploitative technologies: This distinction comes from the defusing versus accelerating technologies, but it treats from the time horizon of farmers and its farming. As discussed in the previous topic, cassava grows well in poor soil and makes the already poor soil more exhausted. Investing in soil regeneration or planting of legumes gives a lower short-term yield but at the same time ensures a livelihood for future generations. The NCA mixed farming mode puts heavy emphasis on the regeneration with the involvement of technologies such as controlling erosion with planting of fodder crops, nutrients recycling, and mutual management of cropping and livestock.

5. Exogenous and indigenous technologies: The difference between exogenous and indigenous technologies is not so strict. It helps in pointing out the difference between solutions that were generated and collected over years by the legacy of farmers, whereas the solutions came from outside. Indigenous technology talks about the potential of creativity and local knowledge that helps in the modification of existing technologies, which can be used locally. With this knowledge farmers can come up with cheaper solutions generated from outside that would not have been possible otherwise. One of the examples of indigenous technologies is the ethnoveterinary medicines whereby woman have the knowledge of curing diseases in some animals using local herbs. With this the farmers also get the knowledge for the best timing to plough and harvest. Indigenous technology has no cure for all – for instance it has no way to cope with infectious diseases and new disorders coming up with the development. Still, the use of local knowledge improves the absorption of development programs.

2.3 SUBSISTENCE FARMING

2.3.1 INTRODUCTION

2.3.1.1 What Is Subsistence Farming?

Subsistence farming is a type of agriculture where farmers produces only the amount of food on their land required to feed their immediate family and their extended family members or a small community nearby. Rural communities across the globe depend majorly on access to land in order to sustain their livelihoods, while farming on communal lands that supports majority of people in the world [8]. The production as well as the output is limited and there is not much focus on trading as the production is for the locals living there. Many consider subsistence farming as living a backward lifestyle since there is not much exposure to the market for sale or trade, and farming communities should be transformed in to industrialized settlement operating commercial farming that can solve the problems of poverty and famine. The main characteristic of this farming is that it has a range of crops sufficient for feeding the locals for the entire year. In this mode of farming not only produces crops but animals, too, that can help the family in dairy, clothing, and so forth.

The annual decisions regarding what crops to cultivate each year is made with a vision of what the family will need in terms of food. In a nutshell, subsistence farmers are those that grow what they eat based on their family decisions, living without buying or selling anything from and to the market. One benefit is that the peasants practicing it choose harmony in human relationships and the environment without focusing on material wealth. Although poverty is an issue that needs to be overcome, the idea behind subsistence farming is ecologically appropriate, which helps in preserving the lives of all people around the world. So, let us go briefly through the features of subsistence farming:

1. Usually it is practiced on smaller pieces of land.
2. Moe involvement of family members in farming.
3. No high skills of specialization required.
4. Use of primitive and local tools such as scythes, hoes, and so forth.
5. The output or returns of this farming are minor.
6. It is usually practiced by peasants.
7. More unskilled laborers are hired.
8. Primary focus is to fulfil the family needs.
9. There is hardly any surplus for sale.
10. As the main focus is to fulfil the food needs of family, the area involved in this mode of agriculture is often small.

2.3.1.2 History of Subsistence Farming

Subsistence farming is still prevalent in parts of the world such as areas of Southeast Asia, sub-Saharan Africa, and parts of South and Central America. This mode of agriculture largely vanished in Europe during World War I, and in America with the departure of tenant farmers from South and Midwest during the years 1930 to 1940. It was the dominant mode of farming until the advent of market-based capitalism. The practice in these regions is an extension of primitive foraging that was carried out by the early civilizations. It was believed that the early farmers practiced subsistence farming in one way or another in order for survival. Communities such as the hunter and gatherer groups depended on hunting animals, collected fruits and vegetables and shared among all the members of the community. So, as time passed and with the evolution of certain plants and animals, there was a development of advanced subsistence society, where the communities practiced small-scale farming that efficiently produced enough to meet the consumption requirements of the community.

During previous times when mostly subsistence agriculture was practiced, there was a lot of freedom and some of these subsistence farming systems had similar structural traits. There was equal access to the lands for all the farmers who practiced this mode of farming, and there was a minimum amount spent the agricultural labor for producing subsistence amounts of foods. However, problems started to emerge as people started to lose their freedom which forced many subsistence farmers to abandon their traditional ways of farming. In Kenya during the twentieth century, the citizens were forced to shift toward commercial farming because there was a lack of land access as the British colonists commercialized certain farmlands.

During the sixteenth century, Japanese commercial farming gradually started dominating as the surpluses generated were far better than subsistence practices as it had been, and nineteenth-century Southern Africa allowed farmers to expend more agricultural labor on certain goods that were kept strictly for trade. As population density grew, and with the development of more intensive techniques in agriculture there was a commencement of a gradual shift from subsistence to commercial farming and industrialization, which then went on to become the most practiced and prominent way of farming. However, some countries such as Zambia, Mexico, Vietnam, Bolivia and few more still practice subsistence agriculture even in the twenty-first century.

2.3.1.3   Types of Subsistence Farming

Subsistence farming/agriculture is mainly divided into two subtypes:

    a.   Primitive Subsistence Farming
    b.   Intensive Subsistence Farming

Let us understand each of the categories of this mode of agriculture.

    a.   Primitive Subsistence Farming
         Primitive agriculture is also termed as simple subsistence cultivation. As discussed in previous topics of subsistence farming is still prevalent. People of this present generation have learned the art of domesticating crops by shifting from primitive gathering. Farmers who belong to this category grow crops only for themselves and their families. Small surpluses are exchanged by a barter system or sold for cash. There is only a very negligible chance of economic improvement but at the same time there is a

sense of independence among the farmers as they are not tied to landlords or any of the trading centers.

Primitive cultivation is generally practiced by various tribes living in South and Central America, Africa and Southeast Asia. Tribes living in the tropical regions practice this form of agriculture. Some of the names are the Ladang tribe in Malaysia, Caingin in the Philippines, Roca in Brazil, Tamrai in Thailand, and Milpa in parts of Central America. Asian tribes such as Chena in Sri Lanka and Poda tribe in India also practice a simple form of subsistence farming.

This mode of farming is usually characterized by certain features that clearly show the difference between a subsistence farm and an intensive farm. In subsistence farming the forests are burned and cleared. The ashes are added to the fertility of the soil. This type of agriculture is termed as slash-and-burn, where the trees that are not burnt are hacked out or sometimes left to decay naturally. The farming usually is done with very primitive tools like hoes and sticks without the involvement of machines or modern day equipment. Few types of crops are raised in these lands. Some of the crops are corn, millet, banana, cassava, beans and tapioca. Here once the crop grows in a shorter period of time, more effort is spent on fallowing so if the farm cannot support enough yield, then the farmers abandon that land and shift to another, which shows that they believe in farm rotation rather than crop rotation.

b. Intensive Subsistence Farming

This form of subsistence farming is completely different that that of the primitive type and, due to the change in the nature of agriculture with the advent of advanced technologies, it is somewhat unfair to now categorize subsistence farming. Yet it can be characterized as higher output per unit of land with a relative lower work per individual. So, even after the changes in intensive agriculture, this mode is still considered more sophisticated than primitive agriculture. This form of agriculture is developed and is especially productive in the monsoon lands of Asia. Therefore, it is found in countries such as India, Sri Lanka, Korea, Japan, Pakistan, China and some of the South-east Asian countries such as Java, Luzon, Malaysia and coastal Sumatra.

Farming in the terraced uplands and wet lowlands is rigorous in order to support dense population. Populations of some agricultural areas of Asia are quite high compared to that of those living in industrial areas in the West. The rigorous practice of tillage of lands is due to the increase in necessities due to the growth in population. A smaller size of farm now has to support more than ten times the number of people. Many of the regions with this mode of subsistence farming have a highly developed society as well as government where some countries such as India and China have a continuous civilization history ranging to more than 4,000 years.

In some areas there have been problems about the dwindling size of the farm plots, and for generations farms have been, causing them to become very small, which made them uneconomic. The average farm in Japan is around 1.5 acres, which is considered quite huge, but for some of the Asian countries such as India, Sri Lanka, and Pakistan that might not be the case. So, the peasants owning these lands grow crops to support their families as well as some for sale, too, if there are any surpluses. In monsoon Asia, the demand for growing food and utilizing every bit of land resources is so strong that the farmers use every bit of tillable land. To satisfy their needs, land is being cleared for cultivation by draining swamp areas, and making hilly farm lands flat for suitable farming. Several crops are grown on the same field by the farmers as the farming has been so intensive, which shows that the farmers in one way or the other believe in mixed farming. During the previous times primitive tools such as cangkul, ploughs, and so forth were used for farming, but now-a-days machines have been developed that have greatly reduced the human labor. Although these machines are not available to all the farmers due to the cost factor, they have gradually been entering the lives of farmers even in Asian countries such as India.

2.3.2 HARMONY BETWEEN MODERN WORLD AND SUBSISTENCE FARMING

With the advent of advanced technologies there has been a revolution in the agricultural field. Many developed nations have adapted to these technologies and implemented them in the farms, which have totally accepted the agricultural revolution and solved many global problems such as starvation and famine. However, for the underdeveloped as well as developing nations, the scenario is somewhat different. These countries are still dependent on subsistence farming despite the difficulties and hardship they face while performing farming activities. For these counties subsistence farming remains the only way to avoid starvation and famine. For subtropical regions such as Papua New Guinea and Colombia, subsistence farming has been ecologically efficient. In these regions rainfall levels are quite high and due to that various crops can be produced in a year. These conditions can prove very beneficial for small subsistence farms.

However, this scenario is not possible for regions such as sub-Saharan Africa where poverty and famine conditions are very high, but the main reason why subsistence farming has failed is that these populations experience growth which did not meet with the production of agricultural output through subsistence farming. Other factors are harsh climatic conditions, lack of proper infrastructural facilities and widespread disease among plants. In Zambia the population also depends on subsistence farming but the irrigation systems are meagre. Due to severe drought the population had to face a decline in food production and starvation issues.

Efforts are being made to shift from subsistence to commercial farming. As in Uganda, commercial farming has been promoted to reduce poverty throughout the subsistence communities. Many economists have started to promote commercial farming rather than subsistence farming in order to bring economic industrialization that will solve worldwide starvation. An alternative view is provided by ecofeminists that understanding sustainable economies is the foremost need. According to them the Western style that is optimal for all should be replaced by an ecological approach by valuing harmony with nature, human dignity and quality of life. They believed that subsistence is the empowerment for all, which showed people cooperation with the nature as well as among themselves. Although subsistence farming is not the ideal model, it works with nature to provide and maintain productivity. In a nutshell sustainability depends on harmony between people and the environment.

2.4 SHIFTING CULTIVATION

2.4.1 INTRODUCTION

2.4.1.1 What is Shifting Cultivation?

This mode of agriculture is also termed as slash-and-burn agriculture or swidden agriculture and is one of the most ancient farming systems [9]. This agriculture is mainly carried out in topical and subtropical areas supporting at least 35 million people [10, 11]. Cultivation involves a practice where a piece of land is alternatively used for crop production and then for the native vegetation for a certain period of years. So, a parcel of land is cleared for vegetation, the crops grow there for a couple of years and then it is left fallow for a period of as much as 10 years. For clearing the land in order to do cultivation, the existing vegetation is cut and debris is burned earning the name slash-and-burn agriculture. It is generally found in regions where techniques involved in farming are not advanced, and the nutrients content of soil is quite low. Due to the native and primitive techniques involved here the nutrients are depleted by cultivating crops, so after few years the land will support minimal plant growth. Then the land is used for native vegetation which takes certain years to concentrate nutrients back to the soil.

This cycle is continuously repeated, and the traditional agricultural system is practiced by self-made nomadic people. In the past when agriculture this mode of agriculture began, the system was practiced worldwide but in modern times it is found mostly in tropical rainforest areas. These farming systems are rapidly intensifying in some areas such as Southeast Asia, where there is shortening of fallow periods [12]. This system is generally practiced where population density is less and there is not much food demand to fulfil. But as the population keeps on rising the demand for food also increases, which eventually leads to the lands that are being abandoned for concentrating nutrients is being taken up to use again, but not given enough time to recover, which leads to the depletion of nutrients and even degradation of forest to scrub or woodland types. There has been several resettlement programs that provide people with livelihood opportunities and weaning shifting cultivations [13]. Although it is not very productive it still provides a living to the people as well as to afford basic fertilizers and tools. Soil erosion is also reduced as most of the time land is not cultivated.

Shifting cultivation has frequently been criticized by agriculturalists due to its obsolete methods, which destroy the soil as well as the underground nutrients. Nevertheless, shifting agriculture is most suitable for tropical conditions, which supports continuous and long-term cultivation without much use of fertilizers – as well, advanced techniques for soil cultivation will be extremely harmful for soil. According to a report by the United Nations more than 250 million people derive subsistence from shifting cultivation, and its ecological consequences can be very harmful. Different regions of the world have different names of shifting cultivation and diverse forms. So, some of the local names of shifting cultivation in the world are Ray in Vietnam, Tavi in Madagascar, Masole in Congo, Comile in Mexico, Milya in Central America and Mexico, Roka in Brazil, Ladang and Humah in Java, Jhum in Northeast India, Konuko in Venezuela, Milpa in Yucatan and Logan in Western Africa. In the developing countries shifting cultivation is a traditional land-use practice in tropical landscapes [14].

2.4.1.2   History of Shifting Agriculture

Shifting cultivation is the oldest and most primitive mode of agriculture and can be traced back to the Neolithic period about 8,000 BC. During that time this mode of agriculture brought a drastic revolutionary shift in the food production – a complete shift from hunter-gatherers to food producers. Right from the beginning, shifting agriculture has been characterized as rotation of fields rather than land, excessive use of human labor, usage of sticks or hoes, absence of manuring, alternative shift from growing crops to leaving the land for a period of 5–10 years in order to concentrate nutrients. Subsistence agriculture as well as the forests near to it tend to provide alternative subsistence sources practicing it. When there is crop failure forest resources increase their food supplies and provide building materials, wood, timber and fuel.

In some of the hilly regions of India such as the "seven sisters" – Assam, Tripura, Mizoram, Nagaland, Meghalaya, Nagaland and Arunachal Pradesh – shifting cultivation is been practiced. Commonly known as *jhum* in India, shifting cultivation continues to be dominant mode of food production as well as the economic mainstay of many rural households. Between October to December the villages that practice this mode of agriculture begin the process of shifting cultivation by selecting land near to a hilly region or forests. This decision is taken sometimes by village elders, clan leaders or even in some tribes this decision is taken by the whole community. While selecting the land the size of plot as well as the workforce in the family is taken in to consideration because, after all, farmer families have to carry out all the farming activities.

The land-clearing process, which is the first step before the commencement of cultivation is very labor intensive, which can take approximately an entire month, done entirely with traditional equipment. Householders remove certain useful biomass such as trunks, big branches, and boles for building and to satisfy firewood and timber requirements while the debris that is remaining and of not much use is left to dry. There is an issue of crops catching fires so special care is taken such that the fire cannot spread much. The ashes are scattered over the ground and, before the advent of monsoon, dibbling of seeds takes place. Planting and dibbling of seeds is the primary job of women. Men broadcast seeds of crops such as millets whereas crops such as maize, cotton, vegetables and pulses are sown by women. Crops are tended regularly by removing weeds and shifting cultivators.

People during these times give major importance to crop protection. Crops are enclosed by bamboo fences in order to protect them from wild animals and stray cattle. Many shifting cultivators also construct huts in the field to look after the crops. Sometimes the shifting cultivators even practiced mixed cultivation where they grew soil-exhausting crops such as millets, maize, rice, and soil-enriching nutrients such as legumes are grown together. This kind of practice is followed for two to three years and then that land is being fallowed for nutrients to concentrate. Some of the cash crops such as linseed, ginger, rapeseed, orange, pineapple and jute are also grown under *jhum* agriculture. These cash crops are generally sold in nearby markets and, in recent years, the sale has been done in markets with urban settlements and in large towns.

2.4.2 Tools Used in Shifting Cultivation

Different communities use various types of tools for day-to-day agricultural practices. These are not very modern tools or machinery but still a lot of people have to engage with these tools in order to carry out the tasks. Some of the tools used in shifting agriculture are as follows:

1. Lepok – Also known as Naga-Dao used for cutting the vegetation. As discussed land needs to be cleared for cultivating crops so this tool helps in removing the vegetation. Removing dry biomass for firewood is important after clearing land. To clear vegetation of around 95,000 ha Jhum land, a work force of 11.9 million is required using Lepok.
2. Kheya – This tool is made from bamboo or wood for removing weeds and unwanted particles in the *jhum* field. In order to remove unwanted particles and plants from a land of 95,000 ha, a workforce of 6.8 million is needed.
3. Spade – Also termed Choktchii and used for land development of *Jhum* land. It is mostly used for digging for preparing the seedbed. To prepare a land of 95,000 ha using choktchii, a total of 9.5 million man days is required.
4. Dibbling/making hole for seed sowing – Dibblers originally made from bamboo or wood are used for planting of seeds for land preparation. A total of 5.9 million man-days is required on *jhum* land for dibbling the seeds of 95,000 ha of land.
5. Kholo – Used for threshing paddy crops this tool is made from wood or bamboo and looks like a wooden stick. It is used as a threshing device that helps in removing paddy from the straw. Approximately a 531,000 workforce annually is required on the *jhum* land for threshing of crops.
6. Vekhuro – Commonly known as a sickle, this tool mainly helps in harvesting the crops in *jhum* land. A total of around 4.7 million man-days is required annually for harvesting the crops in the *jhum* fields.
7. Moro – Made from bamboo and cane; this tool is mainly used for winnowing of threshed crop by separating grains from unwanted particles. Annually a total workforce of 265,000 is required for winnowing the threshed crops in *jhum* land.
8. Ehe – Commonly known as a hand weeder, this tool is also made from wood or bamboo. Annually in the *jhum* field around 5.4 million man-days is required for removing weeds from the crops in *jhum* areas.

2.4.3 Features of Shifting Cultivation

Various land activities are involved in shifting cultivation, due to which this mode of agriculture is cyclical. The stages and features vary in different shifting cultivation cycles but is very difficult to distinguish. For instance in the montane form of shifting agriculture the cycle is comprised of six stages: burning, clearing, planting, weeding, and protecting, harvesting and succession. Figure 2.1 shows the graphic portrayals of the main general stages of shifting cultivation and its relation to village growth.

The cropping cycles of shifting cultivation shows planting, maintenance, harvesting and protection of flora that are being introduced. Varieties of crops and different ways of planting them vary from one shifting cultivator to another. Intercropping of varieties of the same crop species takes place, followed by a fallow period during which natural vegetation of that particular land is allowed to grow, which restores the soil nutrients. Even in the modern times the tribes that follow traditional shifting practices are closely tied to spiritual and cultural activities. For instance religious beliefs are closely linked to swiddening in the upland regions of the Philippines, especially in sites such as land selection, clearing vegetation, firing, planting of crops, and harvesting. Such complexity of culture has been seen in many countries where shifting cultivation is practiced.

2.4.4   PROBLEMS AND PROSPECTS OF SHIFTING CULTIVATION

As discussed previously, the prerequisite of shifting is the land clearance. Clearing of bushes, cutting of trees not only increase soil erosion but also increase the prominence of rainfall variability and can cause droughts or floods. This leads to increase in soil fertility. Due to this the ecosystem loses its resilience. The nutritional standard goes down and there is a shortage of food and fodder among the community practicing shifting agriculture. Fallowing in shifting cultivation is indirectly proportional to the biomass and soil erosion, that is, the more time is given to gathering the nutrients less will be soil erosion and loss of biomass. So, as the shifting cultivation cycles shorten the biomass cultivation time on which humus of soil depends and gets considerably reduced, there are some serious negative impacts, which lead to the loss of biodiversity, too.

There are divergent opinions about the adverse effect of shifting cultivation and what damage it can cause to the environment. Many environmentalists and ecologists holds the view that it is very primitive and depletes the forests, soil and water resources. According to them *jhuming* should be stopped completely as it damages the ecosystem. On the other hand some promote this mode of agriculture and favor the continuance of it. According to them the necessary reforms in shifting cultivation do little damage to the soil erosion as heavy rainfall and high humidity don't permit the soil to remain uncovered for long period of time. They further stated that some vegetation forms cover top soil which checks soil erosion.

While carrying out agricultural operations during shifting agriculture certain tasks such as ploughing, pulverization and hoeing of soil help in making soil compact. *Jhuming* lands are generally steep slopes where sedentary cultivation develops easily. People practice it for their livelihoods, not thinking about its adverse and negative impact on the environment. So, there is an alternative needed to make the process more productive in order to sustain the increasing pressure of the *jhum* population with a reasonably good standards. It can be a good practice to provide *jhumia* with land where each of them can cultivate and derive the profits permanently. Another

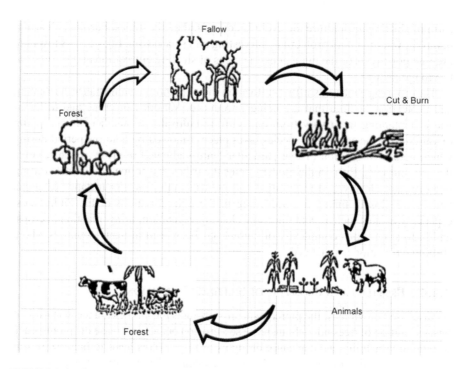

FIGURE 2.1   Stages of shifting cultivation.

main approach to overcoming the issues of shifting cultivation is to modify the *jhuming* lands to sedentary farms.

Terraces should constructed in the hilly areas, which can also prove better for shifting cultivation. Developing terraces varies from one ecosystem to another and these terraces have an advantage of achieving sedentary farming in areas where shifting cultivation is practiced. Most planners believe that terracing plays a major role if agricultural land used in the hilly regions is made more efficient. Apart from terracing, other measures such as trenching, bundling, gully ploughing, protective covers forests, grasses, cash crops and leguminous crops. Although shifting cultivation has no potential over subsistence farming, it provides food, medicines, firewood and other domestic needs to the farmers and their families.

2.5   PLANTATION CULTIVATION

2.5.1   INTRODUCTION

2.5.1.1   What is Plantation Agriculture?

Plantation Agriculture is a form of commercial farming where crops are grown in order to earn profit. This agriculture involves growing and processing of a single cash crop just for sale purposes. This kind of agriculture is mainly practiced in countries that experience tropical climates with high annual rainfall along with high temperatures. Some of the important crops that come under plantation agriculture are coffee, rubber, spices, tea, fruits and coconuts. It is a single and intensive crop farming which requires huge amounts of capital. It is generally practiced in large farms, and all the crops grown are solely for the market. This mode of agriculture requires intensive labor, sophisticated machineries, vast estates, fertilizers, good transport facility, technical knowledge and factories for processing. It is being practiced in almost all the countries across the globe including India, where some of the regions are Nilgiri, north-eastern India, West Bengal and the sub-Himalayan regions. Efficiency of plantation farming is directly proportional to the harvesting period. The longer the harvest period, the better the quality of crops harvested.

In this mode of agriculture large farms in American colonies used slaves as labor to plant and harvest cotton, sugar, rice, tobacco and other farm products for trade and export. Here a single species of crop is grown on a large field. Plantation farming is completely opposite to subsistence farming because here the crops are sold for profit in markets and not used for personal use as it was in subsistence farming. It is focused on mass production of agriculture requiring a large labor workforce. Among the American colonies that practiced plantation farming were Maryland, Georgia, the Carolinas (North and South), and Virginia. As transportation plays a major role in this cultivation so the waterways of South provided a good transportation system.

Vast areas of farms are required for plantation farming, so those farms needed to be cleared for growing cash crops, which require a labor workforce. Generally plantation sizes ranged from 500 to 1,000 acres with each farm containing around 5,000 plants. Crops grown were traded for items such as fine lace, shoes, farm tools and dishes, which were not much produced in plantation country. Plantation farming was generally found in tropical regions, that is. near to the equator so the countries having tropical climates such as Asia, North America, Latin America, and Africa were favored. Coffee, sugarcane, banana and tea plantations occupied the most percentage of plantation farms. Coffee plantations were found in Bolivia, Tanzania, Kenya, Brazil and Paraguay; tea plantations in Sri Lanka, Indonesia and India; sugarcane plantation in Brazil, Peru, Philippines and Cuba; banana plantations in Columbia, Mexico, Costa Rica, Jamaica and Panama. These countries export their crops overseas and the main focus of this cultivation is export-oriented where financial profit is the main objective.

2.5.1.2   History of Plantation Farming

Plantation Agriculture originated in the sixteenth century when the Europeans started dominating the New World. Tropical crops were grown on a larger scale and exported to the temperate world, which constituted the extension of temperate technology to the tropical world. It was termed corporate agriculture, as its primary focus was on commercial production. This system originated in Brazil, with the involvement of Portuguese settlements. The earliest major plantations were in Recife, the Northeast, and then spread to the South, north to the islands of the Caribbean and at last to the American South. Gradually plantation agriculture started spreading into Central America. The Portuguese main interest was at first Asia and Africa and not America. Large landgrants were given by the royalty, establishing plantations along the coastal plains 150 miles wide. Their main focus originally was in gold, but there was no gold to exploit so they focused on tropical crops for their profits.

Sugar was chief crop for the Portuguese who cultivated it in islands to the west of Africa, the Azores and Capo Verde. The Portuguese had learned to cultivate sugar from the Middle East when it was introduced in the Crusades, and its original source was traced to India. The Portuguese had to shift to African slaves, as Indian slaves did not make good laborers. Slaves were used in the sugar industry of Madeira and available from trading stations along the west coast of Africa. The original plantation cultivation was based on European domination of the American colonial system and their labors being exported to Europe. The colonial plantation system reached its development peak in the West Indies in a time of great fortunes and debts. The main reason for collapse of the system was due to the great debt in part because the slave system had been declining. By the eighteenth century plantation society comprised white owners and a large populations of black slaves.

During the colonial period this mode of agriculture existed in various regions of the United States, but it was more synonymous with the South. American colonists manufactured glass, silk by raising mulberry trees, growing grapes for wine production and timber production from harvesting of wood. Tobacco emerged as the crops that offered great potential for profits. However the problem was that the tobacco plants quickly drained the soil nutrients so those fields became unusable and had to be cleared. Gradually the planters started looking for lands in the South and West as the land of Maryland, Virginia and Delaware became unproductive during the colonial period. These plantations were so large that it required a labor force of thousands to carry out day-to-day plantation activities. Slaves had to do a lot of work from sunrise to sunset and got little rest during the entire day with a very minimum wage. Slaves during those times maintained a sense of community among one another and encouraged relationships through family, friends and religion, which helped them survive the brutal labor system. Slavery was ended in the year 1865 but replaced by another form of labor. Many freed slaves returned to work as tenant farmers who rented land from white owners and received part of the crops, not wages. They raised livestock, grew cotton and other agricultural products on those farms.

2.5.2 Characteristics of Plantation Farming

After discussing the meaning and history of plantation agriculture let us understand how different it was from other modes of agriculture. The characteristics of plantation agriculture were as follows:

1. Plantation farming requires scientific methods and highly sophisticated machines for large scale production. The size of the farms is huge, covering thousands of hectares and is generally run by private companies.
2. At any given time a single crop is planted so there is a mono-crop specialization in plantation farming such as tea in India, coffee in Brazil and so forth.
3. Small holdings play a major role in the success of cash crops that are grown in hundreds of acres of lands so the farmers encourage growing such crops on small holdings, which exist side-by-side with the big farms.
4. Farming in estates requires specialized skills with the right application of machinery and fertilizers. This could give high yields, good quality of

production and higher output, most of which gets exported. The final cash crop products such as tea, sheet rubber and palm oil needed to be carefully processed in order to meet the high standards and world demand.

5. The owner of large estates were generally foreigners. Most of the large estates were owned by Europeans. Most Malaysian rubber estates were owned by British companies and were managed by Englishmen. The British established tea gardens in India and Sri Lanka, with banana and sugar farms in the West Indies. The French established coffee and cocoa plantations in West Africa. Some of the large farms of coffee in Brazil are still owned by Portuguese but belong to wealthy Brazilians.

6. Plantation agriculture is both labor- as well as capital intensive. Large numbers of workers are employed, recruited from neighboring countries, which leads to the development of pluralist societies. Apart from labor a lot of capital investment is required in these farms. Plantations generally own huge factories for processing crops, and they have their own infrastructure.

7. Many plantations buy the same product from small-scale farmers in order to increase their output. This agriculture is generally practiced in areas where population is sparse.

8. The crops cultivated are generally exported to other countries in international markets, which requires packaging, a processing facility and, most important, a better communication network. Unlike other forms of agriculture this one is well planned and has facilities such as hospitals, residences, retail markets, and transport for workers and their families. Here cultural exchange also occurs as thousands of workers need to migrate from one place to another for work.

9. It has been proven that even if plantation agriculture was located previously on sparsely or underdeveloped areas, a minimum mode of communication either by road or rail had to be developed with or without government assistance, and which requires large sums of money. These plantations mostly appeared in tropical places where the cost of maintenance is very high. The overall cost of production is very high, especially in Indian and Sri Lanka tea estates due to the unionized laborers.

2.6 TYPES OF PLANTATIONS

Plantation enterprises differed from other land-use enterprises in various ways and also differed from one another. Michel-Rolph Trouillot, an anthropologist spoke about the plantations that these never existed historically not even in the Americas of slavery. Instead, hundreds of plantations existed offering challenges to the plantation ideal. Here we are going to cover four major kinds of plantations, namely sugar, rice, cotton and tobacco, along with their social organization and labor requirements.

1. Sugar Plantations – These were typically one of the largest and were privately owned, with enslaved African populations vastly outnumbering the whites. Nearly two thirds of the Africans entering the United States worked in sugar plantations. Women accounted for more than 50 percent of the total workforce

throughout the Caribbean and played a major role in the production of sugar. Places such as Barbados, St. Kitts, Jamaica, Haiti and Antigua had sugar as a chief commodity and here the African population remained dominant. Sugar plantations were regarded as the most labor-intensive and demanding among all the plantations. It requires both industrial and agricultural component which not only demands high skills but a proper division of labor, too. In order to produce granulated sugar, molasses and other sugar-based products various steps are involved, such as harvesting and grinding cane, boiling extracted juice to high temperatures and producing and curing crystallized sugar . Cane once harvested needs to be process immediately to avoid spoiling. European owners took a lot of benefit and knowledge from African workers, which made their sugar production very smooth but at the same time underscored the heavy toll exacted on African slave life.

2. Rice Plantations – As compared to sugar, tobacco and cotton the rice plantation enterprise was comparatively small, but for 200 years it was important for South Carolina, Florida and Georgia. Merchants and rice planter families created an elite society. The cultivation of rice has added wealth to the provinces and a trade of active commerce started flourishing. Maintenance of rice fields was very important, and the rice fields depended heavily on water as the land must be saturated in order to favor the growth of rice, and lot of work is required for the initial setup of rice field as well as maintenance of fields. In the years 1740–1760 there was an increase in African slave population along with the increase in production of rice, too, and about two-thirds of that population was there in South Carolina.

There were many instances where swamplands were created containing cypress forests that were cleared followed by the construction of canals and ditches to provide huge irrigation system. These systems then required constant maintenance to remain in a working condition and be as efficient as in the beginning. With the increase in African laborers these artificial systems were maintained in a very proper way. An island named Jehossee on the coast of South Carolina had the most successful rice production with the most successful rice business in the world carried out here and about 95 percent of the population was Africans.

3. Cotton Plantations – The domination of cotton as the chief crop in the eighteenth century was due to massive forced migration of enslaved Africans from the coast to the interior regions of America. Before cotton, tobacco was the crop that was flourishing, but it majorly depended on fresh soils and there was very short range migration. In that century more than 800,000 black people migrated to cotton-producing states and many of these Africans were from tobacco areas or the rice areas. Cotton farms ranged from forty to thousands of acres. The chief reason behind that was due to the growing market of cottons in the eighteenth century. During that period the cultivation demand of cotton was far more than tobacco and the market was readily available.

This requires two different types of labor, namely an initial and established form of labors. The initial work of labor is to clear the uncultivated land and make it ready for cultivation, whereas the work of established labor groups is planting and harvesting cotton. Clearing of uncultivated land was generally done by male laborers as it required more strength and not more skills, whereas harvesting was done more by female workers and were ranked more productive than male ones. African slaves were required to work in a tightly supervised group from the sunrise to sunset. The African slaves who were part of the cotton plantation had lives more strict and tough as compared to those African slaves, who worked in tobacco or rice plantations and were not able to utilize their personal skills and knowledge, as workers were required to use a narrow range of skills for maintaining plantation operations due to limited requirements of cotton processing.

4. Tobacco Plantations – In the beginning of eighteenth century the demand for tobacco increased in European markets, especially in France, which caused the planter communities to focus on production in the colonies of Maryland and Virginia. The planters purchased African slaves, which led to the increase in tobacco production in the Piedmont region. The laws were made against black people (mostly Africans) that made their life very tough and increased white power. These laws brought both free and enslaved whites under the same category, and the free black people were treated the same as enslaved ones. Tobacco plantation was regarded as less labor-intensive compared to the other three plantations. These plantations were generally small with less than 30 slaves in a single plantation. Growing tobacco was consistent throughout the year, and there was little to no change in the growth due to seasonal fluctuations.

The leaves of tobacco ripened seasonally and need to be picked at the right time for optimal value. Tobacco plantations were completely dependent on planting and harvesting tobacco leaves, which required constant attention throughout the year. A limited amount of processing and then harvesting is required. Production of tobacco leaves required a constant supply of soil rich in nutrients. But in the middle of the eighteenth century there was a decline in tobacco production with a gradual rise in grain production. Tobacco plantation economy was then dominated by women and their children, who were then considered ideal laborers by the tobacco planters.

2.7 PRECISION FARMING

2.7.1 INTRODUCTION

2.7.1.1 What is Precision Farming?

The precision mode of farming is termed the most advanced form of agricultural practice among all other cultivation. It focuses on managing soil, water and climate with much accuracy in order to grow food with higher productivity by causing less harm to the environment. Modern technologies are involved at every stage of work in this agriculture. Due to the division of zones and with each zone being heterogeneous farmers can efficiently use the pesticides, fertilizers and seeds. While in traditional modes of agriculture farmers apply the same amount of fertilizers, pest control and carry out irrigation activities equally irrespective of the crops growing on any particular field. However, precision farming targets the spatial differences in the farm and optimizes the output. This farming follow the principle of Variable Rate Application which states that inputs are given in the amount needed, the place where it is needed and when it is needed. Precision livestock farming plays an important role in achieving sustainable development of small farms, and there is a rapid need to increase the involvement of intelligent technologies[15].

There have been various stages involved in agriculture, which can be improved using the technologies involved in precision farming while keeping costs low, such as soil sampling, replanting, irrigation, applying fertilizers, pests and disease control, harvesting, transportation and storage. The technologies developed have resulted in a scope of possibilities to improve all the stages aforementioned in precision farming. Some of technologies that have brought an evolution and shaped the agricultural sectors are geo-mapping technology, remote sensing, autonomous steering vehicles, communication technologies integration in machines, various kinds of sensors involved in the agriculture, precision positioning systems such as GPS, GNSS, variable rate technology and many more subtypes of them. The data collected by the sensors and other devices is being analyzed and maintains documentation by computers, mobile devices, tablets which help to manage the farm efficiently.

Precision farming is sometimes complicated for some farmers of any private companies owing large farms as they have not used a particular technology or machine newly introduced before. However, it is not always expensive because there are simple technological solutions available to every farmer. Precision farming can be sometimes expensive and sometimes not. Yes, due to the high cost of special equipment and software for farms, these technologies are generally found in huge farms. Most of the applications are free so farmers need a smart phone and Internet access. Although it was originated in the 1980s the idea behind this agriculture increased only in approximately the past ten years due to the development of mobile technology, access to satellite data to the companies and farmers with high-speed Internet.

2.7.1.2   History of Precision Farming

Precision Farming started in the year 1996 when Louis van den Bourne took the first step in precision farming. An on-board computer named Uni-Control-S was linked to a spray registration system that can be used on many agricultural machines in order to measure, check, control and store the data. This registration was done automatically by measuring fuel consumption for doing personal registration. In 1998 the chip card of the on-board computer was supported by Comwaes. However, Comwaes was no longer able to support the chip card as MS-DOS was shifted to Windows 3.1 due to which the system became useless. In the same year first steps were taken with respect to the registration of field boundaries and a French software named ISAplan was developed for geo data, which made the processing of data possible and the name of program was ISAGPS.

In 1998, with the help of Uni Control S system the first potato disease model was tried out with a weather station set up especially for this. This model worked on the point system, which means since it was a sprayer the plots that are more susceptible to diseases are on the top of the list. Back at the station the computer calculated the amount of spraying per hectare. Later, in 2000, Van der Borne in his college days did an internship at Grimme where the employees were working on yield measurements and the sensors of the harvester were tested on Van der Borne's potatoes so the sensors were purchased and mounted on the potato harvester. In 2004 a fertilizer spreader was bought which could determine the amount of fertilizer that was spread on each plot. This machine was able to spray variable amounts of doses to the left and right. The dosages can be adjusted manually as there is no software that can dose controlled amounts from the left as well as from the right. Later in the same year a hydraulic poter was purchased that allowed 10 percent more seed planting than normal in the middle row in between the two ridges next to the spray paths.

In 2009 focus was primarily on improving the accuracy of the GPS system and how much more deviation the GPS can provide and were fitted in the devices such as Hassia CP. There was an extension of autopilot in the GPS system, which allowed two tractors to move in the same field at the same time, which could cause less harvesting damage. In 2010, an autonomous vehicle was deployed for scanning the soil. It would operate within fixed boundaries and a program was employed to map all the parcels. In 2011, the Hassia CP, which had a section for control technology was equipped with GPS in that year and a software named HMI GPS Planting Comfort was installed, which made sure that the four planting elements were switched at the correct time. Drones were flown for the first time this year, which contained multi-spectral cameras that showed what land needed more or less fertilization.

In 2012, a contract worker named Danny Goris bought a three-axis manure spreader, which helped in spreading variable soil manure and helped in site-specific fertilization. In 2013 a three-axle self-propelled sprayer with double tank with a capacity of 12,000 liters was purchased. In 2016, new drones were bought, with one capable of handling heavy loads and could hang heavy cameras and sensors under it.

2.7.2 CROP GROWTH CYCLE IN PRECISION AGRICULTURE

There are majorly five steps involved in this cycle, namely,

Soil preparation; precision seeding; precision management of crops; precision crop harvesting; data generation and analysis

    a. Soil Preparation – This is the initial step, which is often overlooked by farmers, and the impact of surface water management on the crop growth is also not being taken care of. Preparation of soil needs to be planned properly. There needs to be a detailed study of the soil type and land topography from the survey maps. The soil physical property, such as its texture and water availability for particular plants needs to be checked from the property maps. The last and the most important is the yield maps of the crops that were grown previously in order to find out the condition of the soil and whether the next plantation can be planted here or not. By studying these maps and following right agricultural practices, one can obtain optimum results with the soil preparation.

b. Precision seeding – Sowing of seeds in an optimum manner is the most crucial in a way that if fewer seeds are sown but at a correct depth and with proper row spacing, then those can yield much better results compared to sowing more seeds, and this can save money, too. When geo-mapping is used, more seeds can be planted in soil with chances of a higher yield. Seeds are not wasted in places with less yield production areas and effective VRT (variable rate application) of fertilizers is achieved. Uniform generation is the key for optimum germination of seeds, so effective tillage practices is important to ensure that the farmer is equipped with better technology for optimum yield.

c. Precision management of crops – Managing the fields and making sure that there is no harm to the growth of plants is a crucial part of this process. Farmers should make sure that there is right amount of top-dressing at the right time as well as proper management of weeds, pests and diseases. Various modern devices such as crop sensors, autonomous steering vehicles, and so forth are used for eliminating the risk of under and over fertilization as well as reduced spraying.

d. Precision crop harvesting – As the name suggests, this is the final step of the precision crop production cycle. But at the same time this is the most critical step too as the success of all the previously mentioned steps is determined by three factors, namely, speed, timing and accuracy. The next crop production cycles depend on the success of this crop harvesting step.

e. Data generation and analysis – Although harvesting is considered the final step of production cycles, this cycle officially ends in the data evaluation step. It is necessary to identify various points from the short- and long-term data generated out of this cycle. Such environmental effects this one cycle has caused, and if it is somewhat harmful then the necessary steps taken to reduce the effect, profit or loss in the individual management zones, roles the communication systems, technology, sensors, and so forth, have played in one entire cycle. And the last important point is the new strategy that needs to build up in order to overcome the loss or the disadvantages encountered in the previous crop production cycle.

2.7.3 ADVANCE TECHNOLOGIES INVOLVED IN PRECISION FARMING

In the modern century, with the advent of modern technologies, there has been a drastic revolution in agriculture. With the blend of Artificial Intelligence and Internet of Things the machines that were developed have completely changed the agricultural field. Devices and technologies such as drones, GPS, sensors, robotics, and so forth have not only increased the production of food but also helped in monitoring the crops and their health. Let us consider the list of technologies shaping precision agriculture.

1. Robotics – This term has gained so much importance in the past few years and is being termed by experts as the carrier of future generations. The involvement of these machines in agriculture has really shaped the industry. They

are capable of handling many tasks these days by reducing the work load on human laborers and with a higher success rate sometimes compared to humans. Especially the autonomous vehicles that are controlled using telematics. Controlled remotely these vehicles are capable of doing various tasks such as planting greenhouse crops, pruning vineyards, picking fruits and vegetables such that it does not affect the plants, spraying fertilizers and so forth.

2. Global Positioning System (GPS) – Precision agriculture as the name suggests requires a lot of accuracy. So, the machines in which the GPS technology is involved provide a perfect line of path. This technology made managing the field work of farmers much easier and done with higher accuracy, and global manufacturers have found various ways to tie in to these tools.

3. Mobiles – The development of mobile devices and tablets is the next most best innovation in the past few years, and what an impact it can have on precision farming. Mobile devices has made the work so much easier for us as it helps in connecting various people from different parts of the world; from these devices one can monitor the condition of crops, control various devices connected over IOT, display of technical data about agriculture at the right time to farmers, alarm system in their mobile and tablets whenever there is any danger of wild animals. According to the experts in the present day the number of mobile devices outnumbers the humans.

4. Irrigation – Farmers usually face the scarcity of water due to drought, less water allocation, and sometimes depletion of water underground. So, the with the evolvement of technologies, work has been going on to solve or eradicate this issue of which one recent advancement was that of telemetry and adoption to valley irrigation. Soil moisture monitoring and the facility to monitor weather data have also been included in various devices. These advanced products allow farmers to monitor every flow of irrigation and helps in saving water, time, and also fuel of those vehicles.

5. Sensors – Another important component in agricultural technology is sensors. Various wireless sensors capable of performing different tasks by gathering data for various factors such as soil fertility, soil compaction, plant water status, weather data, and water availability in the soil, infestation of diseases such as weeds and many more. Irrigation scheduling is one of the most important things that needs to be monitored using sensors, especially in countries such as India because of the possibility of water scarcity in some areas and less wastage of water in areas where there is excess.

6. Weather Modelling – Weather trackers installed along with the knowledge of how to use and understand them is very important for farmers in order to maintain better growth of crops as well as their health condition. Weather is the only factor that is highly fluctuating and is the main factor affecting plants and related activities. For instance, a potato grower named Keiser found harvesting potatoes at a certain temperature helped in maintaining integrity and crop quality.

7. Internet of Things (IOT) – Another technology that has been equally as important as Artificial Intelligence in this field and has immense potential of

changing things around is IOT. It connects any device with a switch to the Internet. With this technology the devices could communicate with each other efficiently and help in connecting agricultural components such as field sensors to satellites for monitoring of fields.

REFERENCES

[1] A.V. Henriksen, G.T.C Edwards, L.A. Pesonen, O. Green, C.A.G. Sorensen (2020). "Internet of Things in Arable Farming: Implementation, applications, challenges and potential." *Biosystems Engineering* vol. 191, 60–84. https://doi.org/10.1016/j.biosystemseng.2019.12.013

[2] V. Kuzmanovski, D.E. Larsen, C.B. Henriksen. (2019). "Optimization of arable land use towards meat-free and climate-smart agriculture: A case study in food self-sufficiency of Vietnam." *IEEE Explore*, International Conference on Big Data, Los Angeles, December. https://ieeexplore.ieee.org/document/9006264

[3] T.N. Bwana, N.A. Amuri, E. Semu, L. Elsgaard, K. ButterbachBahl, D.E. Pelster, J.E. Olesen (2021). Soil N2O emission from organic and conventional cotton farming in Northern Tanzania. *Science of the Total Environment* vol. 785, 147301. https://doi.org/10.1016/j.scitotenv.2021.147301

[4] A. Bisson, S. Boudsocq, C. Casenave, S. Barot, R.J. Manlay, J. Vayssieres, D. Masse, T. Daufresne (2019). "West African mixed farming systems as meta-ecosystems: A source-sink modelling approach." *Ecological Modelling* vol. 412, 108803. https://doi.org/10.1016/j.ecolmodel.2019.108803

[5] S. Aravindakshan, T.J Krupnik, J.C.J. Groot, E.N. Speelman, T.S. Amjath-Babu, P. Tittonell (2020). "Multi-level socioecological drivers of agrarian change: Longitudinal evidence from mixed rice-livestock-aquaculture farming systems of Bangladesh." *Agricultural Systems* vol. 177, 102695. https://doi.org/10.1016/j.agsy.2019.102695

[6] G.D. Li, G.D. Schwenke, R.C Hayes, A.J. Lowrie, R.J. Lowrie, A. Price (2021). "Perennial pastures reduce nitrous oxide emissions in mixed farming systems in a semi-arid environment." *Science of the Total Environment* vol. 834, 155304. https://doi.org/10.1016/j.scitotenv.2022.155304

[7] T. Bayissa, B. Dugumaa, K. Desalegn (2022). "Chemical composition of major livestock feed resources in the medium and low agroecological zones in the mixed farming system of Haru District, Ethiopia." *Heliyon* vol. 8, no. 2, e09012. https://doi.org/10.1016/j.heliyon.2022.e09012

[8] Z. Lidzhegu and T. Kabanda (2022). "Declining land for subsistence and small-scale farming in South Africa: A case study of Thulamela local municipality." *Land Use Policy* vol. 119, 106170. https://doi.org/10.1016/j.landusepol.2022.106170

[9] Wapongnungsang, E., Ovung, K.K. Upadhyay, S.K. Tripathi (2021). "Soil fertility and rice productivity in shifting cultivation: impact of fallow lengths and soil amendments in Lengpui, Mizoram, northeast India." *Heliyon* vol. 7, no. 4, e06834. https://doi.org/10.1016/j.heliyon.2021.e06834

[10] N. Arunrat, S. Sereenonchai, R. Hatano (2022). "Effects of fire on soil organic carbon, soil total nitrogen, and soil properties under rotational shifting cultivation in northern Thailand." *Journal of Environmental Management* vol. 302, 113978. https://doi.org/10.1016/j.jenvman.2021.113978

[11] A. Heinimann, O. Mertz, S. Frolking, A.E. Christensen, K. Hurni, F. Sedano, L.P. Chini, R. Sahajpal, M. Hansen, G. Hurtt (2017). "A global view of shifting cultivation: recent,

current, and future extent." *PLoS One* vol. 12, no. 9, e0184479. 10.1371/journal.pone.0184479

[12] T.B. Brunn, C.M. Ryan, A. Neergaard and N.J. Berry (2021). "Soil organic carbon stocks maintained despite intensification of shifting cultivation." *Geoderma*, vol. 388, 114804. https://doi.org/10.1016/j.geoderma.2020.114804

[13] I. Mathur and P. Bhattacharya (2022). "Transition from shifting cultivation to agroforestry: A case study of regrouped villages in Tripura, India." *Environmental Challenges* vol. 7, 100471. https://doi.org/10.1016/j.envc.2022.100471

[14] S.B. Sharma, S. Kumar, E.V. Ovung, B. Konsam (2022). "Vegetation dynamics and soil nutrients across different shifting cultivation fallows in Montane Subtropical Forest of Mizoram, NE India." *Acta Oecologica* vol. 115, 103833. https://doi.org/10.1016/j.actao.2022.103833

[15] M. Zhang, X. Wang, H. Feng, Q. Huang, X. Xiao, X. Zhang (2021). "Wearable Internet of Things enabled precision livestock farming in smart farms: A review of technical solutions for precise perception, biocompatibility, and sustainability monitoring." *Journal of Cleaner Production* vol. 312, 127712. https://doi.org/10.1016/j.jclepro.2021.127712

3 Methods Used Currently Which Incorporate AI and Robotics

3.1 INTRODUCTION

Agriculture is one of the most essential and crucial fields of the economic system. According to Worldbank.org, agricultural development is one of the most critical components for eradicating worldwide poverty, and improvement in this sphere could grow collective wealth and feed the populace. Agriculture accounted for 4 percent of gross domestic product (GDP) in 2018, and in many other developing countries it can account for more than 18 percent of GDP [1].

The global populace has grown to greater than 7.7 billion [2]. The Food and Agriculture Organization has predicted that the world population will reach 9 billion by 2050. Population increase is directly proportional to food demand. The food demand is increasing steadily, and at the same time, the meals supply chain is going through a crisis [3]. United Nations business enterprise states that around 68 percent of the populace practicing agriculture in rural areas will live in urban areas by the year 2050, which prompts a necessity to reduce the burden from the farmers.

Agriculture faces many difficulties, from sowing to harvesting. Significant elements include climate change, international warming, water scarcity, insect infestation, overuse of insecticides, weeds, under-irrigation, and drainage. Together with these, labor scarcity is another critical problem [4]. One of the reasons for labor shortages is that the age of present-day farmers is rising. Once they leave farming activities, the new technology is less likely to replace them, which brings up a sizable issue.

The agriculture enterprise and its contributors are the essential drivers for environmental alternatives, accountable for shifts in land usage, degradation of freshwater supplies [5], contamination of marine and terrestrial environments by different use of nitrogen and phosphorus inputs [6]. This change is mainly because of farming practice, wooded area clearing, heavy use of synthetic fertilizers, and cattle emissions [7]. For much of our history, if we wanted to grow more crops, we deforested territory to obtain more farming land. Agricultural practices have contributed to the destruction of whole ecosystems the world over. Inclusive of tropical forests, various types of forests, including tropical forests, are being deforested at an unprecedented rate. This is concerning because deforestation can have negative impacts on biodiversity, carbon storage, and overall ecosystem health [7]. Today, almost 500 billion hectares of land

DOI: 10.1201/9781003213550-3

are used for agriculture, accounting for nearly 40 percent of the available land. The agricultural regions, a significant consumer of fresh water, accounts for 70 percent of all water use in the world [8]. The European Agricultural Machinery Association (CEMA) [9] predicts that agricultural lands in evolved international locations have reached their height [12].

Conventional farming methods are incapable of producing the daily food required by using the future population of the farming sector, and this shortfall additionally endangers people's fitness and the planet. Agriculture produces unacceptable amounts of pollutants and waste [1]. These issues have driven the agriculture sector into seeking more modern thoughts and strategies for enhancing crop yield and shielding the ecology. For more than a century, agriculture has moved from hard, work-intensive family businesses to mechanization and strength-intensive manufacturing systems. Agriculture has begun to digitize over the past 15 years. However, the development within the area compared to the to be had modern technology could be very minimal [4]. AI and robotics are a rich mixture for automating any mission. In recent years, AI has turned out more and more not to be an unusual presence in robot options, introducing knowledge of and adaptableness skills in previously inflexible packages (limited capabilities) [10].

Artificial intelligence and robotics in agriculture are bringing about a revolution. These technologies enhance crop manufacturing and improve actual-time control, harvesting, processing, and advertising [11]. Various high-tech primarily laptop-based structures are being designed for figuring out plants' illnesses, weed detection and elimination, yield prediction, and crop growth tracking, studying the satisfaction of produced yield. Agriculture is a diverse sector, which means there is need for tailored approaches rather than relying on a single method for all conditions.. The AI and robotics techniques assist one to collect the details of each situation and provide a most fulfilling way to meet the trouble. AI and robotics-based technology can solve those troubles efficiently. This technology can improve crop-yield efficiency, irrigation through less water usage, crop tracking, and the best of the crop. AI and robotics-based technologies can permit farmers to supply higher yields with reduced manufacturing value and explode their profit [12].

3.2   TECHNIQUES OF VERTICAL FARMING

Vertical farming ought to end food scarcity in a green and sustainable way, maintain water and electricity, beautify the economy, lessen pollutants, provide new employment opportunities, restore ecosystems, and offer access to nutritious meals. In a controlled environment, plants might be less affected by infections. The nutrient cycle is maintained, crop rotation is easy, polluted water runoff is cut short, almost zero pesticides and dust [13].

Vertical farms additionally utilize advanced technology and extensive farming methods that may exponentially surge production. Researchers have optimized indoor farming by calibrating, tuning, and adjusting a vast range of variables along with light depth, light color, area temperature, crops and roots, CO_2 contents, soil, water, and air humidity. In addition, vertical farming presents a possibility to help the growth of the local economic system. Abandoned urban homes can be transformed into vertical farms to provide healthful meals in neighborhoods where clean produce is scarce [14].

Some of the advanced techniques are discussed in this section.

3.2.1 HYDROPONICS

Hydroponics is a word not well known, but it's one of the most innovative and futuristic ways to grow crops.

It's also one of the most sustainable and effective forms of agriculture we have today. Hydroponics involves growing crops without soil by using mineral-rich water in a closed system with artificial lighting. Plants grown hydroponically don't need to use all their nutrients to get their roots wet because they are constantly immersed in water. This means that the amount of nutrients used by the plant is significantly reduced. This, in turn, means that crops can be grown in areas where there isn't much arable land because it's too dry or too rocky. But not only are crops raised hydroponically far happier than soil-based ones, but they are also much more productive.

With hydroponics, farmers can grow more food on less land and are able to hold back on bulldozing forests to create a more arable property. This, in turn, means saving the environment. The other significant benefit of hydroponics is that it has allowed scientists to look at new ways to improve plant growth while preserving our natural resources. From the use of new types of fertilizers and soil replacements to the addition of beneficial microbes, there are lots of different ways that scientists are exploring how to make crops grow better without spending too much money or tapping into our non-renewable resources like water and fossil fuels. At the same time, these new methods are making farming more environmentally friendly.

Hydroponics is also known as the "Soil-less plant growing technique." Different available processes for soil-less agriculture are put in practice based on some factors as follows:

1. Amount of available space and other resources
2. Future productivity calculation
3. Availability of suitable growing medium
4. Quality

Hydroponics in practice has different methods to carry it out successfully. Plants grown in solution culture have their roots directly immersed in nutrition. It can be further classified into this:

1. Circulating Methods or Continuous solution flow method:
   We will discuss the two methods that incorporate continuous solution flow, which helps the plant grow at its best.
   (a) Nutrient Film Technique: The design is straightforward, with a very shallow nutrient solution pouring through the tubing. The Plant's roots floating above the solution will absorb the nutrients when they come into contact with the water.

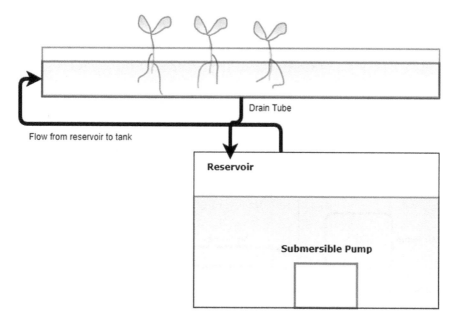

FIGURE 3.1 Nutrient film technique.

From the above diagram, we see that the grow tank is placed in such a way so that the water flows down toward the nutrient return pipe. The excess nutrient solution will flow out the tube into the reservoir again, where it mixes with more nutrients to be recirculated through the pipes over and over.

The underlying foundations of the plants hang down in the tank, where they come in contact with nutrients and ingest the essentials from them. The thin film of the nutrient solution permits the plants to be watered yet not altogether splashed. This thinness likewise allows the upper piece of the roots to stay dry and approach oxygen noticeable all around. It is suitable for lightweight and fast-growing plants.

(b) Deep Flow Technique: In hydroponics, plants are developed with supplement water rather than soil. A few frameworks effectively convey the supplement water to the plant roots to animate development. While different frameworks work by just letting the plant establish sitting endlessly in the supplement water.

DFT tank-farming frameworks do a bit of both. Circulated air through supplement water from a repository is siphoned up into one side of a plate. Plants are placed on the top of the container with their foundations hanging inside. As the water is circulated, it circles, conveying supplements to the plants' underlying foundations. On the furthest edge of the plate, a channel brings the used water down to the supply.

Since DFT gets and reuses water like this, it utilizes very little of it. DFT is like the nutrient film method (NFT) and profound water culture (DWC) tank-farming frameworks.

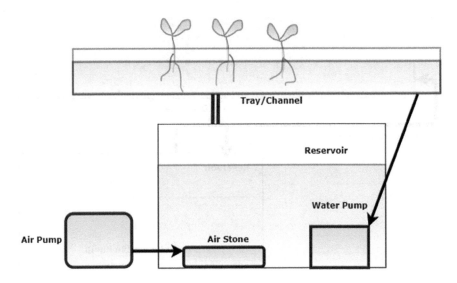

FIGURE 3.2 Deep flow technique.

2. Non-circulating method (open system) / Static Solution Culture
   (a) Root Dipping Technique: Plants are grown in tiny pots loaded up with the minimal developing medium. The pots are lowered so that the bottom 2–3 cm of the pots are submerged in the nutrient solution. A few roots are dunked in the nutrition solution while others linger palpably in the air.
   (b) Floating Technique: This method is similar to the Box method, but this one has shallow containers that may be around 10–15 cm deep. Plants established in small pots are correctly fixed to a Styrofoam sheet. The styrofoam sheet is a product of closed-cell extruded polystyrene foam (XPS). Styrofoam sheet is known as Blue Board, which are used in walls, roofs, and foundations as thermal insulation and water barrier.
   (c) Capillary Action Technique: Planting pots of various sizes and shapes with openings at the base are utilized. Fill these pots with a dormant medium and plant seedlings/seeds in that idle medium. These pots are put in shallow compartments loaded up with supplement arrangements. Nutrient Solution arrives at static medium by slender activity. Air circulation is vital in this procedure. The procedure is appropriate for decorative, bloom, and indoor plants.

3.2.2 AQUAPONICS

Aquaponics is an incorporated arrangement of aquaponics and aquaculture development [15]. Water flows between the parts of the framework (fish tank, biofilter, aquaculture framework), during which the wastes of the fish become compost for the plants [16], and the nitrifying microorganisms in the biofilter convert the nitrogen structure from alkali to nitrate, which is consumed by the plants [17]. The pattern of water and supplements works on the proficiency of water use [18], understands the reuse of hydroponics wastewater [19], and also maintains a strategic distance from the ecological contamination brought about by customary fisheries. Aquaponics has disposed of the reliance on the land and can be developed under various scales and natural conditions. It has appealing potential for metropolitan farming [20].

Current aquaponics is mostly grouped by different aquaculture structures and how the water cycle is shut or not. Media-Based Growing Bed (MBGB), Deep Water Culture (DWC), Nutrient Film Technique (NFT) are normal structures. The three sorts of aquaponics have their qualities: MBGB is space-saving, however, it is hard to keep up with and clean. DWC is simpler to clean and has a higher expulsion pace of nitrate; however, it requires additional biofilters, air circulation gadgets, and a bigger volume of water. NFT has higher effectiveness for water use, however, lower yield [21]. Aquaponics is partitioned into the coupled and decoupled framework dependent on whether the water cycle is shut. The coupled framework puts used water from the tank-farming subsystem promptly back into the aquaponics subsystem, though the decoupled framework breaks this circle and permits water to leave the system. On comparing the coupled system with the decoupled system, we see that decoupled requires more water; however, it has better command over water quality, which prompts further developed vegetable yields [22].

Tilapia, fancy fish, catfish, and verdant vegetables are the most widely recognized fish and plant species for aquaponics cultivation [23]. Aquaculture types, fish, and plant density [24], flow rate, water quality boundary, taking care of, and planting methodologies are significant components influencing yield. Moreover, the dissemination of nitrogen is a basic issue that might influence the degree of maintainability of an aquaponic framework. Besides, pH, DO, and pressure-driven stacking rate was recommended to impact the nitrogen change in an aquaponic framework [25]. There is a distinction in nitrogen usage proficiency (NUE) and N2O discharge between aquaponics with various plants [26].

3.2.3 Aeroponics

Aeroponics is a strategy for developing plants whereby they are moored in openings in Styrofoam boards, and their foundations are suspended noticeably all around underneath the board. The panels form a fixed box to forestall light entrance to energize root development and also forestall green growth development. The supplement arrangement is showered in fine fog structure to the roots. Clouding is accomplished for a couple of pauses, each 2–3 minutes. This is adequate to keep hearts wet, and supplement arrangement circulating air through. The plants acquire supplements and water from the arrangement film that clings to the roots.

The aeroponic culture is usually polished in ensured structures and is reasonable for low verdant vegetables like lettuce, spinach, and so on; the chief benefit of this strategy is the most extreme usage of room. In this strategy, twice as many plants might be obliged per unit floor region as in different frameworks. One more expected utilization of this strategy is in creating plants liberated from soil particles from cuttings for trades.

Aeroponics turned out to have a considerable advantage. It was found out that eliminating the growing medium is very beneficial for a plant: the additional oxygen they are presented to brings about quicker development. Aeroponic frameworks are likewise incredibly water productive. The closed-loop controlled frameworks utilize 95 percent less water than plants filled in soil. Furthermore, since the supplements are held in the water, they get reused, as well.

Notwithstanding these efficiencies, aeroponics eco-accommodating standing is supported by the capacity to develop enormous amounts of food in tiny spaces. The methodology is principally utilized in indoor vertical homesteads, which are progressively normal in urban areas, reducing the natural expenses of getting food from field to plate. Moreover, because aeroponics frameworks are entirely encased, there is no supplement overflow to foul nearby streams. The idea is to grow equipment that can be sterilized when needed rather than treating the plants with harmful chemicals for pests and disease.

Aeroponics frameworks require a bit of artfulness to work adequately. The supplement convergence of the water should be kept up with exact inside boundaries and, surprisingly, a slight glitch of your hardware can cause the loss of an entire crop. If, by any chance, the sprayers don't spray at regular intervals – perhaps due to a power outage, for example – those suspended roots can quickly dry up.

One significant environmental disadvantage is that aeroponic frameworks depend on the electrical ability to siphon water through the little moistening gadgets. And keeping in mind that they can be utilized in normal light, they are all the more regularly used with energy-escalated development lights. Sunlight-based power or other elective energy sources can be tackled to dispense with this disadvantage.

There are two techniques to perform Aeroponics as below:

1. Root Mist Technique
2. Fog Feed Technique

To prevent excess dehydration from the plant, we need to balance humidity and transpiration to allow water and nutrients to help the plant grow. Humidity in the air plays a vital role in the evapotranspiration rate from the leaf surface. In a plant with a thick foliage shelter and the absence of minimum required air movement, a limited layer of dampness develops.

The use of the Fog and Mist technique can be vital when the air temperature increases, and the leaf starts evaporating more moisture. As the environmental temperature rises, it places stress on the plant to fulfill its water needs. If these needs aren't met, the gradual loss of water can adversely affect the crop. The use of aeroponics can diminish the effect of air temperature increase, and as more oxygen and humidity reach the root zone, the roots grow rapidly.

3.2.4 CONTROLLED ENVIRONMENT AGRICULTURE

The upward cultivating model is basically an indoor agriculture practice dependent on an elevated structure staggered like a multi-tiered manufacturing plant plan that is designed to efficiently grow crops in a confined environment. Common provisions incorporate imaginative utilization of reused water expanded by rainwater or water from a desalination plant, programmed air-temperature and moistness control, sunlight-based charger lighting and warming, and tunable 24-hour LED light. The LED gear can be controlled all through a developing season to emanate a customized range of light that is ideal for photosynthesis for various sorts of crops. When combined with guideline of temperature and humidity, the impacts of irregularity can be limited or wiped out.

An indoor vertical homestead may not require soil if aquaculture is utilized. This development procedure includes developing plants in a dirt-free culture with supplement arrangements. The plants are suspended in a medium, like stone fleece or perlite, and provided with nutrients, or the roots are straightforwardly washed in the supplement fluid utilizing the supplement film procedure [27]. Cooling gives a steady stream of air which can be enhanced with carbon dioxide (CO2) to additional plant development and improvement. Both encompassing and supplement temperatures can be held at explicit levels that enhance the pace of plant development. Any supplements and water not consumed by the roots can be reused as opposed to lost to the framework. The methodology is reliable with CGG food creation. It tends to be utilized to grow a wide scope of harvests, drugs, or spices.

A variation of tank-farming is aeroponics, which includes splashing the underlying foundations of plants with atomized supplement arrangements or mists [28]. There is diminished requirement for composts, herbicides, and pesticides in case there is powerful separation from a hostile outside environment. Such a plant would basically kill normal limitations and dangers to efficiency, including warmth and dry spell, nuisances, irregularity, and transportation costs from remote areas. Instability in business sectors can be tended to since instability in business sectors can be mitigated by adjusting production according to demand. There are likewise suggestions for future food security and manageability even with environment change and decreasing area and water assets.

The farming capability of LEDs has been the focal point of exploration in nursery lighting [29]. The much lower energy necessities of LED lighting in mix with photovoltaics has brought about quick arrangement in industrial facility applications. The photoreceptors in plants assimilate the light energy with the end goal of photosynthesis and are influenced by the frequency and power of light. The unearthly spectral composition of light, such as the blue frequency in LED lighting, has been discovered to alter the concentrations of nutritionally important primary and secondary metabolites in specialty vegetable crops [30]. Specifically, plant reaction to various frequencies of light from LED sources calls for exceptionally critical enhancements in efficiency are conceivable. In addition to wavelength, controlled lighting with respect to force and time span is another region where potential enhancement systems are conceivable and requires further examination. In specific, hereditary qualities research plays a potential part to play in coordinating with plants to the accessible light range for further developed yield. Phantom affectability may likewise reach out past the apparent frequencies and into the bright and infrared transfer speeds with likely consequences for development rates.

Genetic designing may likewise have the option to improve development of harvests that are viable with other controlled indoor ecological conditions. For

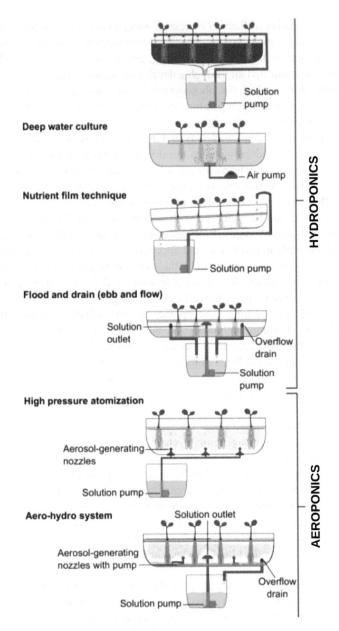

FIGURE 3.3　Hydroponics and Aeroponics.

example, it very well may be feasible to expand crop yield by calibrating factors like temperature, moistness, and CO2 levels. Assurance of a portion reaction model for light-sensitive cells would enthusiastically support network advancement [31].

3.3 HISTORY

3.3.1 PROPOSAL OF VERTICAL FARMING

In the past, the primary way for people to get leafy foods was to gather it. We picked wild foods grown in the harvest time and burrowed or cut verdant vegetables and tubers in the spring. Although agriculture may seem as timely and local as anyone in the modern world would desire, it was destined to undergo change.

People initially began developing vegetables in farming climates around 23,000 years ago. Since then, we've been intentionally choosing what to grow, gather and eat depending on how good the food tastes, how fulfilling or nutritious it is, and how much exertion we need to get a harvestable yield.

Indeed, the products accessible in our cutting-edge stores are immediate after the effect of millennia of determination dependent on a portion of these same elements.

Farmers started to try different things, with shielding crops from the elements until the start of the twentieth century. What began as a plain little box put in the ground and finished off with a level piece of glass immediately turned into limited scope nurseries. With this incredible innovation came an expectation to accumulate information to make ideal development conditions for an enormous assortment of plants.

The primary imaginative renderings of food developed upward were featured in *Life Magazine* in 1909. Although the thought was for vertical residences set sincerely busy cultivating country, it was beginning something new. From that point forward, compositional proposition appeared all through the twentieth century. Yet, these were primarily insightful dreams by visionaries thinking fifty years ahead of the time.

The innovation couldn't uphold these dreams until nursery innovation got up to speed. Around the 1970s, we figured out how to develop crops with no dirt. First utilizing a medium called mineral wool (essentially any fibrous material formed by spinning or drawing molten mineral or rock materials such as slag and ceramics); this innovation decreased the carbon impression and created better quality and yields.

Technological jumps in tank-farming and artificial lighting followed. Driven lighting progressions have just been brought into nurseries in the last decade. Yet, it was significant headway, and because of that, Controlled Environment Agriculture (CEA) was immediately created. This is the interaction where yields are given their own streamlined climate in a controlled indoor framework. This headway straightforwardly prompted developing crops upward in stacked layers.

Although the main genuine illustration of vertical agriculture first evolved in Armenia in 1951, vertical cultivating didn't acquire footing as a plan to support developing populaces until an educator at Columbia University in New York suggested a troublesome conversation starter to a clinical biology class of graduate understudies in 1999.

Professor Dickson Despommier requested that his understudies sort out some way to take care of the whole populace of Manhattan (around 2 million individuals then) utilizing just five hectares of roof gardens. After his group bombed at the task – they just sorted out some way to take care of 2 percent of the populace with housetop gardens – Professor Despommier became energetic with regards to the thought. He determined that while we were unable to take care of the whole populace of Manhattan, we could take care of 50,000 utilizing one city block and an entire 30-story building, not simply the roof.

His unique thought was to commit the structure's upper floors to create hydroponically developed harvests and the lower floors were committed to chickens and fish, consuming the natural waste from the plants in the floors above. By 2001, Professor Despommier had the main authority framework of a vertical business ranch, itemizing the particulars of water and supplement frameworks and other early innovation frameworks of current indoor vertical homesteads.

To those who have never seen vertical farming, the thought may appear to be exceptionally futuristic and unnatural, particularly when contrasted with conventional open-field agriculture. Be that as it may, history is brimming with instances of how agribusiness has consistently been founded on innovation – even the Romans utilized reservoir conduits to enhance water to their fields.

The paper that came about because of that one alumni class proceeded to promote the possibility that food creation could be considered compared to conventional, open-field farming. Likewise, with numerous mechanical jumps, the concept was generously tested from the start. In any case, from that point forward, the business and the innovative headways, have sped up. Today, indoor vertical cultivation is nearly reshaping the worldwide food model and is relied upon to be valued at US$9.96 billion by 2025.

3.3.2 IMPLEMENTATION OF VERTICAL FARMING

We will now study how to implement a vertical farm to supply 15,000 individuals with food. This planned elevated structure is included with these properties: the size of the vertical homestead: 93 ha, 37 stories, 25 of which are only for harvesting crops and 3 for hydroponics. Additionally, 3 levels of a similar appropriation are for changing the climate; 2 found underground are utilized to control the waste. Moreover, one story is assigned to the cleansing of the development plate, appearing just as germination. One storey is for the pressing and preparing of the vegetables or fish. Another floor is for the selling of the items grown underground. This makes the general height of the structure 167.5 meters and its length and width equivalent to 44 meters. The viewpoint proportion will be 3.81. The facility is outfitted with a roomy lift in the center large enough to accommodate a forklift truck. This assists with moving the crops down to other floors. Every day, approximately 217,000 gallons of water are required for the system; 14,000 of that is absorbed and utilized by the framework, leaving the remaining water as waste. The water not consumed by the vegetables is at that point, flowed again in a framework accountable for reusing water. It is handled and showered again, and the controlled feedback loop is closed [32].

Additionally, authors of [33] referenced the design as particular floors for model creation, lab, framework, poultry, and general store [33]. To submit to a vital job in neighborhood food creation, the ground floor of vertical agriculture should be a supermarket or an eatery. The items are offered for sale to the general population. What makes vertical farming interesting is its newness since the produce is distributed to the customers as it is being harvested on upper floors. The produce is likewise a lot less expensive than regular harvests because the expense excludes transportation or storage.

3.4 TYPES OF VERTICAL FARMING

Vertical farming systems can be further classified by the type of structure that houses the system. We will discuss two classifications below: Building-based vertical farms and Deep Farms.

3.4.1 BUILDING-BASED VERTICAL FARMS

Organizations keen on vertical cultivating are multiplying throughout the planet. For instance, Nuvege in Kyoto, Japan, is a 2,787 m² (30,000 ft²) aqua-farming complex with 5,295 m² (57,000 ft²) of vertical development space that delivers an assortment of lettuces in a climate protected from the close-by Fukushima atomic plant [34]. PlantLab in Den Bosch, Holland, is a three-story underground vertical ranch that utilizes progressive LED innovation that aligns light organization and power to exact requirements, eliminating the episodes of daylight that could slow plant development [34]. The building-based vertical farm utilizes a computerized framework that screens and controls various factors, including moistness, CO2, light power, light tone, air-speed, water system, dietary benefit, and air temperature [34]. The cutting-edge vertical farm delivers a yield multiple times the measure of the typical nursery while reducing water use by 90 percent.

3.4.1.1 Sky Greens

Singapore's Sky Green is one of the marvelous structures practicing vertical farming. As a small island, but with a population of more than 5 million, Singapore faces food security issues. With land at a higher cost than normal, accessible space for cultivating is restricted. Singapore creates just 7 percent of the food it consumes, and just 250 sections of the island's land are given over to cultivating. The remaining need is provided by food imports from everywhere in the world. In any case, the transportation expenses of food are turning out to be progressively restrictive. Consequently, Singapore has been viewing vertical cultivation seriously.

Sky Greens is Singapore's first "tropical vegetable metropolitan vertical cultivation farm to accomplish improved green, feasible creation of protected, new and scrumptious vegetables, utilizing negligible land, water, and energy assets" [35]. The five-year-old farmstead is 3-stories tall (9 m or 30 ft) and utilizes a technique called "A-Go-Gro (AGG) Vertical Farming" that uses clear nurseries to develop verdant tropical vegetables all year at fundamentally more significant returns than conventional cultivating strategies. Sky Greens is equipped for delivering one ton of new vegetables every other day. It supplies an assortment of tropical vegetables, including Chinese cabbage, spinach, lettuce, Xiao Bai Cai, Bayam, Kang Kong, Cai Xin, Gai Lan, and Nai Bai. The farmstead has flourished and means to extend its operation by

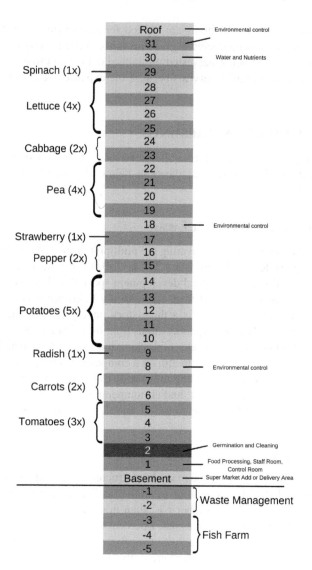

FIGURE 3.4 Vertical farming structure.

selling its goods at moderately reasonable prices, giving a more extensive assortment of vegetables.

The AGG framework primarily comprises aluminum A-forms that can be as high as 9 m (30 ft) tall with 38 levels of a box that contains different developing media – soil and aquaculture. The A-outline framework takes up just 5.6 m² (60 ft²), making it multiple times more proficient than traditional cultivating [35]. The box gradually turns around the aluminum outline (about three pivots each day) to guarantee that the plants get uniform daylight. Such consistent openness lessens or even removes the requirement for artificial lighting in certain spaces of the structure. Pivot is fueled by a protected low-carbon water-powered framework that contains a plate of plants. The pressure-driven framework is a traditional innovation with an advanced curve; it is a shut circle that utilizes gravity and requires little energy. Every 9m (30 ft) tower utilizes just 60 W of energy and, hence, the proprietor goes through just about "$360/month ($3/tower) on power" to serve the ranch [35].

As well as offering business benefits, Sky Greens is occupied with instructive projects in the encompassing neighborhoods, where understudies visit the ranch, getting advice and involvement with relocating, gathering, and understanding the force of science and innovation in making green metropolitan arrangements. The venture began as a model that grew mutually with Agri-Food and the Veterinary Authority of Singapore (AVA) in 2010. Sky Greens, along with AVA, won the Minister for National Development's Research and Development Award 2011 (Merit Award) for Vertical Farming. Sky Greens vows to turn into a suitable food-providing choice [35, 36].

3.4.1.2   Green Spirit Farms

Situated in New Buffalo, Michigan, Green Spirit Farms (GSF) is an expert food organization that has straightforwardly accepted vertical cultivating. The New Buffalo office has outgrown a previous plastic manufacturing plant. The structure contains 3,716 m^2 (40,000 ft^2) of space and sits on an 11-ha (27-ac) site. As standard practice, GSF will enter more seasonal empty modern or business structures to supply produce close by metropolitan business sectors. GSF intends to give nearby business sectors top-caliber, sans pesticide, non-genetically changed (GMO) food varieties at reasonable cost. The organization developed high neighborhood request items like lettuce, basil, spinach, kale, arugula, peppers, tomatoes, stevia, strawberries, and Brussel sprouts. Whatever is produced by them, they sell locally to supermarkets and cafés and to a large group of little "Gather Markets" that sells directly to shoppers. GSF runs vertical natural farmsteads in Atlanta and Philadelphia, as well as in Canada and the United Kingdom [35]. The organization has solid confidence in vertical cultivating. As per Green Spirit Farms' Research and Development Manager Daniel Kluko, the eventual fate of producing is going one unambiguous way: vertically.

GSF has advanced a few innovations to develop vegetables. These incorporate the Volksgarden Rotary Garden unit, termed a Rotary Vertical Growing Station (RVGS), and a staggering plate framework, termed a Vertical Growing Station (VGS). GSF has of late marketed rotational and vertical cultivating frameworks utilizing protected methods to develop regionally popular vegetables, spices, and a few organic products and has opened vertical farmsteads in repurposed mechanical structures, restoring one for East Benton, Pennsylvania. The new facility of GSF produces more compared to what 81 ha (200 ac) of farmland collected all year. This is empowered by the operation's proficiency, which employs "98 percent less water, 96 percent less land, and 40 percent less energy" than would be needed by traditional farming [37]. Typically, the office will take more than a hundred duties to help the neighborhood economy. GSF has contributed about $27 million to build up the upward vertical farming and received a monetary grants, including a $300,000 Pennsylvania First Program award, $303,000 in Job Creation Tax Credits, and a $45,450 Guaranteed Free Training award to prepare new workers [38, 35]. The area has engaged Green Spirit due to its nearness to enormous neighborhood markets, with a significant portion of its produce selling inside roughly 75 miles of the operation [38]. In synopsis, the vertical farming project gives a helpful illustration of versatile recycling set up through a solid public–private association. This has been made conceivable through a coordinated effort among GSF and a few organizations, including the Commonwealth of Pennsylvania, Lackawanna County, Benton Township, and the Greater Scranton Chamber of Commerce.

3.4.2 Deep Farms

In these long stretches of expanded worry about environmental change, two of the foremost weaknesses influencing our present food creation are the accessibility of arable land and the openness of harvests to outrageous varieties in climate. Another cultivation idea from scientists at the UK University of Nottingham might give a strategy – even though it might appear absurd – to protect a few harvests from the whims of the land market and the climate.

The concepts of "deep farms" are being advanced by Professors Saffa Riffat, fellow of the European Academy of Sciences and president of the World Society of Sustainable Technologies, and Professor Yijun Yuan, Marie Curie Research Fellow.

Savvy profound shafts for crop establishment would be built utilizing new tedious procedures. Existing coal mining and typical air protection burrows, a significant number of which are presently deserted could likewise be utilized for crop creation. The new profound vertical farms could be utilized for extreme yield cultivating to care for rising metropolitan populaces.

The recently protected idea for deep farms is an elective way to deal with colossal scope crop creation. When you think about it, standard cultivating is quite wasteful, requiring huge scope utilization of assets, including land, manures, synthetics, and water. Furthermore, surface soils can assimilate unsafe materials. Developed land and water are thoroughly contaminated in numerous nations. Riffat writes that around one-fifth of arable land in China is defiled with levels of poisons higher than government norms (2014 information) and that 14 percent of homegrown grain contains substantial metals, including lead, arsenic, and cadmium (2015).

The deep farms are generally created near populated areas to reduce transportation costs and CO_2 emissions. A wide range of crops can be grown in deep farms using hydroponics or aeroponics techniques. We can also use high lumen LED lights in the absence of sunlight. This also helps the growth in places where there is not much sunlight all year long. A significant benefit of this approach is that crop production is largely unaffected by climatic or seasonal factors – one of the most important limitations of conventional farming methods.

Carbon dioxide (CO_2) is essential for plant photosynthesis, and deep farms has designed carbon storage spaces to use it effectively.

The carbon capture system used by deep farms has the added benefit of reducing CO_2 content in the environment. Materials in the ground also adsorb carbon. The automated system incorporated with robots, control systems, and sensors can be used for planting and harvesting. Data generated from those sensors can be used to create trends and perform data analysis on them. Everything used in deep farms is renewable and, most importantly, electricity is used to power LED lighting for crops.

To sum up, LED lighting, water/supplement shower units, and CO2 carbon catch gadgets are essential for deep farms, which would empower harvests to be developed utilizing an aeroponic technique, where water and supplements are splashed on the plant roots. Aquaponics techniques can do crop planting. For this situation, the plant's underlying foundations can be set in water and supplement tanks. Yield reaping would be completed utilizing a mechanical means of turning/lifting gadgets. The crops can be grown in the vertical farm and harvested at the top of the tower after a period of ten days or more, depending on the type of crop planted.

Sustainable power could undoubtedly be utilized to control the developing framework using both LED lighting and a sun-oriented concentrator joined with optic fiber lighting. Sunlight-based energy would be used during the day, and LEDs would be used around evening or when sun-powered radiation is low.

3.5 ADVANTAGES

The advantages of developing most of our harvests inside as far as possible in vertical farming are many [39]. The majority of them likewise apply to controlled-climate farming in single-story nurseries. The distinctions connect with food gathering, stockpiling, and transporting issues, just as the size of their individual natural impressions. Land prices on the outskirts of populated areas are relatively less so major high-tech greenhouses lie on the outskirts. The further away food creation gets from the metropolitan focus, the bigger its natural impression. Without a doubt, there are quite a large number of other valid justifications for building up vertical farming that will become clear after a few operations are going. Estimating carbon at its actual worth would make a monetary motivating force for farmers, the majority of whom are just squeezing out a living, to at last be well remunerated and simultaneously help to reestablish harmed environments.

Permitting the trees to grow back would assist delayed down environment with changing by sequestering carbon from the climate and further the biodiversity of ruined, divided up forests. To the extent the costs caused in the "innovation" of a vertical farm, I would dare to estimate that any first release of innovation will cost a great deal. As the startup becomes acknowledged and interest for it develops, the cost of everything goes down. Take any of our cutting-edge accommodations – air travel, the crossover vehicle, plasma screen TVs, the wireless, the hand-held adding machine – and you understand. I completely expect that upward homesteads will succeed when we understand their actual worth, for us as well as for the rest of nature. In outline, development of the upward ranch utilizing enormous scope aquaculture and also aeroponics inside the cityscape is a possible answer for two issues: creation of fresh food harvests to the metropolitan populace without further harming the climate, and freeing up farmland, permitting it to get back to its original state. By and large, this implies the rebuilding of hardwood forests.

Some of the advantages as mentioned by author in [39] are worth discussing:

1. Year-Round Crop Production
   Since the beginning, agriculture has been heavily dependent on the seasons. Due to the yearly increase in carbon content in environment, we are experiencing

seasonal changes that are directly affecting crop cultivation. All around the globe we have certain growing season for each crop, and if that is affected by adverse weather like reduced or increased rainfall, the growing season arrives late or early, and many other cases we do not get a maximum crop yield. The increase of urbanization in recent years and reduction in farming land day by day puts serious pressure on the arable land to produce enough yield. This unwanted consequence can easily be avoided but putting vertical farming into action. Vertical farms can be grown in city limits as well to avoid the shortage and transportation cost.

The upside of not being worried about conditions outside is self-evident to everybody. A farmer can develop any yield and any place. In addition to the fact that this is a superior, more dependable procedure for practical food creation, it likewise permits the farmer to exploit business sectors that might allow a yield to be sold at a lot higher price than the typical cost. A genuine model happens in Europe every year during the pre-fall months in regard to the offer of tomatoes. At the point when the yields are in season, economic deals become real that incline toward the offer of neighborhood produce. At the point when deals drop off as the season advances, taxes go down. This is when CEA sparkles, since a farmer in Morocco, for example, can plant tank-farming tomatoes to develop at the perfect time to have the option to sell them at their highest price in Spain, lengthening the season for tomatoes.

2. Efficiency

Today, conventional horticulture utilizes some 70 percent of all the accessible fresh water on Earth and in doing so contaminates it, delivering it unusable for those living downstream. Interestingly, aqua-farming and, all the more as of late, aeroponic horticultural advancements have reformed the manner in which water is utilized to develop plants without the harmful side impact of horticultural spillover. At the point when these two techniques are utilized a tremendous measure of water is moderated, up to 95 percent in a few extreme cases. These two strategies for development are the response for maintainable food creation by the National Aeronautics and Space Administration (NASA) and the European Space Agency and will empower space explorers to ultimately deliver food on the Moon or Mars. Additionally, once vertical cultivating is widely practiced, food creation on Earth could happen anywhere. That will be the result of the vertical farming project.

Vertical farming increases efficiency in a way that we are no longer subject to weather-related crop failure as we can grow whichever crop we want, and in any season. There is no agricultural runoff in vertical farming. Irrigation methods have changed a lot in traditional farming, but there is considerable loss of water by each technique. One of the main concerns of majority irrigation practice is agricultural runoff. Runoff is actually unpreventable, given the fact that in order to increase the yield every crop would need extra water. Runoff at the end pollutes water with pesticides, silt, fertilizer, and herbicides which end up in a river. Vertical farming also ensures more control of food safety and security, and we can use any abandoned city properties to start a vertical farm so a vertical farm can be started anywhere.

3.6 PROBLEMS WITH VERTICAL FARMING

1. Expert Needed to Maintain a Vertical Farm

   Since vertical cultivating projects are typically very perplexing, industry specialists are expected to set up an upward planting framework in an appropriate way. Nonetheless, since the innovation behind vertical cultivating is fairly new, it very well may be hard to track down somebody in your vicinity who has the fundamental degree of mastery in this field.

   Consequently, it very well may be difficult to come by qualified staff to set up vertical cultivating projects.

2. High Upfront and Maintenance Cost

   One more inconvenience of vertical cultivating is that the underlying expenses of development and establishment can be very high. Since vertical cultivating frameworks are frequently mind-boggling and require a lot of arranging, the underlying expenses can be immense.

   Consequently, organizations need to take serious consideration with regard to the choice of whether or not upward cultivating will be reasonable for them, since wrong choices can prompt genuine monetary disadvantages in this field. Also, traditional farmers cannot easily adapt to vertical farming concepts so the high initial investment would be a big problem for them. Operating costs are very high as it requires high attention in order to be sure of high yield. Since vertical cultivating frameworks are generally very intricate, there will be the requirement for exceptionally qualified employees, who need to screen these cultivating processes consistently.

   These high endeavors likewise infer critical work costs connected with vertical cultivating.

   Hence, much of the time, vertical cultivating won't be sensible according to a monetary point of view by any means. Also, the maintenance efforts for vertical farming are very challenging. The conditions inside the cultivating framework are controlled in an artificial way through lighting and adjusting the dampness level, a portion of the gadgets that are utilized to control these boundaries might separate over the long haul.

   Consequently, these gadgets must be replaced and this might require significant expenses.

3. High Energy Consumption

   One more drawback of vertical cultivating is that it requires huge quantities of energy. Since many layers of plants must be covered by appropriate lighting, the power bill will increase steadily over the long run.

   Consequently, contrasted with outside cultivating, the expenses for energy will typically be a lot higher with vertical cultivating.

   The colossal energy utilization can likewise be viewed as a natural issue since the majority of our energy is as yet created out of petroleum derivatives, which thus infers genuine ozone-harming substance outflows.

4. Nutrient Deficient Plants

   There may likewise be the issue that vertical cultivating frameworks might contain fewer supplements contrasted with plants that are raised outside on the field.

Since plants that are raised outside need to safeguard against bugs and other hurtful elements, these plants frequently produce specific substances that may be helpful to human wellbeing. In any case, plants from vertical cultivating frameworks won't deliver those substances.

Consequently, certain minerals in plants that are filled in vertical cultivating frameworks may be missing compared with plants that are developed outside.

REFERENCES

[1] The world bank.org. (Sep. 30, 2020). "Agriculture overview." www.worldbank.org/en/topic/agriculture/overview.

[2] United Nations Department of Economic and Social Affairs (2017). "World population projected to reach 9.8 billion in 2050, and 11.2 billion in 2100 | UN DESA | United Nations Department of Economic and Social Affairs," Jun. 21.

[3] United Nations Department of Economic and Social Affairs (2018). "68% of the world population projected to live in urban areas by 2050," says UN | UN DESA | United Nations Department of Economic and Social Affairs, Apr. 16.

[4] V. Marinoudi, C.G. Sørensen, S. Pearson, D. Bochtis (2019). "ScienceDirect Robotics and labour in agriculture. A context consideration." *Biosystems Engineering Journal*, vol. 184, 111–121. doi: 10.1016/j.biosystemseng.2019.06.013

[5] FAO (2009). Water at a Glance. The relationship between water, agriculture, food security and poverty, 87–110. doi: 10.1787/9789264059221-5-en

[6] M. Springmann et al. (2018). "Options for keeping the food system within environmental limits." *Nature*, vol. 562, no. 7728, 519–525. doi: 10.1038/s41586-018-0594-0

[7] H. Ai. (2020). "Artificial intelligence in the design of the transitions to sustainable food systems." *Journal of Cleaner Production*, vol. 271, 122574. doi: 10.1016/j.jclepro.2020.122574

[8] P. Gonzalez-de-santos, R. Fern, D. Sep, E. Navas, L. Emmi, M. Armada. (2020). "Field robots for intelligent farms – Inhering features from industry." Agronomy vol. 10, 1638.

[9] CEMA–European Agricultural Machinery – Home (2020). www.cema-agri.org/ (accessed Dec. 14).

[10] Robotics online. (2018). How AI is Used in Today's Robots | RIA Blog | RIA Robotics Blog, Nov. 09, 2018. www.robotics.org/blog-article.cfm/How-Artificial-Intelligence-is-Used-in-Today-s-Robots/117 (accessed Dec. 14, 2020).

[11] T. Talaviya, D. Shah, N. Patel, H. Yagnik, M. Shah (2020). "Artificial intelligence in agriculture: Implementation of artificial intelligence in agriculture for optimization of irrigation and application of pesticides and herbicides. *Science Direct* vol. 4, 58–73, doi: 10.1016/j.aiia.2020.04.002

[12] A.P. Shet et al. (2020). "Artificial intelligence and robotics in the field of agriculture." doi: 10.13140/RG.2.2.10162.84167

[13] D. Touliatos, I.C. Dodd, M. Ainsh (2016). Vertical farming increases lettuce yield per unit area compared to conventional horizontal hydroponics. *Food Energy Security* vol. 5, 184–191.

[14] A. Padmavathy, G. Poyyamoli (2016). Enumeration of arthropods in context to plant diversity and agricultural (organic and conventional) management systems. *International Journal of Agriculture and Environmental Research* vol. 6, 805–818.

[15] J.E. Rakocy (1994). "The integration of fish and vegetable culture in recirculating systems." In *Proceedings of the Caribbean FoodCrops Society*, 30th Annual Meeting, Virgin Islands, USA, 31 July–5 August.

[16] M.A. Nichols, N.A. Savidov (2012). *Aquaponics: A Nutrient and Water Efficient Production System*. Leuven, Belgium: International Society for Horticultural Science (ISHS).

[17] S. Wongkiew, Z. Hu, K. Chandran, J.W. Lee, S.K. Khanal (2017). "Nitrogen transformations in aquaponic systems: A review." *Aquacultural Engineering Journal* vol. 76, 9–19.

[18] D.C Love, M.S. Uhl, L. Genello (2015). "Energy and water use of a small-scale raft aquaponics system in Baltimore, MD." *Aquacultural Engineering Journal*, vol. 68, 19–27.

[19] A. Endut, A. Jusoh, N. Ali, W.B.W Nik (2011). "Nutrient removal from aquaculture wastewater by vegetable production in aquaponics recirculation system." *Desalination and Water Treatment*, vol. 32, 422–430.

[20] L. Palma, M.J. Dos Santos (2016). "Smart cities and urban areas-Aquaponics as innovative urban agriculture." *Urban Forestry and Urban Greening*, vol. 20, 402–406.

[21] S. Goddek, B. Delaide, U. Mankasingh, K.V. Ragnarsdottir, M.H. Jijakli, R. Thorarinsdottir (2015). "Challenges of sustainable and commercial aquaponics." *Sustainabilty*, vol. 7, 4199–4224.

[22] G.M. Gibbons (2020). An Economic Comparison of Two Leading Aquaponic Technologies Using Cost Benefit Analysis: The Coupled and Decoupled Systems. Master's Thesis, Utah State University, Logan, UT, August.

[23] D.C. Love, J.P. Fry, L. Genello, E.S. Hill, J.A. Frederick, X. Li, K. Semmens (2014). "An international survey of aquaponics practitioners." *PLoS ONE*, vol. 9, e102662.

[24] S.R. Surnar, O.P. Sharma, V.P. Saini (2017). "Nutrient harvesting through aquaponics: Growth of *Labeo rohita* and production of plant (spinach)." *Journal of Experimental Zoology, India,* vol. 20, 389–396.

[25] Z. Hu, Z.J.W. Lee, K. Chandran, S. Kim, S.K. Khanal (2012). "Nitrous oxide (N2O) emission from aquaculture: A review." *Environmental Science & Technology*, vol. 46, 6470–6480.

[26] S. Wongkiew, B.N. Popp, S.K. Khanal (2018). "Nitrogen recovery and nitrous oxide (N2O) emissions from aquaponic systems: Influence of plant species and dissolved oxygen." *International Biodeterioration & Biodegradation Journal*, vol. 134, 117–126.

[27] J. Jones (2016). *Hydroponics: A Practical Guide for the Soilless Grower*. Boca Raton, FL: CRC Press.

[28] C. Christie, M. Nichols (2004). "Aeroponics: A Production System and Research Tool." In *South Pacific Soilless Culture Conference–SPSCC*, M. Nichols, ed., vol. 648, 185–190.

[29] N. Yeh, J. Chung (2009). "High-brightness LEDs: Energy Efficient Lighting Sources and Their Potential in Indoor Plant Cultivation." *Renewable and Sustainable Energy Reviews* vol. 13, 2175–2180.

[30] D. Kopsell, C. Sams, R. Morrow (2015). "Blue wavelengths from LED lighting increase nutritionally important metabolites in specialty crops." *HortScience* vol. 50, 1285–1288.

[31] K. K. Benke, K. E. Benke (2013). "Uncertainty in health risks from artificial lighting due to disruption of circadian rhythm and melatonin secretion: A review." *Human and Ecological Risk Assessment* vol. 19, 916–929.

[32] C. Banerjee, L. Adenaeuer (2014). "Up, Up and Away! The economics of vertical farming." *Journal of Agricultural Studies*, vol. 2, no. 1, 40.

[33] M. Cicekli, N. T. Barlas (2014). "Transformation of today greenhouses into high tech-nology vertical farming systems for metropolitan regions." *Journal of Environmental Protection and Ecology*, vol. 15, no. 4, 1779–1785.

[34] R. Cho. (2011). "Vertical farms: From vision to reality." *State of the Planet, Blogs from the Earth Institute*, 13 October.

[35] K. Al-Kodmany (2018). "The vertical farm: A review of developments and implications for the vertical city." *Buildings*, vol. 8, no. 2, 24.

[36] M. Aiken (2014). "Vertical farming powering urban food sources." *Diplomatic Courier*, 3 April.

[37] J. Smiechowski (2013). "Vertical farming venture achieves sustainability and success in New Buffalo, Michigan." *SeedStock*, 10 June.

[38] L. Frank (2013). Pennsylvania Governor Corbett Partners with Innovative Farm to Establish Operations in Lackawanna County, Creating 101 Jobs. 13 December.

[39] K. Benke, B. Tomkins (2017). "Future food-production systems: vertical farming and controlled-environment agriculture." *Sustainability: Science, Practice and Policy*, vol. 13, no. 1, 13–26. doi: 10.1080/15487733.2017.1394054

4 Understanding Irrigated Agriculture

4.1 INTRODUCTION

The current worldwide setting is adapted by the development of the total populace and the reformist, and the nonstop disintegration of the climate. This makes the test of guaranteeing the inventory of fundamental assets, like food and water, and feasible turns of events, where water assumes a fundamental part in the endurance of human civilization and adds to the arrangement of a wide scope of regulations on which the prosperity of society is based. But the water bodies are subject to serious damage due to many factors, such as the consequences of global climate change, day to day man-made activities, increases in agriculture practices and urban expansion, and exploitation of water bodies due to economic development [1].

Agricultural practice is the most essential concern for any country, and they all consume a lot from the water resources on a global level. A research study at the University of Wisconsin–Madison states that about 40 percent of total land is dedicated for agriculture. This number has been increasing day by day, which directly means that in order to meet the global food needs many forests are cleared in order to accommodate agriculture practice. Statistics from the UN Food and Agriculture Organization in 2018 show that the land area of the world is 13,003 million ha. and out of that 4,889 million ha. are classified as agricultural land, which is about 37.6 percent. This clearly shows that in order to meet food demands many forests are deforested, which in the end threatens biodiversity and reduces wilderness. The idea for understanding irrigated agriculture is to find an optimal use of resources we have (land, water, fertilizers, etc.) and increasing productivity of land makes it possible to produce food with much less inputs and reducing the impact on the environment (see Figure 4.1).

Below we see a general overview by authors Hannah Ritchie and Max Roser in 2019 for global land use for food production [2].

Presently, various methodologies are being utilized to address the difficulties of food arrangement and the supply of water for various utilizations and to keep a natural equilibrium. A few works highlight the improvement of measures to control request with the goal that water system water manageability can be reached. The advancement of proficient water markets can be an ideal measure in immature regions and with a significant degree of water shortage, as in South Africa [1]. Different ways

DOI: 10.1201/9781003213550-4

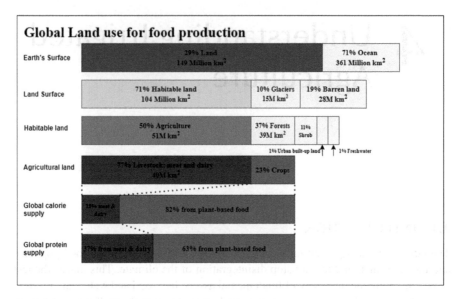

FIGURE 4.1   Global land use for food production.

to minimize agricultural water use and to develop effective ways to harvest are being developed all around the globe, but all of them are traditional methods in force, which are effective up to certain extent but fail to give results when the amount of control parameters increases.

Certain research discusses phases of irrigation in agriculture. Zhang et al. discusses the following three stages in water systems: The first incorporates the extraction of water from the source and its exchange through channels to the place of utilization; the second comprises the dissemination of water to the root framework to work with its assimilation by crops (this incorporates both customary water systems utilizing floods and furrows and present-day water systems through trickle frameworks and micro sprinklers); and the third covers the entire yield developing interaction, whereby the water is moved from the roots to the remainder of the plant. The objective is to save assets through limiting water mishaps during these three stages and to work on the efficiency in the utilization of water assets [3].

Lately, there has been an expansion in the number of studies dissecting agricultural water systems according to the viewpoint of maintainability with attention to its natural, monetary, and social effects. The target of this investigation is to dissect the elements of the exploration of the practical water systems in agribusiness in the course of the most recent twenty years. To satisfy this levelheaded approach, a two-overlap examination was embraced: quantitatively, through a bibliometric examination, and subjectively, through a fundamental survey dependent on watchword investigation. The examination breaks down the advancement of the number of articles distributed, the primary writers, establishments, and nations that advance this exploration field, the disciplines engaged with the research, the main lines of exploration, the distinctions in scholastic methodology and the nations considered, and the primary issues that influence the examination in this field [1].

Increasing the rate and accuracy of robots for farming programs are the primary troubles to be addressed for the generalization of robotics structures, but as compared to the commercial and military instances, the shortage of substantial studies investment and budgets in agriculture has decelerated this technique. For the case of robotic harvesting, enhancing sensing (fruit detection), acting (manipulator movement, fruit attachment, detaching, and gathering), and growing device (go away pruning and plant reshaping) is suggested to increase the efficiency. It must be cited that the development of a lower-priced and powerful agriculture robotic requires a multidisciplinary collaboration in several regions together with horticultural engineering, pc science, mechatronics, dynamic management, deep learning and intelligent structures, sensors and instrumentation, software layout, system integration, and crop management. We highlighted a number of the demanding situations inside the context of utilizing sensors and robotics for precision agriculture and virtual farming as object identification, challenge planning algorithms, digitalization, and optimization of sensors.

In this chapter we will discuss about different methods of irrigation and then we move forward to the need for smart irrigation in today's world. We discuss how robotics and AI can help us to expedite the farming process with less manpower.

4.2 TYPES OF IRRIGATION

In order to decide upon an irrigation system on a piece of land we require a great deal of planning and financial management. On most of the agricultural land, the number of irrigated acres is usually much less than the dryland acreage. Therefore, irrigation must be integrated into the total farm enterprise.

Irrigation requires intensive fertility control, progressed weed and insect manipulate, well timed identity of disease troubles and, especially, correct recordkeeping. Allocating the time for coping with the irrigation gadget is a key aspect inside the success of any irrigation assignment. The want of records and help from public and private sources turns into a greater vital aspect underneath irrigation.

When thinking about investment in irrigation, one of the first questions to ask is, "Why do I want to irrigate?" The number one purpose should be to stimulate larger net farm earnings over dryland production.

Increased income may also be an end result from the ability to grow longer-season plants or a high-price specialty crop, offer an assured forage supply for animal operations or to enhance crop rotations. Irrigating as insurance against insufficient rainfall just due to the fact the water is available or because you've got fields with irrigable soils are terrible motives. The higher yields viable with irrigation require greater management competencies and inputs within the shape of fertilizer, seed, and probable pest control.

A simple checklist has been developed by North Dakota State University which might help to guide the irrigation development process according to different farming enterprises.

Steps to follow [4]:

1. Determine if your soils are irrigable.
2. Determine the quantity and quality of water required.
3. Determine the availability of power and the type of irrigation equipment you'll need.
4. Determine whether irrigation will be cost-effective in your farm enterprise.
5. Determine whether you can obtain financing.
6. Select and manage your irrigated crops.

Let us discuss more briefly each step mentioned above.

Step 1: Determine if your soils are irrigable

Not all soils may be irrigated due to diverse physical issues, which include an excessive amount of slope, low infiltration costs or poor internal drainage that can promote salt buildup. Soils are classified as irrigable, conditional, or non-irrigable and are described in the following manner:

Irrigable soils haven't any regulations for sustained irrigation, the usage of right software quotes, quantities, and water satisfaction.

Conditional soils have regulations for sustained successful irrigation due to many environmental reasons.

Non-irrigable soils have intense regulations on irrigation and ought to be developed only where they are minor inclusions into irrigable soils.

Step 2: Determine the quantity and quality of water required

The water supply is the heart of any irrigation system development. We always measure the amount of water needed per acre, but the most important thing is the quality of water as well. Along with good fertilizers we also need quality checks for water so that the crops have the best of all.

If surface water (pond, lake, river, and so forth) is the source, whether sufficient water will be available during the summer months must be determined. If ground water is the source, online and published aquifer information can be obtained from the state government website. That data can be used to determine the location, size, and estimated production capacity for the ground water source at the field to be irrigated.

Step 3: Determine the availability of power and the type of irrigation equipment you'll need.

Electricity is normally the favored source of power. However, if current power lines are more than a mile from the pump site, using an inner combustion engine can be more cost-efficient. Electricity has some advantages over engines, consisting of decrease pumping expenses, much less upkeep, reliability, and simplicity of operation.

Construction fees and compensation for the extension of power strains range with each electric issuer. An estimation of annual power use, charges, and production repayment is important to decide the maximum reasonably priced electricity supply.

For electrically powered pumps, 3-phase power is favored, but regularly isn't always available or is too pricey to convey to the pump site. Variable-frequency drives (VFDs) and rotary or static segment converters will transform unmarried-segment electricity to three-section strength. Early touch with the strength supplier is necessary to allow time to devise and assemble centers.

Step 4: Determine whether irrigation will be cost-effective in your farm enterprise.

Detailed crop budgets overlaying economic and cash charges need to be organized for the proposed irrigated cropping system. If the budgets display a good enough return to labor, capital and control, then a total enterprise evaluation should be made to decide how irrigation fits the farm. Further, when different types of irrigations are discussed, we also have to decide upon the cost-effectiveness of each one based on the farming needs and come to a middle ground before deciding. Middle ground is decided based on the maximum stretch of the budget and irrigation system needed for the crop.

Step 5: Determine whether you can obtain financing

Legitimate arranging before reaching a monetary foundation can limit the issue of satisfactory financing. Accomplishment in water systems relies to a great extent upon your administration capacity. A sign of that capacity can be communicated surprisingly readily as homestead records, benefit and shortfall explanations, total assets proclamations and income articulations. Notwithstanding these records, you ought to be ready to supply your acknowledged organization for an assessment of the potential restitution limit of the water system speculation. This is the place where the yield spending plans, and all out big business examination, are exceptionally useful.

Step 6: Select and Manage your Irrigated crops

Crops chosen for water systems should deliver a monetary yield increment. This implies the normal yearly yield increment over dryland creation should be adequate to pay for the interest in the water system and expanded creation costs just as some extra benefit. Generally, watering corn (for silage or grain), sugar beets, potatoes, and dry consumable beans has been beneficial for acceptable water system directors.

Irrigation gives a climate helpful for expanded plant creation for long-season crops; notwithstanding, it likewise offers a good environment for infection, insects, and weeds. The irrigator should realize how to deal with the water system framework and harvest pivots to limit possible issues. By exploring the field consistently and utilizing incorporated bug-the-board strategies and best administration rehearsals, the irrigator ought to have the option to deal with the water system framework beneficially.

The irrigator should know about agronomic practices that favor water systems and are crop-explicit, like legitimate half-breed determination, line widths, proper plant populaces, higher compost necessities, and split uses of manure to limit draining potential.

Flooded harvest water the executives is critical to forestall yield misfortune because of dampness stress, limit siphoning costs and forestall filtering of supplements. A technique for water system planning should be utilized. Soil dampness observed by the vibe technique regularly is utilized, yet more exact strategies, like the checkbook strategy, are accessible. Whichever technique is utilized, it will require expanded administration abilities and extra time. Water system booking is a day-by-day measure (see Figure 4.2).

Now we will discuss irrigation system selection based on various specific requirements. There are many kinds of water system frameworks available that are reasonable for vegetable production. Frameworks shift significantly in costs and have distinctive activity and site necessities. Many variables figure out which situation is appropriate for you. Texas A&M AgriLife Extension has developed a very simple table based on factors to consider and data needed for proper irrigation system design [5].

FIGURE 4.2   Agricultural irrigation.

TABLE 4.1
Principal Data Needed For Irrigation System Design

Data	Specific Requirements
Crop	• Distribution and area of each crop to be grown.
	• Suitability of each crop to climate, soils, farming practices, markets.
	• Planting dates for each crop to be grown over the expected life of the project.
Soil	• Area distribution of soils,
	• Water holding and infiltration characteristics,
	• Depth,
	• Drainage requirements,
	• Salinity,
	• Erosion potential of each soil
Water Requirement	• Data for estimating daily and seasonal water requirements for each crop
Water Supply	• Location of water source,
	• Amount of water or pumping capacity, water surface elevation.
	• Hydrologic and water quality information for assessing the availability, costs, and suitability of the water for irrigation.
	• Water rights information
Energy Source	• Location, availability, and type of source(s).
	• Cost information
Capital and Labor	• Capital available for system development,
	• Level of technical skill,
	• Cost of labor
Other	• Topographic map showing location of roads, buildings, drain ways, and other physical features that influence design, financial situation of farmer, or farmer preferences.

TABLE 4.2
Typical Overall On-farm Efficiencies for Various Types of Irrigation Systems

System	Overall Efficiency (%)
Surface	50–80
1. Average	50
2. Land Leveling and delivery pipeline	70
3. Combination level and graded flow irrigation	80–95
4. Surge	60–90
Sprinkler	55–75
Center Pivot	55–75
Lower Electric Power Application	95–98
1. Bubble Mode	80–85
2. Spray Mode	
Drip	80–90

Another table for general overview of effectiveness for various types of irrigation system is as follows.

4.2.1 SURFACE IRRIGATION

A surface water system utilizes gravitational force to spread water over a field. A decent stockpile of water (stream size) in GPM (gallons per minute) is required. Surface frameworks are the most economical to introduce, however, they have high maintenance needs. Talented irrigators likewise are required to get excellent efficiencies. Regardless of whether appropriately planned, surface frameworks will in general have low water application efficiencies. Low efficiencies result in higher pumping (or water costs) because of the expanded measures of water required (see Figure 4.3).

The two most common surface systems used for irrigation are level basin and furrow systems. With the level basin method, water is distributed over a small period of time to a completely flat area enclosed by borders. The floor might be level, furrowed or molded into beds. The basin water system is the best on uniform soils accurately evened out when huge stream sizes (in GPM) comparative with basin region are accessible. On the off chance that appropriately planned and worked, level basin frameworks can achieve high water application efficiencies [5].

Furrows are little, uniformly dispersed, shallow directs shaped in the dirt. Ideal furrow lengths are fundamentally constrained by the dirt admission rate, furrow slope, set time and stream size. For most applications, the stream size ought to be just about as extensive as conceivable without causing disintegration.

Mix level and reviewed stream water systems are utilized in the Lower Rio Grande Valley. They have a most extreme incline of 0.1 ft per 100 ft (0.1%) and block closes. With legitimate stream size, these frameworks can have excellent water application efficiencies.

FIGURE 4.3   Surface irrigation field view.

Benefits of surface frameworks are water shortfalls that can be defeated quickly; most affordable of the significant sorts of water systems frameworks; low support, and generally require the least degree of the executives [5].

Disadvantages of surface frameworks are estimated as having the least water use effectiveness; need consistency in water appropriation, increment infection frequency particularly in vining crops, and occasional consumption of soil oxygen, which can cause yield decrease.

Around 94 percent of surface irrigation application is where water is spread over the field by gravity. The other majority of the remaining 6 percent is irrigated by methods that need energy, pressure and pipe systems such as sprinkler irrigation and drip irrigation [6].

The main idea for surface irrigation is to serve water across the field and as a surface through which infiltration occurs [7]. In different irrigation techniques soil infiltration characteristics serve to determine the level of performance achievable by surface irrigation.

Now, that we understand that surface irrigation's end goal is to irrigate the field at its optimal capacity so that crops neither receive less water for the growth nor more water, which would create flooding and invite more crop diseases. We know that traditional agriculture methods do not help much to achieve such high goals as there are always human errors, but robotics and AI can create a controlled environment and function at optimal capacity.

4.2.2 LOCALIZED IRRIGATION

Localized or micro irrigation is the system of applying water that results in allowing only a certain small area of the soil around the surface to get wet and many times it's sent directly to the roots only. This process helps plants to absorb just the required amount of water directly into the roots and thus prevents the surface waterlogs found in surface irrigation. There are different subtypes of micro or localized irrigation, including micro jets, surface drip, and subsurface drip irrigation.

Subsurface irrigation is probably the most common type of localized irrigation for agricultural purposes. In Oklahoma, about 2 percent of our irrigated lands are under localized irrigation and most of them are under subsurface drip irrigation. Under this type of irrigation, the subsurface drip irrigation, drip lines are buried about 12 to 18 inches below the soil surface. There are tiny emitters in this drip line that apply water in small amounts mostly on a daily basis. So, with subsurface drip irrigation, we're basically spoon feeding the crops and we're minimizing the evaporation of water and other losses such as deep percolation and surface runoff. A well-maintained and well-designed subsurface drip irrigation system can have efficiencies of 95 percent or above. This means only a very small fraction of water is lost due to reasons mentioned, and almost all the water that we apply is used by the crop for production of agricultural products.

Water is by and large applied at a low stream rate, in limited quantities, and very frequently. The idea here is to give less water with more frequency instead of giving more at a single time which might get evaporated from the surface as well. The application gadgets might be little cylinders, openings, spouts, or punctured lines. The water may either be applied above or underneath the dirt surface. The principle segments of a confined water system framework are the water supply (counting stream and pressing factor controllers), the filtration framework, primary lines, sub-fundamental lines, laterals, and merchants (see Figure 4.4).

The number one blessings of localized irrigation systems are the high-performance rates that can be accomplished, now and again as high as 90 percent. High efficiency may additionally result in very extensive water savings. Often a localized irrigation device will permit a farmer to irrigate twice the location viable with floor irrigation. Precise manipulate of water and nutrient application frequently affects in a good deal better yields and first-class. Control of weeds and pests may be higher as the complete soil floor is not wetted. A localized irrigation system might also permit using extra saline water and may be used correctly with low infiltration soils that cannot be sprinkler irrigated. Some dangers are the better initial expenses of the systems, salinity buildups, extra limited root improvement, and better technical necessities. Later savings may be offset with the aid of higher maintenance prices. There are low-value strategies, but, for irrigating garden-sized plots with localized irrigation.

Drip or trickle irrigation is a localized irrigation method that applies water at very low float rates. Pressing factors needed in a trickle water system are ordinarily somewhere in the range of 0.7 and 1.4 kg/cm2 (10 and 20 psi). Drip water system is reasonable for greatest soil sorts and most sorts of geography. It could be pleasantly ideal in circumstances of restricted water materials or unnecessary water charges. Its high

FIGURE 4.4 Localized irrigation.

worth ($2,000-$5,000/hectare) can be defended best in plantation plants or diverse significant expense plants.

There are two essential techniques for dribble or stream utility line supply (utilized explicitly for column yields) and point supply (utilized much of the time for tree plants). The line supply technique comprises of a couple of chamber polyethylene-type plastic tubing, 4–15 mm thick, and with little openings (by and large laser cut) each 20 to 60 cm. The single outlet type utilizes producers, typically a catch type plastic device with a pointed turning into that appends to a polyethylene sidelong hose having a measurement of 0.5" to 1."

Localized irrigation can be precisely explained with drip irrigation. It is one of the highly practiced methods out of all localized irrigation. One of the main problems with localized irrigation is soil-wetting and inadequate wetting of the roots can limit growth. A minimum of 33 percent wetting of the total surface area is at least required for proper growth of the plant.

4.2.3 DRIP IRRIGATION

Drip or trickle irrigation is the gradual, standard application of water to the soil through emitters or tubing. At its simplest, a small area is wetted; drip irrigation is especially proper for conditions where the water supply is confined. Drip tubing is often used to supply water below plastic mulches. Drip structures tend to be very

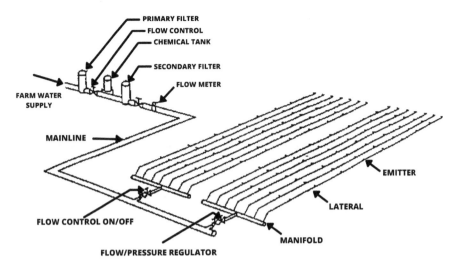

FIGURE 4.5 Drip irrigation.

efficient and can be automatic. Applying nutrients via the trickle machine could be very powerful and reduce the whole quantities of fertilizer wanted. Drip is the maximum ideal for excessive cost plants, including the vegetables, of the irrigation systems available. Properly controlled structures enable the production of maximum yields with a minimal quantity of water. These benefits often help justify the high fees and control requirements [5].

A typical drip irrigation system is shown in the figure below. There are many types of drip products on the market designed to meet the demands of just about any application (see Figure 4.5).

Drip irrigation applies water very slowly, allowing the water to slowly enter the soil where you want it without running off or blowing away; the problem with drip irrigation is that people think they can place one or two emitters beside a plant and expect the plant to grow generally for many years. This placement of one to several emitters per plant is called point source drip irrigation. When a plant is first planted in the soil and a couple of adrift emitters are added, the roots will grow with moisture over time; the roots will likely fill in the wetted area. Remember plant roots do not search for water; therefore, the roots will not grow beyond the wetted size; however, two things start to happen over time: first, if the plant is watered too frequently, the area sometimes can become supersaturated to the point of choking the soil of gaseous oxygen that the plant roots need; second for a plant to grow larger, its roots must have room to grow. If the wetted area remains the same, the root growth area remains the same, so it is like growing your plant in a pot. The plant will never reach mature size.

These problems can be seen in the landscape where shrubs and trees are irrigated with one or two emitters each overtime. The landscape will die out. What is the solution? Drip irrigation is an efficient way of applying water, but the number of drip emitters must increase to stay ahead of root growth as the plant grows. This can be accomplished by adding more emitters to each plant or by adding or initially starting with a grid layout of emitters. Another question is that why do we need to irrigate? The sole reason is to provide water to plants when rainfall is not enough. Drip irrigation is not like rainfall; it concentrates water in specific areas. If it is applied too frequently drip irrigation can cause shallow rooting. So, It needs to be used infrequently but long enough to give the rooting area a good soaking.

Trees and shrubs can root one and a half to three feet deep. Since, drip irrigation is typically used to irrigate shrubs and trees, longer watering times will be needed to water these deeper levels, but the watering frequency should be no more than once a week. New plantings will need more frequent irrigation when it is really hot in the summer and little to no irrigation in the winter.

There are a lot of variables with drip irrigation, including emitter flow rate and soil type. A row of shrubs can be easily irrigated with one or two strips of drift line. A single tree or large tree will require lots of emitters. Here's an example: if a tree or shrub is rooted two feet deep, with one-gallon water per hour and drip emitters spaced 12 inches apart and tubing spaced 18 inches apart, then you will need to water for about two hours if you have heavy clay soil. On the other hand, if you have sandy soil, you will only need to water one hour, while clay soil needs twice as much water as sandy soil. Because the sandy soil drains fast, it will need more frequent watering compared to the clay soil. Clay soil can stay wet for many days or even weeks.

Further, the question arises is that how do we know the emitter spacing and other variables like emitter flow rate, wall thickness, emitter diameter? For a proper practice a list is usually made so that it can help to decide based on the need. Below is an example discussed by Oregon State University in a table [8].

TABLE 4.3
A Listing of Different Manufacturers and Specification of Drip Irrigation System

Manufacturer	Diameter(inches)	Wall thickness (mil)	Emitter Spacing (in)	Emitter flow rates (gal/h)
Chapin Watermatics	5/8,7/8	4,6,8,10,15	2,4,8,9,12,16,24	0.125–0.65
Drip Tape Man. and Eng. Inc.	5/8, 7/8	5,6,7–8,10,15	4.25, 8.5, 12.75, 17.25	0.15,0.21,0.28
Eurodrip	5/8,7/8,1	6,8,10,12,15	8.48	0.16,0.25, 0.40,0.60,1.00
Netafim	5/8, 7/8, 1	6,8,10,13,15	7	0.16,0.21,0.24, 0.33,0.48, 0.60
Roberts Irrigation Products	5/8, 3/4, 7/8	5,6,8,10,13,15	4,8,12,16,24	0.13,0.18,0.20 0.24,0.27,0.34, 0.50
T-Systems International	3/8, 5/8, 7/8, 1 3/8	4, 5, 6, 7, 8, 10, 15, 20	4, 6, 8, 12, 16, 18, 24	0.14, 0.17, 0.20, 0.22, 0.27, 0.28, 0.34, 0.40, 0.44, 0.45, 0.67
ToroAg	5/8, 7/8, 1 3/8	4, 6, 8, 10,12, 15	4, 8, 12, 16, 24	0.13, 0.15, 0.20, 0.27, 0.34

4.2.4 SPRINKLER IRRIGATION

A sprinkler irrigation system is a compressed framework where water is distributed through an organization of lines to and in the field and applied through chosen sprinkler heads or water applicators with a pressurized system. Sprinkler frameworks are more costly than surface irrigation systems yet offer considerably more adaptability and control. They are reasonable for most soil and geological conditions and can likewise be utilized for cooling and ice/freeze security. Some of the basic components necessary for sprinkler systems are a pump to send water out in the fields, water reservoir, a pipe distributed network for water to flow, sprinklers to spray the water over the ground, valves for the control systems. There are many types of sprinkler systems as listed below [5].

1. Hand-Move and Portable Sprinklers: These frameworks utilize a parallel pipeline with sprinklers introduced at normal spans. The parallel line is frequently made of aluminum and comes in 20-, 30-, or 40-foot segments with unique speedy coupling connectors at each line joint. The sprinkler parallel is set in one area and worked until the ideal water application has been made. Then, at that point, the parallel line is dismantled and moved to the following situation to be inundated. The sprinkler spout is replaceable and should be coordinated to the stream rate, riser tallness, dividing, and region to be covered. The maker's determinations on size and separating should be followed to guarantee legitimate cross-over of shower example and uniform application.
2. Solid Set or Permanent Sprinklers: Such systems are not moved from one place to other, thus there is a great reduction in the cost. However, they have much higher initial cost. This system incorporates many numerous mainlines, laterals, risers, and nozzles. Mainlines and laterals are sometimes placed inside the soil to prevent interference with mechanical field operations.
3. Side Roll System: With side rolls, the parallel line is mounted on wheels, with the line framing the pivot. A drive unit, typically a gas motor, moves the framework starting with one water system position then onto the next one. The side roll framework is most appropriate for rectangular fields and is restricted to short harvests (generally 4 feet or less). Water is provided to the framework through an adaptable hose associated with risers deliberately situated along the edge of the field.

Portable Gun System: Portable guns come in two kinds: hard hose or hose reel framework, and the link tow or hose-drag framework. Both of them are labor-intensive and utilize a lot of energy because of their high working factors. For the most part, gun systems are not utilized for vegetable yields because of their inefficient water application proficiency, enormous drops, high working pressing factors, and high application rates.

Some of the advantage of sprinkler systems are: automated easily, control systems can implemented, reduced labor requirements needed for irrigation, and are adaptable to wide range of soil and topographic condition. Disadvantages of the sprinkler system is that it has initial high installation cost and high maintenance.

4.2.5 CENTER-PIVOT IRRIGATION

From the dawn of civilization humans have searched for ways to grow crops more efficiently, increasing yields while using fewer resources, including conservation of water. Fast forward a few thousand years that quest to produce more with less led to the innovation of center-pivot irrigation. The system consists of a pumping station which captures water from a source such as a river, well, dam, or reservoir. The pump transports the water from the source through the pipes to the central tower or pivot point. Water is passed through the range construction and circulated to the sprinklers, which apply water drops of the right size to boost assimilation into the dirt the middle turn moves consequently fueled by a profoundly effective partial strength electric engine continuing on wheels intended to deal with even troublesome landscapes. Center pivots can be used on nearly any type of agricultural crops; the system is customizable to the size shape and terrain of individual fields plus variable rate irrigation allows for application of water even more precisely based on different topography and soil types even within the same field to enhance productivity the benefits of center pivot irrigation (see Figure 4.6).

Increased yields in less cultivated area protect against drought-decreased production costs, while larger scale and greater efficiency make multiple harvests per year possible. In addition, center pivots use 25 to 50 percent less water than traditional irrigation and offer better precision; they apply the exact amount of water. Where it is required, center pivots are the solution to preserving resources and maximizing efficiency. Growers can apply fertilizer and pesticide through their center pivots and can irrigate multiple crops at the same time with the latest technological advancements

FIGURE 4.6   Center-pivot irrigation.

growers can accurately manage their irrigation from a control panel located at the pivot point or even from miles away via PC tablet or smartphone all of these factors add up to make center pivots a superior method of irrigation.

Center pivot watering system refers to the modern mechanized irrigation system that can help to irrigate crops by maintaining a round pattern around a central pivot. Mostly, the system has a lengthy radial pipe that is supported by sprinkling towers. The same principle as sprinkler irrigation is implemented here as well but the towers pivot around a center point of the whole mechanism. This system also gives irrigation effectiveness by applying suitable amount of water required on the top of crop to create wetness to the wanted level.

Center pivot irrigation has benefits, such as requiring much less labor than many other surface irrigation methods, such as furrow irrigation. The lower labor cost is because it does not require continuous maintenance. The system operators on its on and also covers the whole field. It also reduces the amount of soil tillage, and it has good uniformity in water application. This system is very reliable and it its feasible to apply for shallow depths. On the other hand, there are many negatives for center pivot systems such as high initial cost, high maintenance cost, which includes a trained technician who knows ins and outs of the system. It requires flat fields, and it is not suitable for rectangular or square shape fields.

4.2.6 Lateral Move Irrigation

The linear circulate (from time to time called a lateral flow) irrigation system is built identical to a center pivot with moving towers and spans of pipe connecting the buildings. The critical difference is that each tower flows at an equal speed and inside an identical direction. The flow of water is either through the center or from the ends. Water may be furnished to the linear machine both thru a canal, by dragging supply hoses connected to a mainline, or by clicking and disconnecting from hydrants as the linear actions down the sector. The lateral motion makes it hard to power a linear flow sufficient with energy. Usually, a diesel motor with a generator is mounted on the primary pressure tower and supplies the strength had to function the irrigation machine. The primary gain of the linear is that it could irrigate rectangular fields up to 625 meter length and 312.5 meter wide. Due to the high capital investment cost, lateral irrigation is used on excessive fee crops [9].

Typical capital costs associated with Center Pivot/ Lateral Move irrigation systems range from $2,500 to $5,500/ha. The main difference between center pivot and lateral move irrigation is that the center pivot sprinkler is anchored at one end and rotates around a fixed point, while a lateral move system is not anchored, and both the ends of the machine move at a constant speed. Lateral irrigation system covers approximately 98 percent of a rectangular and square field with a uniform sprinkler pattern. This system is usually used as an alternative to a center pivot system. As the land prices are so high it is very important to utilize each and every piece of land in order to increase the production. Lateral move irrigation comes with an easy-to-use control panel and has accurate guidance and real-time irrigation adjustments.

Two models to match as per water supply are:

Hose Fed: The best-known machine is the hose-fed system, which sprays water via a vast hose attached to a pressurized mainline. General lateral use of a 2-wheel or 4-wheel cart (depending on field length) with four-inch, 6-inch, and eight-inch hoses and consists of towing options to be used on adjacent fields for expanded assurance.

Ditch Fed: Ditch-fed systems can draw water from a current ditch within the center of the sector or at the circle's edge. Ditch-fed laterals are the simplest available as a four-wheel cart and are much less popular and more steeply priced to put into service than a hose-fed device. The benefit of ditch-fed laterals is they do not require a supply hose or electrical changeover.

Lateral-move irrigation shares the same advantages and disadvantages as center-pivot irrigation but the only one added disadvantage is that it is very difficult to apply on a circular field.

4.2.7 SUB-IRRIGATION

In agricultural production fields, sub-irrigation is an irrigation practice to control the water table at certain levels by elevating or lowering it. Sub-irrigation is accomplished by artificially adding water to the soil profile underground to moisten the crop root-zone for a determined period.

Sub-irrigation is a greenhouse irrigation method that relies on capillary action to provide plant life with water and nutrients underneath their boxes. The first documented sub-irrigation machine was defined in 1895, and numerous variations of the fundamental design have been used for studies purposes earlier than the current ebb-and-glide kind systems that emerged in 1974. Most sub-irrigation procedures apply the fertilizer strategy to a water-resistant bench or greenhouse segment, permitting the substrate to take in the water through holes within the bottom of the boxes. Because there is minimal leaching, sub-irrigation generally allows for using decreased fertilizer concentrations [10]. Although excess fertilizer salts typically gather inside the pinnacle layer of the substrate, this does not appear to have a harmful effect on flora. Sub-irrigation can preserve nutrients and water, reduce hard work costs, and help growers meet environmental policies. An undertaking with sub-irrigation is the capability to unfold pathogens through the fertilizer solution. Effective disinfection strategies consisting of ultraviolet radiation, chlorine, or ozone should be used when issued. Sensor-based total irrigation management has currently been implemented in sub-irrigation to improve nutrient and water use efficiencies further. Better control of irrigation may reduce the appearance of pathogens while at the same time enhancing crops. The primary financial advantage of sub-irrigation is reducing labor prices, which is the best expenditure for many growers (see Figure 4.7).

4.3 SMART IRRIGATION SYSTEM

In the United States, outdoor water use averages more than 9 billion gallons every day, especially for landscape irrigation. As much as 50 percent of this water is wasted due to overwatering resulting from inefficiencies in traditional irrigation techniques and structures. Innovative irrigation generation is the answer.

FIGURE 4.7   Sub irrigation.

Intelligent irrigation systems tailor watering schedules and run times robotically to meet particular panorama desires. These controllers significantly enhance outdoor water use efficiencies.

Unlike conventional irrigation controllers that function on a preset programmed schedule and timers, intelligent irrigation controllers screen weather, soil conditions, evaporation, and plant water use to automatically adjust the watering timetable to natural needs.

For instance, as outdoor temperatures increase or rainfall decreases, clever irrigation controllers consider web site-precise variables, consisting of soil type, sprinklers' application price, and so on. To adjust the watering run times or schedules, there are numerous options for smart irrigation controllers.

Weather-Based and Soil Moisture Sensors
Essentially there are two styles of smart irrigation controllers: primarily weather-based (ET) and on-website online soil moisture sensors. The proper solution depends on your geographic location and landscape.

Weather-Based Totally Smart Irrigation Controllers
Evapotranspiration (ET) or weather-based controllers, use local weather statistics to manage irrigation schedules. Evapotranspiration has evaporization from soil floor and transpiration by plant substances. These controllers accumulate neighborhood climate data and make irrigation run-time modifications, so the panorama receives the ideal amount of water.

ET climate facts use four weather parameters: temperature, wind, solar radiation, and humidity. It's the maximum correct manner to calculate panorama water desires.

There are three simple styles of those weather-based ET controllers:

- Signal: primarily based controllers use meteorological statistics from a publicly available supply, and the ET price is calculated for a grass floor on the website. The ET statistics are then dispatched to the controller by way of a wi-fi connection.
- Historic ET controllers use a pre-programmed water use curve, based totally on historical water use in special areas. The curve may be adjusted for temperature and solar radiation.
- On-website climate measurement controllers use weather facts amassed on-web pages to calculate non-stop ET measurements and water.

Soil Moisture Sensors Used with Smart Irrigation Controllers
Soil moisture sensor-based totally smart irrigation controllers use installed technologies to monitor soil-moisture content material. When buried inside the root sector of turf, bushes, or shrubs, the sensors correctly determine the moisture stage in the soil and transmit this reading to the controller.

There are different soil moisture sensor-based structures available:

- Suspended cycle irrigation structures can be set like traditional timer controllers, with watering schedules, begin instances, and length. The distinction is that the machine will forestall the next scheduled irrigation while there may be sufficient moisture within the soil.
- Water on demand irrigation requires no programming of irrigation duration (best begin instances and days of the week to water). It has a consumer-set lower and higher threshold, which initiates irrigation while the soil moisture degree fails to satisfy the one's stages.

Smart Irrigation Controllers Save Water and Money
The specialists agree that clever irrigation structures and controllers versus conventional irrigation controllers preserve water throughout several scenarios. Several managed research studies suggest excellent financial savings anywhere from 30 to 50 percent.

Tests at the Irrigation Association (IA) and the International Center for Water Technology at California State University in Fresno have shown clever irrigation controllers to store up to 20 percent more water than conventional irrigation controllers.

Another test examined a prototype controller/receiver machine, which includes a conventional irrigation controller changed to get hold of a sign broadcast via satellite. Outdoor water financial savings have been calculated primarily based on two years of pre-set-up utilization and were adjusted for climate conditions. The stated common doors savings is 16 percent, and it is also said this represents 85 percent of ability savings based totally on reference ET.

Water-efficient irrigation takes a look at the Saving Water Partnership, a coalition of 24 water purveyors in Washington State's Puget Sound. Water financial savings have been calculated primarily based on historical intake, and changes have been made for climate conditions. The pronounced water financial savings were 20,735 gallons per 12 months in line with websites online for websites with rain sensors controllers and 10,071 gallons per year according to the website for websites using conventional controllers.

4.3.1 NEED OF SMART IRRIGATION

As we know that smart irrigation usually involves a combination of advanced technology, such as sprinkler with nozzles, that are able to improve the range and coverage of water flow. Basically, implementing AI and robotics techniques to monitor the weather, soil conditions, evaporation, and plant water use. By monitoring these details, we get a large data set for each sensor we monitor. Through these previous trends we can implement statistical models to get future predictions. With these future predictions we can train the robot to perform is certain manner based on the environmental condition.

Without smart irrigation there is large water wastage. On an average, about 1.7 trillion gallons of water is wasted every year [11]. Here are some of the methods that traditional irrigation structures wastewater:

Sprinkler heads: These can readily malfunction; they're easy for humans to kick and ride over, and they become much more fragile the longer they are left in the baking sun. A few common symptoms of a sprinkler head being broken is they don't pop up while watering, spraying either an excessive amount of or too little water, and finally not spraying at all.

Broken water lines: If a major location of your irrigation tool isn't always running, it may be because of faulty or damaged water traces. A few common symptoms include depression inside the floor, water effervescence up, or a completely wet patch.

Improper scheduling: A principal reason we need clever irrigation is its potential to sense the quality of time to water the land. Traditional irrigation systems can't inform whether it has rained recently or how whether a lot of moisture is in the ground. They are virtually set to work at a particular time of day. This makes no difference if it has just rained. Integrating a smart irrigation gadget will save a lot of cash and water.

4.3.2 OVER-WATERING

For maximum production, growers need to avoid drought stress all through the growing season due to the fact it may quickly reduce yield and cause a misshapen, undersized, and early ripened crop. Applying more water as insurance against these problems makes sense because it could also offer a time buffer if the subsequent irrigation is behind schedule because of a breakdown or an unexpectedly required chemical application.

"A little more" will become "an excessive amount" when the irrigation increases soil moisture in the energetic root zone above area capacity. Soil can store water for crop use, and field ability is the upper limit of this storage. Any additional watering carried out past this restriction starts to drain immediately with the aid of gravity out of the foundation zone, misplaced for crop use, and leaching valuable nitrogen.

Excess soil moisture also promotes root illnesses like armillaria root rot and phytophthora root and crown rot. These sicknesses are found in almost all orchard soils and might significantly shorten the efficient existence of bushes.

Other losses as a result of over-irrigation include:

- Water misplaced to leaching
- Nitrogen lost to leaching and/or de-nitrification
- Increased pumping expenses
- Lower yield
- Reduced tree vigor and lifespan because of illnesses
- Increased weed strain

Artificial Intelligence and Robotics help a lot in preventing over-watering. Firms can use thermal imaging, as an example, to see if vegetation is getting enough water. Thirsty vegetation tends to be a little hotter than others. That's due to the fact, and commonly, vegetation launches some of the water they take in through their roots out via tiny pores on the underside of their leaves. When that water evaporates, it cools off the plant, just as sweating cools off people. Thirsty flora, however, close off those pores to keep from losing water, which leaves them a touch warmer. If farmers can perceive precisely which vegetation is parched, they simply need to irrigate these plants, which helps them keep water, which becomes more difficult as weather exchanges bring about longer and more extreme droughts.

Firms are gathering pictures from cameras mounted to sprinkler frameworks, robots, planes, and satellites and are utilizing PCs to examine those pictures to distinguish which harvests are assaulted by caterpillars, encircled by weeds, or shrouded in a parasite. PCs then, at that point, advise producers to shower those plants – and just those plants – with insect spray, herbicides, or fungicides.

These assist cultivators with utilizing less water and fewer synthetics, which saves cash and keeps farms in business. Utilizing less insect poison, for instance, helps protect bumblebees, which are needed to fertilize many crops. Utilizing less engineered compost can eliminate contamination. Manure on farms will result in general advance into streams and, at last, the sea, where it obliterates ocean life.

4.3.3   UNDER-WATERING

The alerts we receive from a plant for under-watering are like the indicators received when we overwater flowers. Under-watering and over-watering flowers frequently reach the same final results – unwell or dead flowers. The symptoms to look for to know whether we are under-watering, or over-watering are listed below:

4.3.3.1   Your Plant is Wilting

Shriveling or wilting is an indication of both under-watering and over-watering. On account of under-watering the plant's leaves, you can know they're fresh if they are not limp. Withering in the present circumstance is an indication of a deficiency of water passing through by means of the pores of a plant. On the outside of leaves plants have pores called stoma. They allow air to enter vegetation. At the point when vegetation no longer has sufficient water, they close their stoma to stop declining, prompting shriveling. Foliage likewise shrivels due to different actions, including over-watering, an exorbitant amount of sunlight, root-bound, an excessive amount of manure, and so forth.

4.3.3.2 The Soil Is Dry

A simple tool for looking at soil dampness is a long screwdriver. Press a screwdriver into the ground. At the point when the dirt is clammy, the screwdriver ought to infiltrate the dirt without issues. The power of infiltration will differ by utilizing the dirt kind, screwdriver length, and energy. As the dirt evaporates, the screwdriver might be harder to drive into the ground.

4.3.3.3 Slowed Growth

A slowdown in a boom is an indication a plant isn't receiving sufficient water. This can be a temporary or prolonged state of affairs. If the plant studies a short lower water supply, the increase may also simply last for a short duration. If the issue seems permanent, you may see the new leaf being smaller than usual.

4.3.3.4 Discolored Leaves

The decrease in leaves commonly appears first, becoming yellowed and curled. The leaves can also expand dry edges.

A simple robotics system designed with electronics and mechanical chassis can easily help to control the soil moisture level. Using soil moisture sensor and a alarm with electronics circuit can notify the growers if the soil moisture level falls below the threshold. It is very important as under-watering can cause loss in market value through yield reduction and reduction in fruit size and quality.

4.3.4 IRRIGATION SCHEDULING

Irrigation scheduling is the process by which an irrigator determines the timing and quantity of water to be applied to the crop or pasture. The challenge is to estimate crop water requirements for different growth stages and climatic conditions.

To avoid over- or under-watering, it is important to know how much water is available to the plant and how efficiently the plant can use it. The methods available to measure this include:

- plant observation
- feel and appearance of the soil
- soil moisture monitoring devices
- available water from weather data.

Irrigation scheduling is based on historical data collected over time by sensing different parameters based on the agricultural needs. With the appearance of the cloud era, the capacity to seize and record statistics produced by irrigation hardware has by no means been greater. This, combined with new sensor improvement, analytics, and satellites, gives irrigators significant possibilities to drive effects and production enhancements via smart scheduling.

To date, there are four primary strategies used to schedule irrigation: climate-based, soil moisture tracking, remote sensing, and plant sensors. Here are some of the pros and cons of each type [12, 13].

4.3.4.1 Climate-Based Scheduling

Primarily climate-based scheduling is based totally on figuring out day-by-day evapo-transpiration and multiplying this via the crop coefficient for a selected plant at a specific growth degree. Previously tested harvest coefficients are openly accessible and utilized universally to set water system benchmarks in a range of areas. The primary issues faced with the aid of this method are that it may be labor-intensive to stay on top of it, and that the combined effect of small differences in types, rootstocks, crop load, soil kind, and root intensity will have a dramatic impact on the water necessities of a crop.

4.3.4.2 Soil Moisture Tracking

Soil moisture probes (whether or not they be tension meters, gypsum blocks, or capacitance probes) have been available for over 30 years. To date, they were a widely utilized way to get further information on plant water use dynamics in the soil medium. The recent migration of their facts to the "cloud" has allowed for clean facts logging and comparatively cheap monitoring of the soil moisture stability in irrigated plant life.

Major issues with in-area hardware are that they frequently stop working, batteries go flat, or they're no longer calibrated/set up correctly, or are now not installed in a specific region. We regularly find that while the developments proven by way of probes are consistent with our modeling, the numbers are of little use, as they simply don't constitute what is definitely taking place in the soil throughout the whole subject.

4.3.4.3 Remote Sensing

Satellite/remote sensing-based irrigation scheduling is pretty new and gives great opportunities because it is simple to put into effect and can be of low cost. However, scheduling by way of this approach is fairly problematic due to bad picture quality caused by to cloud cowl or infrequent picture captures. While there are first-rate possibilities here, we feel it ought to best constitute part of the irrigation management suite. Unless plant-unique info is recognized, then components like drainage and runoff can't be modeled or absolutely preferred.

4.3.4.4 Plant Sensors

The trendy fashion is totally plant-based sensors to reveal sap float and cover temperature, and dendrometers for without delay measuring increase (and contraction) of stems and culmination. These were available for some time, however, they have only lately found utility in irrigation-scheduling systems. These sensors are very good at letting a supervisor realize precisely what's occurring with the plant; however, they encounter similar challenges when it comes to maintaining the equipment used in the field. They also are high-priced, which in all likelihood limits sample length and requires exceedingly specialized species-unique interpretation and formats for accurate management insights.

4.3.5 Artificial Intelligence Techniques Used to Conserve Water

Agricultural practices account for around 70 percent of all water withdrawals globally according to the Food and Agriculture Organization (FAO) of the United Nations. About 60 percent of that is wasted, largely due to inefficient applications in line with the UN's Food and Agriculture Organization (FAO). With water increasingly valuable in opposition to the backdrop of a growing human populace and weather exchange, can AI be used to prevent water wastage?

Simple strategies like rainwater harvesting and wastewater recycling are already being used in lots of areas to lessen water consumption. And many farms have realized the blessings of changing their floor and sprinkler irrigation systems with greater efficient drip irrigation structures.

But there's another area that would provide bigger advantages to farms across the world: Artificial Intelligence. There are various discussions of Artificial Intelligence (AI) techniques all around the globe; some of them are below.

In [14] the author discusses the specific irrigation methods with the primary reason for growing a tool with decreased resource usage and increased performance. Devices like a fertility meter or a PH meter are set up in the sector to decide the fertility of the soil by way of detecting the percentage of the number one components of the ground like potassium, phosphorous, nitrogen. Automatic plant irrigators are planted in the sector through wireless technology for drip irrigation. This method guarantees the fertility of the soil and ensures the effective use of water sources.

The technology of intelligent irrigation is developed to increase production without the involvement of considerable manpower by detecting the level of water, the temperature of the soil, nutrient content, and climate forecasting. The actuation is done according to the microcontroller by turning the irrigator pump on and off. The M2M, that is, Machine to Machine technology, has been developed to ease the verbal exchange and information sharing among each different actor and to the server or the cloud thru the central community between all the nodes of the agricultural field [15]. They evolved an automatic robot model for the detection of the moisture content material and temperature of the Arduino and Raspberry pi3. The records are taken at regular periods and are sent to the microcontroller of Arduino (which has an edge-level hardware linked to it); it similarly converts the input analog to digital. The sign is dispatched to the Raspberry pi3 (embedded with the KNN algorithm), and it sends the signal to Arduino to start the water supply for irrigation. The water could be furnished by means of a helpful resource in keeping with the requirement, and it's going to additionally update and store the sensor values. In [16] the authors also developed an automatic irrigation machine with the generation of Arduino for lowering the manpower and time intake inside the process of irrigation.

Authors in [17] additionally advanced the idea of an efficient and automated irrigation system with the aid of growing far-flung sensors the usage of the generation of Arduino, which can increase around 40 percent of production. Another system for automatic irrigation changed into given via another group of researchers. In this method, unique sensors had been constructed for exclusive functions like the soil moisture sensor to discover the moisture content material in the soil, the temperature sensor to discover the temperature, the stress regulator sensor to reduce strain, and the molecular sensor for better crop boom. The installation of virtual cameras. The output of most of these gadgets is transformed into a virtual signal, and it is sent to the multi-plexer via a wireless network together with Zigbee and hotspot [18].

The first approach was the subsurface drip irrigation system, which minimized the amount of water loss due to evaporation and runoff as it is without delay buried under the crop. Later, researchers got here with exclusive sensors, which were used to find the need for water supply to the fields as soil moisture sensor and raindrop sensor, which we're told via the wi-fi broadband network and powered through solar panels. The raindrop sensor and soil moisture sensor tell the farmer about the mois-ture content inside the soil via SMS in their cellular smartphone the usage of the GSM module.

Accordingly, the farmer can give commands for SMS to turn ON and OFF the water delivery. Thus, we remember this system will detect components or sites inside the fields that required greater watering and the farmer can hold off watering while it's raining

Soil moisture sensors are one of the several technologies used to measure the soil moisture content. It is buried near the root zones of the vegetation [18]. The sensors assist in accurately figuring out the moisture stage and transmits this analysis to the controller for irrigation. Soil moisture sensors additionally assist in protecting water [18]. One method of moisture, is the water on demand irrigation in which we set the edge according to the soil's field capacity, and these sensors permit the controller to water only when required. When the scheduled time arrives, the sensor reads the moisture content or level for that particular zone, and watering will be allowed in that zone only if the moisture content is below the threshold. The other is the suspended cycle irrigation, which requires irrigation duration, unlike the water-on-demand irri-gation. It requires the start time and the duration for each zone.

All the above discussion gives an idea that there is already a lot of development in this field, but still we have not reached the level where we can choose the methods for each different crop. Still a lot of research has been going on in this field to get the best results.

4.3.6 EMBEDDED SYSTEMS AND ITS INTEGRATION

The proposed idea is to develop a system that is a combination of electronics and AI with an end goal to monitor many important aspects of the agricultural field to form a sustainable agricultural environment. To achieve the purpose, the system has a Wireless Sensor Network (WSN) to accumulate the vital facts and send them via LoRa and MQTT to the server. MQTT is a publish-subscribe network protocol that sends and receives messages between devices or, in short, it's a standard for IoT messaging. This same WSN also has the capability of receiving messages from the

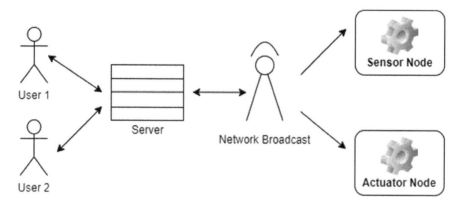

FIGURE 4.8 System architecture.

server to carry out the necessary responsibilities, such as starting the water pumps for the duration of the required time, collecting the sensor data, and transferring it to the database and alerting the growers with the present health of the farm (see Figure 4.8).

1 System Architecture

Keeping this in mind, it became essential to create several nodes, each one for a specific venture, that together creates a WSN, with a star topology, letting them proportion the vital facts among each other. The system desires to encompass numerous Sensor Nodes, for statistics series, an Actuator Node, to turn ON/OFF the irrigation machine, and a Network Broadcast, to manipulate the network and send/acquire messages from the server.

Although each hub has great qualities, there are certain specs that are normal to all, for example, the microcontroller and the correspondence module that gives the verbal trade inside the subject local area. Therefore, all of the nodes proportion a commonplace base, composed of an ESP32, a twin-middle microcontroller produced by authors [19] and a RFM95W LoRa transceiver.

The LoRa protocol ensures interaction between all the nodes of the network has been particularly used due to its low energy intake, lengthy variety, low price of the gadgets, and is a protocol that supports bi-directional communications [20]. The RFM95W module permits long-distance, up to 2 km, verbal exchange with a low intake relation. Taking into consideration that this core system and the needs of the system, each of the developed nodes, their charter, responsibilities, and features are described within the following subsections.

2 Network Broadcast

The network broadcast system is the one responsible for exchanging records from the other types of nodes of the network and in the end with the server. As defined above, the core of the node is composed of an ESP32 and an RFM95W LORA module, to permit the change of messages many of the nodes within the network and to speak with the server MQTT was used.

An Internet connection is necessary for utilizing MQTT. Consequently, a cellular solution was chosen as a suitable option. In this scenario, NB-IoT technology was employed due to the expanding coverage in Portugal. This technology was designed specifically for situations like this, where it can transmit small data packets through a cellular network. This enables small devices to establish an internet connection anywhere in the world.

To utilize NB-IoT, the SIM7000E module was connected to the aggregation node. This enabled the mobile network to establish an Internet connection. This connection has the capability to function using either NB-IoT or 2G technology. The truth that this module can work, the use of 2G brings blessings as agricultural fields are characterized utilizing low community coverage.

3   Sensor Node

Sensors play the main role in this whole embedded system. They are responsible for gathering field statistics. These systems need to have the important sensors to gather the facts, for example, a LoRa module in order to send the real-time sensed data to the network broadcast system, a control board, and a power supply.

The ESP32 microcontroller is used to manipulate all the modules, similar to the network broadcast system. It is possible to turn ESP32 into sleep mode in order to save energy, but a network broadcast system always runs.

Regarding the statistics series, numerous sensors have been used, which include:

- SI7021, a temperature and humidity sensor, able to collect temperature and moisture values with excessive precision (±3%RH, ±0.4°C), in a selection between −40°C and 125°C in terms of temperature and zero to 100 percent in humidity values [21].
- DS18B20, a water-proof soil temperature sensor, able to acquire facts between −55°C and 125°C with an accuracy of 0.5°C for −10°C to 85°C intervals, easy to put in force, with one wire connection [22].
- SparkFun Soil Moisture Sensor just needs to be connected to VCC and GND pins to Arduino based device. There is also a SIG connection that gives SIG out depending on the amount of water present in the soil.
- DHT11 is an ultra-low cost 3 to 5V temperature and humidity sensor. It uses 2.5mA max current during conversion and it is good for 20–80 percent humidity readings with 5 percent accuracy and 0.50°C temperature readings with 2 percent accuracy.
- To hold the data of the field beneath evaluation updated, a group is made each 10 min. Between every collection and with a view to shop the battery that powers the node, the circuit is positioned in Deep Sleep mode, wherein the strength intake is reduced to 100A. Towards the end of every Deep Sleep time, the node wakes up and runs all the code once more, gets all the new statistics (new readings), and sends new data back.
- To power the nodes, because of their low strength intake, it will become feasible to use batteries. In order to make the system more sustainable and decrease the need for maintenance, a solar panel can be extensively utilized to charge the battery, ensuring that they'll always have sufficient power to

electricity the node even at some stage in lengthy intervals of the absence of solar publicity.

4 Actuator Node

The Actuator Node is in charge of acting consistently with the accumulated records utilizing the Sensor Node. This node includes a microcontroller, ESP32 (Wifi Module), a LoRa radio module, RFM95W, the weather station, and the irrigation pumps. As defined earlier, the RFM95W (transceiver from LoRaTM long range modem) will be accountable for exchanging messages among the node and the network broadcast system, receiving the irrigation commands, and sending the current status of every pump.

The microcontroller will get hold of the update messages for irrigation and process them to control the pumps at some stage for the defined time for each section. It may also be connected to a climate station, the SEN 0186 (Weather Sensor), is able to gather measured wind velocity, wind route, and precipitation values. These sensors aren't linked to a Sensor Node since they want to continuously accumulate statistics, now not capable of working with batteries.

Regarding the node power consumption, and because irrigation pumps work at 12 V, it was no longer feasible to charge the node with batteries or solar panels, much like the Sensor Node. Therefore, the node will be powered by an electrical socket with a transformer that converts the 220 V of the local electric modern to 12 V wanted. Also, a modern-day converter, the LM2596 (regulator), was used to transform the 12 V coming from the transformer to 5 V to be able to strengthen the ESP32 and the whole circuit. Since ESP32 now does not have enough strength to supply the water pumps, the Panasonic AQY212EHAT Solid State Relays (SSR) are used, making it viable, through an easy digital circuit and HIGH and LOW alerts from ESP32, to replace ON or OFF the 12 V deliver to the water pumps, switching their popularity.

5 Big Picture

We can discuss a small smart irrigation system that includes AI and electronics by combining all of the above. The idea is to train the model in any such manner that it identifies flowers or other plant life when any image is fed to the model in the future. VGG16 or VGG19 is used to train the version as it's by far the simplest version among all other convolutional networks. This network is recognized for its simplicity, employing only 3 × 3 convolutional layers that are arranged one on top of the other, with increasing complexity. Reducing length is handled by way of max pooling. Two completely linked layers, each with 4096 nodes, are then accompanied by a SoftMax classifier. In VGG16, '16' stands for the number of weight layers within the community. Keras library in python consists of VGG, ResNet, Inception, and Xception network architectures. Huge image facts of various flora and exceptional flowers are used to teach the model and test the accuracy. The version then correctly predicts the plant or flower when any random photograph is fed into the device.

This machine is important for the agricultural sector as every plant has some specific need for the surroundings. A constant amount of water at regular instances and favorable environmental gases help the plant to grow perfectly healthy by category, via deep learning, it turns into smooth for the farmers or botanist to grow the plant as, by way of the identity of the plant and its favorable situations, farmers and botanist can provide such environment and right irrigation [23].

4.3.7 BENEFITS OF SMART IRRIGATION CONTROLLERS

In the present world situation, everything is about upgrading to the "smart" generation. You can deck your house and existence out in clever devices that range the spectrum from smart thermostats to smartwatches to clever shades. As the era advances, increasingly, methods within the home become computerized and smart. This is for an amazing purpose–clever devices generally tend to lower waste and growth efficiency, maximizing talents even as minimizing price. Many human beings might not comprehend that has emerged as "smart" is their irrigation device in a single location. An irrigation device is important to any homeowner's landscape as it keeps the landscape well irrigated on a regular agenda so that a homeowner no longer has to try to not forget when they last watered the lawn or the rose trees. But now, irrigation has become even more state-of-the-art with clever irrigation.

Smart irrigation structures provide a variety of benefits over traditional irrigation systems. Smart irrigation systems can optimize water tiers based totally on matters inclusive of soil moisture and weather predictions. This is completed with wireless moisture sensors that talk with the smart irrigation controls and help tell the system whether or not the panorama is in want of water. Additionally, the smart irrigation control gets nearby climate information that can assist it in deciding whether a landscape ought to be watered. If you have ever been back home when a storm is coming on and see your sprinklers spraying water, you understand how beneficial that is. Rather than wasting water assets and your money on watering, you can benefit from the natural moisture from the storm and save your water for another day when it is needed. The blessings of these smart irrigation structures are extensive. The smart irrigation gadget will assist you in controlling your landscape and irrigation whether you are home or are away. You will save in water bills via sensible control and automation. Your clever irrigation gadget will optimize sources so that the whole property receives what it needs without pointless waste.

Additionally, we've all seen many locations in the United States that have experienced droughts, and we realize that our water resources are treasured. With smart irrigation structures, we can better use resources that are better for the environment. The opportunity to have better control, and be extra green while maintaining a lush and exquisite landscape are only some blessings a smart irrigation machine presents and makes an exceptional addition to any home.

REFERENCES

[1] J.F. Velasco-Munoz et al. (2019). "Sustainable Irrigation in Agriculture: An Analysis of Global Research." *Water* vol. 11, no. 9, 1758.

[2] H. Ritchie, M. Roser (2013). "Land Use". Published online at OurWorldInData.org. Retrieved from: https://ourworldindata.org/land-use [Online Resource].

[3] B. Zhang, Z. Fu, Wang, J., Zhang, L. (2019). "Farmers' adoption of water-saving irrigation technology alleviates water scarcity in metropolis suburbs: A case study of Beijing, China." *Agricultural Water Management* vol. 212, 349–357.

[4] North Dakota State University (2022) www.ag.ndsu.edu/publications/crops/planning-to-irrigate-a-checklist.

[5] Texas A&M Agrilife Extension. (n.d.) https://aggie-horticulture.tamu.edu/vegetable/guides/texas-vegetable-growers-handbook/chapter-v-irrigation/.

[6] A. Nabil El-Hazek (2016). "Challenges for Optimum Design of Surface Irrigation Systems." *Journal of Scientific Research and Reports* vol. 11, no. 6, 1–9.

[7] C.B. Hedley, J.W. Knox, S.R. Raine, R. Smith (2014). "Water: Advanced irrigation technologies." In *Encyclopedia of Agriculture and Food Systems* (378–406). Elsevier. https://doi.org/10.1016/B978-0-444-52512-3.00087-5

[8] Oregon State University. (n.d.) https://agsci.oregonstate.edu/mes/irrigation/introduction-drip-irrigation.

[9] A.R. Warade et al. (2018). "Center pivot and lateral move irrigation system." *International Journal of Advanced Research, Ideas and Innovations in Technology* vol. 4, 557–559.

[10] F. Rhuanito et al. (2015). "Sub-Irrigation: Historical Overview, Challenges, and Future Prospects." *HortTechnology* vol. 25, no. 3, 262–276.

[11] K. Browning (2022). Why Do We Need Smart Irrigation? (All You Need To Know). *ClimateBiz*. May 27. https://climatebiz.com/why-do-we-need-smart-irrigation/

[12] Swan Systems (2020). The Pros and Cons of Different Irrigation Methods. www.swansystems.com.au/irrigation-scheduling-methods/

[13] T.A. Howell (1996). *Irrigation Scheduling Research and Its Impact on Water Use.* Proceedings of the International Conference, Nov. 3–6, 1996, San Antonio, TX, American Society of Agricultural Engineers, St. Joseph, MI.

[14] G. Kumar. (2014). "Research paper on water irrigation by using wireless sensor network." *International Journal of Scientific Engineering and Technology*, IEERT conference Paper, 123–125.

[15] Y. Shekhar, E. Dagur, S. Mishra, R.J. Tom, M. Veeramanikandan, S. Sankaranarayanan (2017). "Intelligent IoT based automated irrigation system." *International Journal of Applied Engineering Research* vol. 12, no. 18, 7306–7320.

[16] K. Jha, A. Doshi, P. Patel, M. Shah (2019). "A comprehensive review on automation in agriculture using artificial intelligence". *Artificial Intelligence in Agriculture* vol. 2, 1–12.

[17] M. Savitha, O.P. UmaMaheshwari (2018). "Smart crop field irrigation in IOT architecture using sensors". *International Journal of Advanced Research in Computer Science* vol. 9, no. 1, 302–306.

[18] T. Talaviya et. al. (2019). "Implementation of artificial intelligence in agriculture for optimisation of irrigation and application of pesticides and herbicides". https://doi.org/10.1016/j.aiia.2020.04.002

[19] Espressif Systems. (2018). ESP32 Series Datasheet. Available online: www.espressif.com/sites/default/files/documentation/esp32_datasheet_en.pdf.

[20] A.I. Ali, S.Z. Partal, S. Kepke, H.P. Partal (2019). ZigBee and LoRa based Wireless Sensors for Smart Environment and IoT Applications. In Proceedings of the 2019 IEEE 1st Global Power, Energy and Communication Conference (GPECOM2019), Nevsehir, Turkey, 12–15 June 2019; pp. 19–23.

[21] Silicon Labs. (2019). Si7021-A20 Datasheet. Available online: www.silabs.com/documents/public/data sheets/Si7021-A20.pdf.

[22] Dallas Semiconductor Electronics. (2019). DS18B20 Datasheet. Available online: https://pdf1.alldatasheet.com/datasheet pdf/view/227472/DALLAS/DS18B20.html.

[23] K. Jha, A. Doshi, P. Patel, M. Shah. (2019). "A comprehensive review on automation in agriculture using artificial intelligence". *Artificial Intelligence in Agriculture* vol. 2, 1–12.

5 A Systematic Review of the Automation of the Agricultural Sector Using Various Modern Technical Approaches

5.1 INTRODUCTION

A recent survey found that in order to satisfy the needs of the world's ever-increasing population, the food supply would have to be increased by a whopping 70 percent. The issue is exacerbated by a shortage of natural resources like fresh water and arable land, as well as by falling production patterns in main staple crops. In addition, the situation is made worse by decreasing production patterns in important staple crops. Alterations in the composition of agricultural labour forces are another factor that gives the farming business cause for worry. In most nations, the number of people working in agriculture has also decreased. Because of a shortage of people willing to work in agriculture, there has been an increase in the number of farming enterprises that make use of Internet connection technologies [1].

Humans have extended the horizons of our thinking processes with the arrival of technology in this digital era, aiming to connect a human brain with an artificial one. Artificial intelligence arose from this continued research. It's the method by which a human can create an intelligent machine. AI is a subset of computer science that can detect its environment and thrive to increase its chances of success. AI should be capable of performing tasks based on prior knowledge.

The fields like finance, medical science, agriculture, education, and numerous other fields have all been changed somehow using artificial intelligence. Machine learning (ML) is involved in AI implementation. This leads us to the "machine learning" subdomain of AI. The basic purpose of training is to provide data from prior experiences and statistical data to the machine so that it can complete its given task of solving a specific problem. Machine learning is responsible for substantial improvements in big data and data science computing. Data analysis based on previous data and experience, product suggestions, weather prediction, image recognition, and medical diagnostics are all examples of current applications. Machine learning algorithms are used for creating intelligent machines in which data is fed to solve problems.

Additionally, the majority of artificial intelligence and machine learning is built on theories and hypotheses. Algorithms and programming are two examples. For implementing these algorithms and logic-based conceptions, there needs to be

DOI: 10.1201/9781003213550-5

a hardware-software interface. The system that makes this possible is known as "embedded systems." they are hardware-based systems with proprietary software that is made up of memory chips.

As a result of the rapid increase in the worldwide population, the agricultural sector is facing a number of deficiency issues, some of which include a lack of fruits and veggies, a lack of soil nutrients, the detrimental consequences of chemical pesticides and fertilizers used to combat crop diseases, a shortage of labor, and operating for reduced hours in the field as a result of environmental conditions [2].

Agriculture developments play a critical part in a country's economy, so it is critical to solving these challenges. Agriculture, like other branches of research such as medical science, automation, and other industries, can benefit from using robots to supplement human labor.

Various unique pieces of technology have evolved in recent years to assist farmers with their work. The development and application of various drone and robotic technology have made it easier for farmers to deal with the demanding nature of their work.

A considerable number of companies are developing drones, automated machine harvesters, automated watering machines, and autonomous tractors. Despite the fact that these technologies are yet in their infancy, an increasing number of conventional agricultural firms are integrating farm automation into their day-to-day operations. There are numerous advantages of agricultural automation such as:

- **Consumer benefit**: Organically manufactured things are in high demand these days, and they are becoming increasingly popular every day. The goods that are created can be delivered to customers more quickly, effectively, and sustainably thanks to advances in automation technologies. The increased yield and production rate that result from increased productivity brought about by automation results in cheaper prices for consumers.
- **Labour Efficiency**: More than half of the cost of farming is accounted for by labour, and more than half of farmers think there is a problem with labour shortages. As a direct consequence of this, 31 percent of farmers are transitioning to crops that need less labour. On the other hand, harvesting robots have a great deal of untapped potential. Robotics technology has the ability to automate regular procedures, which may cut down on labour costs and the number of workers required in the agricultural business, which is now facing a workforce deficit [3].
- **Reduced Environmental Footprint**: Farm automation can boost profits while lowering the environmental impact of farming. Fertilizers and pesticides are applied less frequently, and greenhouse gas emissions are reduced as a result of site-specific application software.

5.2   DISCUSSION

Within the scope of this chapter, we will investigate many forms of automated technology, including the Internet of Things, machine learning, and blockchain.

5.2.1 INTERNET OF THINGS (IoT)

Farmers may employ Internet of Things technology to ensure good harvests, increased profitability, and preservation of the environment, which can help reduce the supply demand imbalance. The term "precision agriculture" refers to a system that makes use of the Internet of Things (IoT) to assure the most effective use of available resources, hence increasing crop yields while simultaneously reducing operational expenses. The Internet of Things in agriculture consists of tools that have wireless connection as well as information technology services.

The results of a study indicate that the number of Internet of Things devices used in the agricultural sector will reach 75 million by the year 2020, representing an annual growth rate of 20 percent. At the same time, it is anticipated that the worldwide market for smart agriculture would treble in size by the year 2025, reaching a total of $15.3 billion [1].

Farmers will be able to cut waste and increase efficiency in several regions by using IoT technologies. IoT smart farming is an example of this type of technology; in this case, farmers may monitor field conditions from wherever they want. They have the option of choosing between manual or automated solutions for operations that are data-driven (see Figure 5.1). If, for example, the moisture in the soil level is too low for the crop that was sown, the farmer may use sensors to trigger the beginning of the irrigation process. Farming that uses modern techniques is much more productive than farming that uses older methods.

The main purpose of farm automation technology is to take care of the daily farming chores. The following are some of the most prevalent technologies used by farmers.

Harvest Automation: Produce harvesting, including but not limited to fruits and vegetables, has traditionally been a challenging process to automate. When harvesting

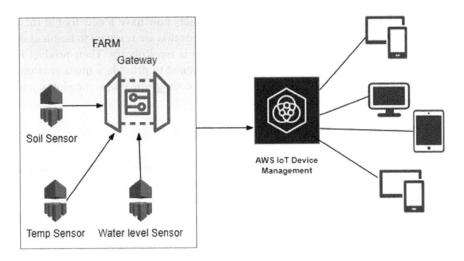

FIGURE 5.1   The IOT devices being used in farm.

vegetables, robots need to be careful not to bruise or otherwise harm the produce. Agrobot has created the first robot that is capable of gently harvesting strawberries regardless of where or how they are cultivated. This robot was built by Agrobot. Up to 24 robotic manipulators collaborate, working from a platform that may be moved, to choose fruit that satisfies the quality requirements of the farmer. The apple harvester developed by Abundant Robotics is the world's first robotic commercial harvester. Their robots don't have claws or other hand-like graspers; instead, they utilize a vacuum to pull apples off the branch.

5.2.2 Autonomous Tractors

The autonomy provided by autonomous tractors may come from the farmer's ability to operate them remotely or even to pre-program their behaviour. Row crop growers may realise value from the autonomous tractor offered by Rabbit Tractor not only because it reduces their costs of manpower but also because it increases their operational efficiency and their output. Bear Flag Robotics is also creating tractor automation kits, which makes automation more accessible for farmers by retrofitting existing tractors with cutting-edge autonomous technology and adding control [3]. These kits are being developed by Bear Flag Robotics.

5.2.3 Seeding and Weeding

Robotic systems that have been developed for sowing seeds and pulling weeds may target particular sections of a crop. On a farm, seeding may simply cut down on the amount of work and duties that are considered tedious. With the use of computer vision, weeding robots may be very precise and significantly cut down on the amount of pesticides needed. Blue River Technology utilises computer vision and robotics technology to accurately spray herbicides just where they are needed and with the exact amount that is required. Farmers now have a new tool at their disposal to combat and prevent the growth of weeds that are resistant to herbicides. Another firm that manufactures a weeding robot is EcoRobotix. Their product is the world's first fully autonomous machine designed to provide a more environmentally friendly and cost-effective method of weeding row crops, meadows, and intercropping cultures [3].

5.2.4 Drones

Drones have the potential to be utilised for a variety of applications, including the remote monitoring of conditions and the application of various treatments such as pesticides, fertilisers, and more. They also have the ability to employ imaging and infrared analysis to quickly and cost-effectively detect issue zones, which enables farmers to address problems at an earlier stage. American Robotics is in the process of constructing a fully autonomous robot that will provide farmers with insights at resolutions, frequency, and speeds that have never been seen before [3]. This robot will feature an autonomous drone, base station, and analytics platform.

5.2.5 MATERIAL HANDLING

Working alongside laborers, robots can perform demanding physical labor duties. They are able to handle heavy goods and carry out activities such as plant spacing with high accuracy, which allows them to make the most of the available space and improve the quality of the plants while simultaneously reducing the cost of production [4].

IoT has the potential to switch the agricultural sector into many aspects:

(1) Managing the health of the crop by using ground and air-based drones, which will keep an eye on the crop's health, soil and field analysis, and it includes lot more practices.
(2) Smart Greenhouse: An Internet of Things (IoT)-based smart greenhouse eliminates the need for human involvement by automatically monitoring and controlling the surrounding environment.
(3) The importance of crop prediction lies in the fact that it assists farmers in making future choices about the production of crops, storage of those crops, marketing strategies, and risk management. The data collected from farm sensors is fed into artificial neural networks, which are then utilised to make cropyield predictions. This data takes into account a variety of parameters, including the soil, temperature, pressure, precipitation, and humidity. Farmers have the option of using either the dashboard or a mobile application that has been specifically designed for them to collect reliable soil data.

5.3 BLOCKCHAIN

A blockchain is a distributed ledger that allows participants to record information on the matter of producing, exchanging, and consuming a good or service. Cooperative administration of a distributed ledger database by all parties concerned is often carried through a peer-to-peer network. Before being added to the blockchain, a new record must be confirmed by the network. Any changes to the recorded data should be decided by consensus, which means that the majority of the parties concerned must agree. Additionally, any change to one entry will affect all subsequent entries in the chain. As a result, changing data recorded in a blockchain is nearly impossible in practice.

In the agriculture sector, blockchain technology allows pupil transactions to take place without the need for a middleman. The establishment of religion now takes place in a peer-to-peer architecture rather than via an authority. This is made possible since the technology does away with the need for a centralised power source. As a consequence of this, it helps in the restoration of confidence between producers and consumers, resulting in a decrease in the transaction costs that are associated with the agro-food industry [5]. It establishes trust between customers and manufacturers. A method for tracking individual transactions is also provided. This approach makes detecting fraud and scams relatively simple. Customers will have faith in the food quality and safety as a result of the tracking and reporting of these issues, which is a major concern element for everyone [5].

We will discuss a few applications where blockchain has been applied.

5.3.1 AGRICULTURAL INSURANCE

The weather has a huge impact on the crops and cattle that are affected. As a consequence of this, agro-insurance may be used to reduce the risks associated with the weather. Before planting their crops, farmers may get insurance that will provide them with compensation in the event that their farm is damaged or destroyed. Farmers are able to better strengthen their financial sensitivity to weather extremes, as well as financial losses caused by weather extremes, as a consequence of the insurer assuming full responsibility for the insured risk. Therefore, in the case of weather risks that impact all insured farmers on a systemic level, the insurer may further hedge the systemic part of the loss by purchasing coverage from a reinsurance company [6].

5.3.2 E-COMMERCE OF AGRICULTURAL PRODUCTS

The following issues are addressed by blockchain technology:

(1) Information security
(2) Managing the supply chain
(3) Methods of payment
(4) Consumer assurance
(5) Farmers' costs should be reduced

Information Security: The technique provides private key encryption, which is an important instrument for satisfying the requirements for authentication. It is able to connect data in such a way that it is safe and cannot be undone, and it does this for all aspects of agricultural product growing and harvesting.

Management of the Supply Chain: Blockchain technology may make management more effective than the many monitoring methods that are already in use since it lowers the cost of sending signals for each individual company. Each connection in the supply chain may be thought of as a "block" of data, which brings with it the advantages of transparency, validation, automation, or robustness.

Various means of payment: A digital payment system with no transaction fees is made available via the blockchain. In addition, the use of crypto currencies in the trading of agricultural goods will drastically reduce the expenses associated with the transaction.

The blockchain's global accounting system is time-stamped through the decentralised process, which ensures that all information on the chain is accessible and unchangeable. This provides consumers with the confidence that they need. Consumers will be protected from con artists and will regain their trust in online shopping.

Reduced Farmers Cost: Many different types of agricultural goods are produced by households. Because of their low transaction volume and small size, conventional forms of e-commerce are either reluctant or unable to provide services for these businesses, which eliminates them from competition in the market. The use of blockchain technology may make it possible to substantially cut transaction costs while simultaneously reintroducing them into the market.

Although some businesses have already begun experimenting with this technology, its effects may not be seen until much later in the process. The use of technologies in online commerce and the exchange of agricultural commodities is still in its infancy, and the present state of affairs is not even close to being perfect [5].

5.3.3   MACHINE LEARNING: LIVESTOCK HANDLING

Animal species are grown for human consumption, such as meat and milk, in conventional livestock husbandry.

Global demand for animal products is predicted to increase by more than 70 percent. We certainly know that when populations and wealth have increased, so has meat consumption. With limited space, water, as well as other natural resources, humans now need to breed more animals [7].

As the world's population grows, we must devise new methods and systems to assist us to achieve larger benefits in animal production.

Several industries are already being transformed by technology such as Blockchain, machine learning, and artificial intelligence. They improve productivity and efficiency. This is why we must evaluate how advanced technologies can assist us to improve animal husbandry efficiency and yields.

In total, livestock accounts for 33 percent of the protein consumed in the human diet [8]. Precision Livestock Farming (PLF) is a new concept that combines ICT with livestock farming to optimize the process. ICT is information and communication technology. PLF employs ICT to save investment costs while also increasing productivity and animal health.

The main purpose of PLF is to:

(1) Improve animal health
(2) Improve crop efficiency
(3) Manage livestock feeding

The production systems of PLF must be more efficient. It's critical to manage data created every day in livestock farms effectively in order to increase efficiency (see Figure 5.2). To handle data, such systems must undertake information gathering, processing, analysis, and distribution. In terms of livestock nutrition, and animal health, proper data management can result in increased productivity.

Technology has greatly simplified the collection and processing of animal-related data. The use of ICT in livestock has made it feasible to predict and process data in order to increase the efficiency of animal production [9].

The author used a mechanistic model to solve animal farming problems. They used this model to collect a large dataset with a variety of specifications. It contained weather data, animal behaviour, and a large amount of data. They also used sensors to collect data in real time. The milking robots, the system of feeding animals based on their species are all developed using the sensors and the model.

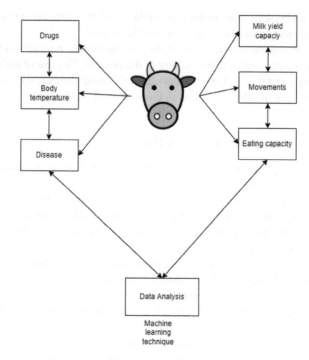

FIGURE 5.2   Interpretation of data using ML techniques.

ML algorithms can use this massive amount of data to analyze, predict, and alert farmers if anything unusual occurs. Big data is important in implementing the latest systems to animal farming practices because it provides a scalable solution for storing vast volumes of data on a remote server. As a result, all the above-mentioned algorithms work together to provide a complete solution in the perspective of animal farming.

It also aids in the identification of diseases in animals; traditionally, farmers would leave the animals in poor condition or seek veterinarian assistance to cure them. However, modern approaches can now continuously monitor animal health, normalcy, and abnormality.

5.3.4   DEEP LEARNING AND COMPUTER VISION

5.3.4.1   Identification of Plant Disease and Plant Health

In the realm of machine vision, the detection of plant diseases is critical. An imaging technique that utilizes the tools of machine vision in order to examine plant images for diseases has been developed [10]. There is already a growing demand for machine vision-based plant disease technology in agriculture, with some degree of success.

Classic machine vision-based plant disease detection methods frequently employ conventional image processing algorithms or human-created features and classifiers. Plant diseases have unique qualities that can be used to construct an imaging scheme and choose a suitable light source and shooting angle, which is beneficial in obtaining photos with uniform illumination. However, while properly built imaging systems can significantly reduce the difficulty of classical algorithm design, they can increase the cost of application implementation. Many of the previous methods that were designed to reduce the impact of scene changes on recognition results are impracticable when applied in a real-world setting.

Numerous issues arise when trying to identify plant diseases in the real world, including low contrast, significant changes in the size and kinds (as well as a high level of noise) in images of disease lesions. In addition, there is a great deal of turbulence while photographing plant diseases and pests in natural light. It is now impossible to achieve improved detection results using typical classical approaches [11].

Using the deep learning model represented by a convolutional neural network, for example, medical expression identification, image recognition, scenario text detection, traffic detection, and face recognition have all been successfully applied in recent years (CNN). To assist farmers in detecting plant illnesses and pests, a number of deep learning-based detection algorithms have been put into use in real-world farming environments [11]. Additionally, a number of domestic and international companies have created WeChat applets and photo recognition APPs to help farmers detect diseases and pests. As a result, a plant disease and pests detection system based on deep learning offers both vital academic and commercial significance.

5.3.5   CROP IDENTIFICATION

Because of the huge advancements in deep learning algorithms and hardware-processing technologies, computer vision is constantly improving. These days, one of the most potent tools for farmers to solve and facilitate several agricultural applications is deep learning-based computer vision.

Traditional machine learning approaches, such as SVM, Decision Trees, and Random Forest, are used to solve the challenge of automatic crop categorization and recognition. However, there are a number of performance issues with these methods. Using deep learning algorithms, farmers can now make critical decisions at the correct time in a wide range of agricultural applications. They have a number of advantages over traditional machine learning algorithms, including the capacity to automatically identify and extract the most relevant features [12]. Because of the abundance of data and recent developments in hardware and software, it is now possible to train and use such potent methods. Several substantial efforts have been made to improve this problem using modern deep learning algorithms, with a significant growth in the use of deep learning algorithms in crop classification tasks in the previous few years.

Several studies have used deep learning algorithms to analyses satellite photos in order to create smart and precise agriculture. As a result, most of the satellite photos are not suited for analyzing small-scale plants because of their low spatial and temporal resolutions [13]. High altitudes and sensor types lead to low spatial resolution satellite photos, while weather conditions and long return times lead to low temporal resolution satellite images that may be lacking data for a whole growth season. The performance of the deep learning model can be affected by missing spatial and temporal information. Satellites and airborne are getting better and better at achieving high spatial and temporal resolutions. With a 0.3-meter spatial resolution and less than 1-day return frequency, the WorldView-3 satellite, for example, delivers a high spatial resolution [13]. The high cost and weather sensitivity that could impair the deep learning model's efficiency remain despite these impressive developments. Consequently, low-altitude UAV systems can gather more precise information on crop types and conditions that satellite data could not.

5.3.6 WEED IDENTIFICATION

The rapid advancement and wide availability of image-capture equipment have simplified the process of taking pictures. Although computer hardware costs have decreased significantly, GPU computing capability has substantially increased. In agriculture, deep learning has been applied. A number of weed identification and classification methods based on deep learning have shown promise. Many advances have been made to standard machine learning approaches, although they are only tested in low-density photos. Detection and localization in natural environments are complicated by occlusion, grouping, and shifting illumination conditions.

Deep learning has a distinct network feature structure, making it more effective to extract features using various deep learning approaches than to do so manually.

Local features can be learned from the bottom and then synthesized at the top to obtain higher-level features. Various jobs can be fulfilled by a variety of features at different levels. Weed detection uses deep learning approaches to distinguish between crops and weeds, and these methods can improve the accuracy of weed identification and detection significantly. CNNs and fully convolutional networks have been popular deep learning networks for weed detection in recent years (FCNs). Several approaches for reducing labelling costs in semi- and unsupervised fields have also been developed. Using deep learning algorithms, classification results can be improved over standard methods in many circumstances. Traditional algorithms are still challenging to utilize to accurately classify different types of crops. The difficulties of gathering crop and weed photographs also shows the disadvantages of using deep learning approaches for weed detection in the context of a big dataset.

5.3.7 DETECTION AND IDENTIFICATION OF WEEDS, ACCORDING TO CNN

Fast and robust vegetation segmentation was achieved using a lightweight CNN, which was then utilized to classify the extracted pixels into crops and weeds. There were two weed-detection algorithms, ANN and Alex Net, that were tested by Beeharry and Bassoo. Weed recognition accuracy was 99.9 percent with Alex Net compared to only 48.9 percent for the same dataset when using an artificial neural network (ANN). Using an aerial image weed segmentation model, Ramirez et al. compared it to SegNet and U-Net. A better balance of data and greater spatial semantic information improved the accuracy of experimental outcomes, according to research findings. Early cranesbill seedlings were extracted using an enhanced Mask RCNN model proposed by Ferentinosn (2018) [13]. They can be used to treat rheumatoid arthritis. Using the proposed method, the weeds could be totally removed from the original image so that they could collect all of the nutrients and boost yield.

Methods of Weed Control and Prevention Automated feature learning, and end-to-end process implementation are made possible through the use of FCNs. Computer vision and remote sensing have benefited greatly from FCN advances in the last few years, particularly in the former. Too et al. (2019) [12] used an FCN to classify pixels in a high-resolution UAV image of a rice field. Rice field weed detection was addressed. SegNet semantic segmentation algorithm based on FCNs. It was found that the suggested method had a much greater accuracy and was able to accurately categories the pixels of rice seedlings, background, and weeds in rice field photos. Early-stage weed detection and identification is critical for successful weed management.

5.3.8 USING FEATURE LEARNING FROM SEMI- AND UNSUPERVISED SOURCES

A large number of annotated photos is still necessary for the supervised training process of deep neural networks, even when using data improvement techniques like rotation and cropping. According to relevant academics, they began to investigate semi- and unsupervised feature learning without data labelling. Hu et al. proposed the Graph Weed Network, a new image-based deep learning architecture (GWN). Images of complex pastures are to be used to identify multiple sorts of weeds. GWN is a semi-supervised learning system that simplifies the work of annotating large datasets. At the time, a precision of 98.1 percent was achieved in the analysis of the Deep Weeds dataset.

5.3.9 DIGITAL AGRICULTURE

5.3.9.1 Machine Learning

Farm management decisions can be supported by data-driven insights from digital farming, allowing for greater crop production precision.

Farming contributes to both the global food and biofuel markets, but ML is changing the way farmers do it [14].

Farmer's risk, long-term viability, and financial returns are all affected by the hundreds of decisions they make each year. Now, farmers may use sensors in the field and ML-enabled digital tools to predict harvest yields, evaluate crop quality, identify plant species, and detect agricultural disease and weed infestations in their fields.

5.3.10 AI AND CLOUD COMPUTING

Artificial Intelligence (AI) techniques and cloud computing technology are becoming increasingly important components in a wide range of applications, including digital agriculture. For explanatory, accurate, and normative analytics, cloud computing makes it possible to store large amounts of data quickly and easily [15]. There have been promising results from AI techniques like deep neural networks in disease detection and yield prediction, as well as other applications. Only a few cloud-based and AI-powered agricultural systems have been made available to farmers for practical use.

5.3.11 AGRICULTURAL REVOLUTION

In the eighteenth century, agriculture began to undergo a major shift. Farming in Britain was revolutionized by increased economic activity, with a rising need for food due to an expanding population, and the British aristocracy's desire to enhance their country estates so that they could provide opulent country homes for their aristocratic family members. Despite the fact that this was a British development, it is crucial to highlight that it is a sign of the increasing strains of industrialization there even before the Industrial Revolution, whereas other European countries, save for the Netherlands, did nothing to promote agricultural output. When it came to the transformation, it wasn't complete until the end of the nineteenth century. In part, the "enclosure" movement was used to reorganize land ownership so that farms might be more compact and efficient to run. In part, this was due to the increased investment in farming improvements, which encouraged landowners to invest money in their estates rather than simply taking rents from them. Aside from that, this money was used for technological advancements, like Jethro Tull's mechanical seeder and better drainage, as well as scientific methods for raising the quality of animals, as well as new crops. Despite the fact that the process is typically referred to as an agrarian revolution, it is more accurate to view it as a precursor to and a component of the Industrial Revolution [16].

5.4 CONCLUSION

Machine learning techniques have shown significant improvements in agricultural operations as technology has advanced in this area.

Blockchain, the Internet of Things, and Machine Learning are all discussed in this article. To keep up with the rising number of people, traditional farming methods are no longer practical. Innovative solutions are needed to deal with today's challenges, and one of these is smart farming. To improve and automate farming operations, Agri-automation combines numerous technical advances. With the help of this technology, farmers all over the world can do labor-intensive agricultural tasks more quickly and efficiently. Farmers can focus more time on and put resources into their properties with the help of farm automation farming and agricultural technology improvements.

Agricultural operations have become increasingly concerned about pesticides that are damaging to human health, about controlled irrigation, pollution control, and environmental consequences. Automatic farming processes have been shown to increase yields and improve soil quality. With the help of several scholars' efforts, this chapter attempts to quickly summaries the present state of agriculture automation.

The usage of Deep Learning and Computer Vision is highlighted for crop and weed identification, and determining plant disease and plant health. Moreover, the emphasis has been put on digital farming and how machine learning and cloud computing can be implemented in digital farming.

REFERENCES

[1] IoT. (2023).Transforming the Future of Agriculture.
www.iotsworldcongress.com/iot-transforming-the-future-of-agriculture/#:~:text=IoT%20smart%20farming%20solutions%20is,the%20field%20conditions%20from%20anywhere.

[2] IoT. (2023).Transforming the Future of Agriculture. www.iotsworldcongress.com/iot-transforming-the-future-of-agriculture/#:~:text=IoT%20smart%20farming%20solutions%20is,the%20field%20conditions%20from%20anywhere.

[3] M.H. Saleem, J. Potgieter, K.M. Arif. (2021). "Automation in agriculture by machine and deep learning techniques: A review of recent developments." *Precision Agriculture* vol. 22, no. 6, 2053–2091.

[4] L. Ku, I. Sema. (2023) The Impact of Automated Farming on the Agriculture Industry. *Plug and Play Tech Center.*
www.cropin.com/iot-in-agriculture.
www.plugandplaytechcenter.com/resources/how-automation-transforming-farming-industry/.

[5] Cropin. (n.d.) Internet of Things in Agriculture: What is IoT and how is it implemented in agriculture? www.cropin.com/iot-in-agriculture.

[6] H. Xiong, T. Dalhaus, P. Wang, J. Huang (2020). "Blockchain technology for agriculture: applications and rationale." *Frontiers in Blockchain* vol. 3, no. 7. DOI: 10.3389/fbloc.2020.00007.

[7] M.J. Miranda, J.W. Glauber (1997). "Systemic risk, reinsurance, and the failure of crop insurance markets." *American Journal of Agricultural Economics* vol. 79, no.1, 206–215.

[8] S. Neethirajan (2020). "The role of sensors, big data and machine learning in modern animal farming." *Sensing and Bio-Sensing Research*, vol. 29, 100367.

[9] K.R. Suryawanshi, S.M. Redpath, Y.V. Bhatnagar, U. Ramakrishnan, V. Chaturvedi, S.C. Smout, C. Mishra (2017). "Impact of wild prey availability on livestock predation by snow leopards." *Royal Society Open Science* vol. 4, no. 6, 170026.

[10] H. Rodríguez Espinosa, A. Bastidas Duque, J.E. Naranjo Arroyave (2016). "Application of Geographic Information Systems (GIS) for the implementation of precision farming." *Livestock Research for Rural Development*, 28(8), Article 144.

[11] S.H. Lee, H. Goëau, P. Bonnet, A. Joly (2020). "New perspectives on plant disease characterization based on deep learning." *Computers and Electronics in Agriculture* vol. 170, 105220.

[12] E.C. Too, L. Yujian, S. Njuki, L. Yingchun (2019). "A comparative study of fine-tuning deep learning models for plant disease identification." *Computers and Electronics in Agriculture* vol. 161, 272–279.

[13] K.P. Ferentinos (2018). "Deep learning models for plant disease detection and diagnosis." *Computers and Electronics in Agriculture* vol. 145, 311–318.

[14] L. Zhong, L. Hu, H. Zhou (2019). "Deep learning based multi-temporal crop classification." *Remote Sensing of Environment* vol. 221, 430–443.

[15] K.A. Vasilyevich (2018). "Machine learning methods in digital agriculture: algorithms and cases." *International Journal of Advanced Studies* vol. 8, no. 1, 11–26.

[16] J. Triplett, B. Bosworth (2008). "The State of Data for Services Productivity Measurement in the United States." *International Productivity Monitor* vol. 16, 53–71.

6 Use of Hardware in Agricultural Automation

6.1 NETWORK ARCHITECTURE MASSIVE

6.1.1 GATEWAYS

Sensors, actuators, and smart devices that are cloud-linked are connected by a physical device known as a "gateway". It collects a massive amount of data from the components and thoroughly processes it before passing it to any cloud platform. The processed data will be transformed into meaningful information. In the following Figure 6.1, the end nodes are sending the information to the established gateway in the farm, and thereafter the gateway will transmit the collected information to the AWS cloud to store and process; next the processed information is sent to the farmer's dashboard. Farmers can access this dashboard from anywhere around the world.

6.1.2 ZIGBEE

ZigBee standard is a development of an alliance of more than a hundred companies like Amazon, Legrand, and so forth. This alliance was established to set a few standards for IoT devices; its mission is to assist in the simplification, harmonization, and development of international standard protocols for the Internet of Things. This was done to develop a reliable, low-cost and highly reliable product to monitor product worldwide. A ZigBee device consists of three things: coordinator device, the router, and the end device [1].

- **Coordinator device**: This device is used to connect the devices, and further communicate with the router.
- **Routers**: The transmission of data between the devices is done through this.
- **End device**: The device that is to be controlled.

ZigBee is designed to be a device that uses low power, has low costs, is highly reliable, and has a secure wireless connectivity standard for use in home automation, meter readings, and other similar applications. Sensors are deployed in various places in the field to sense temperature, moisture, level of water, pH level, and other

DOI: 10.1201/9781003213550-6

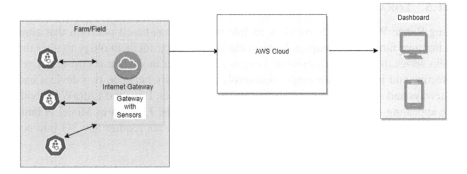

FIGURE 6.1   The Gateway transmits the information to the cloud and then to the Dashboard.

parameters in agricultural monitoring. The data collected is next transmitted to the access point.

6.1.2.1   A Sample Process in an Agriculture Field

1. Activate sensors in the field
2. Collect the data based on the location
3. Transmit the data to the access point
4. The data will process and, based on the processed data, decisions regarding the farm will be taken.

The general sensors are very easy to find, but the ZigBee sensor is used to wirelessly transmit data from the field to the access point. This technology allows for the acquisition of real-time data from any field, even in adverse conditions. It aids in preventing adverse conditions by automating pest control, irrigation, soil quality maintenance, and much more. Because of the mesh network topology, ZigBee can create its network and set data exchange in the network, as well as create a large network with reliable data.

6.1.3   ROUTERS

The world's 4G and 5G trends are gaining traction, and nearly everyone is adopting them. The use of high-speed automation in the agricultural industry will usher in a new age. The routers will aid in the connection of IoT devices that have been deployed in the field, aiding in the reception and transmission of data between devices.

6.1.4   SMART HUBS

A smart hub is a piece of equipment that links a wide range of devices and manages communication between them. Smart hubs are useful for the IoT technology devices that use ZigBee or Bluetooth and connect regionally or to the cloud. A smart hub gathers and interprets data from smart devices using various protocols.

6.1.5 LoRaWAN

Long Range Wide Area Network is an Internet of Things-based platform that aims to improve farming techniques. It uses chip spread spectrum technology to alter the radio waves to encrypt information. Lora is a low-power mode that is cost-effective-effective and has a greater range. It controls connectivity between two devices and gateways and wirelessly integrates devices to the Internet. Lora and LoRaWAN both are appealing choices for smart farming techniques. The LoRaFarm Model is built around the model of LoRaWAN. The LoRaWAN does not require any 3G Internet and Wi-Fi to connect to the Internet.

6.2 SENSORS

The sensors and microcontrollers in combination can help in improving the efficiency of the crop and reduces water wastage. The sensors like DHT11, soil moisture sensor, and a lot more, and the microcontrollers like Arduino, ARM, Atmel, and others.

6.2.1 DHT11–Temperature and Humidity Sensors

These sensors measure the temperature and humidity of the field; it is an 8-bit microcontroller that outputs the value of provided parameters in serial data (see Figure 6.2). It's based on the Negative Temperature Coefficient (NTC), which indicates that as the temperature rises, so does the resistance. With a precision of (-1 percent to +1 percent), this sensor can detect temperatures up to 50 degrees Celsius and humidity levels between 20 and 90 percent [2]. Only three of the sensor's four pins are useful: the first is Vcc, the second is Data, the third is NC, and the fourth is Ground. The VCC pin offers a 3.5V to 5.5V power supply, the data pin provides serial data output, the NC pin stands for No Connection and is therefore useless, and the last ground pin connects to the Earth to complete the circuit. Few equivalent Sensors are DHT22 and SHT71. It can connect to microcontrollers such as Raspberry Pi, ARM, and others. It is inexpensive and durable, allowing it to be readily changed with a different sensor in the future. The sensor will detect the temperature and humidity in the surrounding region and provide information to farmers so that they can maintain their farms suitably.

6.2.1.1 Few Specifications

- The voltage of this device varies from 3.5 V to 5.5 V
- Operating current: 0.3mA
- The output comes up in Serial data
- Low power
- Highly reliable

6.2.2 MQ4 Natural Gas Sensors

The concentration of gases in the air is detected by this sensor. The greenhouse systems measure and control the temperature and CO_2 concentration for optimal

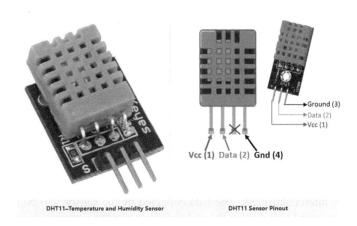

Ground (3)
Data (2)
Vcc (1)

Vcc (1) Data (2) Gnd (4)

DHT11–Temperature and Humidity Sensor   DHT11 Sensor Pinout

FIGURE 6.2 The DHT11 sensor for temperature and humidity measurement.

crop development, and they have a variety of applications. CO2 sensors can detect the deterioration of grains that have been kept. The sensor detects the presence of methane gas in the atmosphere. The sensor's output is read as an analog voltage. It can detect concentrations ranging from 300 to 10,000 parts per million [3]. The supplied voltage can vary up to 24 volts (see Figure 6.3). The sensor consists of four pins, namely, VCC, GND, Digital Output (DO), and Analog Output (AO). The VCC pin gives a power supply to the sensor, the operating voltage is +5V. The GND pin is connected to the Earth to complete the circuit. The DO, digital output pin, is used to obtain the digital output from the pin; it can be done by setting the threshold. The last pin, which is the Analog Output pin, gives the output based on the intensity of the gas in the surroundings [4].

6.2.2.1 Some Specifications

- Durable
- Low cost
- Simple and easy circuit
- Sensitivity to natural gas
- Load resistance is 20-kilo ohm

6.2.3 MQ7 CARBON MONOXIDE SENSOR

This sensor is used to detect the presence of carbon monoxide in the air (see Figure 6.4). The concentration of this gas can range from 10 to 500 parts per million. The sensor's sensitivity to carbon monoxide gas is extremely high. It has a rapid response time and an analog output. The circuit is quite basic, with a 5V power source. If inhaled in significant amounts, CO is a very dangerous gas. It's the most fatal air poisoning in various countries. Without the sensors, it is impossible to detect the gas because it has no color or odor. This sensor works with Arduino, ARM, and

MQ-4 Methane Gas Sensor Module   MQ-4 Gas Sensor Module and Sensor Pinout

FIGURE 6.3   The MQ4 sensor for methane gas detection.

Raspberry Pi microcontrollers. The data collected by the sensor will be transmitted to the webserver and will display the real-time data and the concentrations of the gas in the field's environment [5]. The output voltage rises in accordance with the concentration level.

GND, DOUT, AOUT, and VCC are the four pins of this sensor. The VCC pin provides a 5V power source, and the GND pin connects to the ground to complete the circuit. The analog output works until a defined threshold is met; when the threshold is reached, the sensor transforms the output through the DOUT pin, and the high output is shown. The Arduino will light up the LED to indicate that the CO threshold has been met and that the CO level has now risen above the limit [6].

6.2.3.1   Some Specifications
- Simple circuit
- Detection of CO
- Operating current: 140mA
- Durable
- Low cost
- Sensitivity to natural gas

6.2.4   SOIL MOISTURE SENSOR

The quantity and quality of water in the soil are measured by this sensor (see Figure 6.5). It does not directly measure water in the soil; instead, it continuously monitors the soil and changes in soil properties to forecast water content. There are various types of technologies in these sensors, namely ground sensor, aerial sensor, and satellite sensor. For the ground sensor to work, it must be completely enclosed by soil, with no gaps between the pins and the soil. The aerial sensor retrieves the data with Unmanned Aerial Vehicle (UAV) and maps the soil moisture in the field. The satellite sensor estimates the field situation from the space, helps in cost savings, and with no installations [7]. The sensor consists of four pins, VCC, GND, DO, and AO. The Vcc gives a power supply of up to 5V to the sensor. The GND connects the sensor to the ground and completes the circuit of the Digital Output and the Analog output for the output based on the condition of the field [8].

FIGURE 6.4   The MQ-7 sensor for carbon monoxide detection.

FIGURE 6.5   The soil moisture sensor.

6.2.4.1   Some Specifications

- The operating voltage of a device varies from 3.3V to 5V
- The operating current is 15mA
- The sensor is inexpensive
- Easily available and small
- Connects with microcontrollers

6.2.5   LHT65 LoRaWAN Temperature and Humidity Sensor

The LHT65 Sensor is an external sensor that measures the temperature, and humidity around the soil and of the soil (see Figure 6.6). This sensor has a very long range and sends data quickly. The sensor has a built-in battery of 2400mAh which can be used

FIGURE 6.6   The LHT65 sensor.

for up to 10 years or more. This sensor is fully compatible with gateways like the LoRaWAN gateway [9].

6.2.5.1 Some Specifications
- The voltage supply varies from 2.35V to 5V
- Built-in non-chargeable 2400mAh battery
- 3200 data time stamps can be collected
- It has a built-in monitor for Temperature and Humidity

6.2.6 GLOBAL POSITIONING SYSTEM

The GPS has enhanced farming precision; this technology aids in the collection of real-time data with precise location information. The field mapping, tractor guidance, and many more practices are done with the help of GPS (see Figure 6.7). This allows the farmers to find particular locations in the field. The GPS navigation was used by the farmers to navigate to certain spots in the field to take samples of soil or monitor crop health. Crop dusters with GPS trackers can accurately spread swaths across the field, spraying chemicals only where they're needed, limiting chemical drift, and cutting the number of chemicals needed, all of which benefit the environment and allows for more precise material usage.

6.2.7 ACCELEROMETER

This sensor is utilized to keep the sector's moving components in good working order (see Figure 6.8). The tiniest deviation in movement and vibration determines whether or not standard maintenance is required. It looks after the moving agricultural equipment in the agricultural sector.

FIGURE 6.7   The GPS sensor.

FIGURE 6.8   The accelerometer sensor.

6.2.8   Depth Cameras

The farmers won't be able to invest the high amount in the cameras, so the introduction of low-depth cameras has been introduced to be used in agricultural practices with the sensor being low in cost, reliable, and have a speedy output. This sensor is used to determine the structure and characteristics of several crops (see Figure 6.9). There are numerous depth cameras like Microsoft Kinect and Intel D435. Regarding the Intel D435 depth camera, it gives a clear view up to 10 meters, has low cost, is lightweight, and durable [10].

6.2.8.1   Some Specifications
- Good for low light

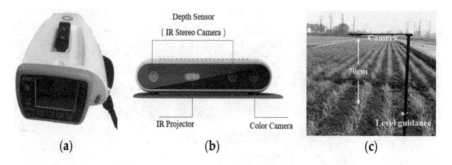

FIGURE 6.9   The depth camera sensor.

FIGURE 6.10   The airflow ensor.

- Good for a wide view of the field
- On-chip calibrations

6.2.9   AIRFLOW SENSORS

Airflow sensors are used to determine the air-bearing capacity of the soil, which means how much air can be passed through the soil (see Figure 6.10). Measurements can be taken at specific sites or in real time while navigating. The effort needed to push a set volume of air further into the ground at a specified depth is the desired output. The power supply of this 30MHz device is 24 V. It works perfectly fine while the weather conditions are in the particular range, for example, humidity varies from 10 to 95 percent, the temperature varies from –20 degrees Celsius to 60 degrees Celsius, and the storage temperature varies from –30 degrees Celsius to 60 degrees Celsius [11].

6.2.9.1   Some Specifications
- Wireless
- Durable
- The range of capturing the real-time data is 0 to 2 meters per second
- This data helps in monitoring the storage, processing, and other conditions.

6.3 CONTROLLERS

6.3.1 Raspberry Pi

The controllers along with the sensors help in improving the crop efficiency, increasing productivity and saving water (see Figure 6.11). The sensors integrated with the controller will modernize the crop.

A processor is about the size of a bank card. The Raspberry Pi is being required to develop machines that perform better. All the sensors integrated with the controller will collect the real-time data and transmit the data to the controller, and post that data processes and asks the farmers to take action accordingly to improvise the crop and field's health or the message will be transferred to the machine to switch on the motors to water the crops. If the soil moisture is less, then the processed data will be forwarded to the farmer asking him to water the crops [12].

6.3.1.1 Some Specifications
- The speed of the CPU ranges from 700 MHz–1.2GHz
- The random access memory varies from 256 MB to 1 GB

6.3.2 Arduino Board

Sensors such as the DHT11 and LHT65 are used with controllers such as Arduino to collect data from the sensors and then process it for output (see Figure 6.12). The Arduino can read the input to see if the light attached to the sensor is turned on, and the output will reflect turning on the LED light or activating a certain feature that is needed in the field. The Arduino is extremely simple to use, affordable, and widely available. It is compatible with all operating systems. If the water level in the field falls below a certain level, the sensor will detect it and relay it to the controller, which will process it before informing the farmer or activating the valves to water the crops [13]. The sensors like Temperature Sensors, Water Level Sensors, Soil Moisture Sensors, and many more are connected to a single Arduino board. The data collected by the sensors are transmitted to the Arduino board, and it shows the output, keeping the farmers updated about their crop status even when they are away.

6.3.2.1 Some Specifications
- Low in cost
- Easily available
- Simple to use
- Open source

6.3.3 ARM Microcontrollers

Advanced RISC Machine (ARM), with a 32-bit data bus and a 32-bit microprocessor, ARM is performance-oriented. There is a separate space for the data and the program. The project includes the use of an ARM CPU and a Communication module. It demonstrates the impact of sensors in the agricultural field while the processor is

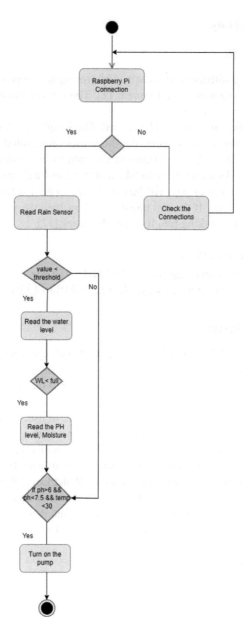

FIGURE 6.11   Working of a sensor integrated with Raspberry Pi.

used. For the most part, the framework succeeds in upgrading the agronomic situation to minimize medieval farming. The sensors read the characteristics and relay the information to the controller, which processes the information before sending it to the farmer [14].

6.3.4 ATMEL MICROCONTROLLERS

The Atmel controller is an 8-bit microcontroller that belongs to the AVR family. The data and the program each has its own space. This includes 120 data instruction sets and memory sizes ranging from 4K to 256K bytes. There are various Atmel microcontrollers, like ATmega168PA and a lot more [15, 16]. This sensor is primarily used to minimize water waste; if the soil moisture level is low, then the crops will be irrigated; otherwise, the excessive water may harm the crop in a multitude of ways, and this is how the microcontroller minimizes the wastage of water.

6.3.4.1 ATmega168PA Specifications

- Used in Arduino board
- The operating voltage varies from 1.8V to 5.5V
- The flash memory is 16Kb
- Can be utilized in the AVR microcontroller project

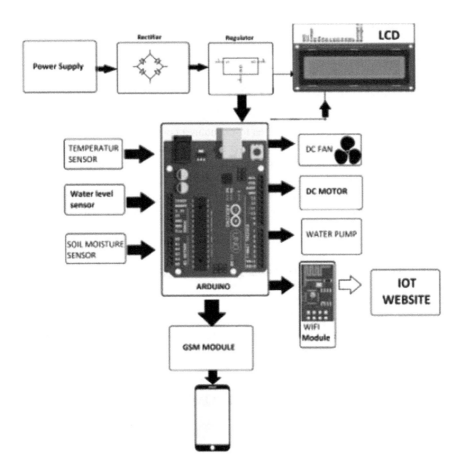

FIGURE 6.12   Working of sensors integrated with Arduino board.

6.4   ACTUATORS

Actuators aid the machine's physical actions by converting applied energy into motion. It essentially allows any machine to move. There are numerous types of actuators depending on the machine type; for example, if we talk about the agricultural sector, the actuators in that area are meant to withstand extreme conditions. It gives farmers a sense of flexibility because practically every current device has an actuator inside it. Actuators can be found in harvesters, spreaders, tractors, seed drills, and a variety of other machines. The spreaders spray pesticides and fertilizers in the field, and the actuators assist the machinery in spraying the fertilizers in the correct amount and direction with help of a machine [17]. The actuator is comprised of a power source that supplies power to an actuator, a power converter that receives power from the source, an actuator that converts energy into mechanical form, a mechanical load that uses the energy to function, and a controller that ensures that the functions of a system run smoothly [18].

Some specifications:

- The higher the weight, the less the speed
- Durable
- Energy efficient

6.5   REGULATORS AND SERVOS

In agricultural automation, it's necessary to differentiate whether the system is basically a regulator or a servo. A regulator tries to maintain a consistent system result, while a servo has a desirable result that changes over time. A greenhouse, keeps the temperature to a known constant and is intended to remain constant even when the outside weather conditions are unfavorable; in this case, the temperature is controlled by a regulator [19]. Servo drives control motion by finely predicting the course, speed, location, and strength required to complete certain farming tasks and then sends commands to the motor [20].

6.6   MOTORS

Electric motors are being increasingly utilized to power machines, while the electricity-powered agricultural gear is becoming more common. There are various sorts of motors being used in the agricultural automation sector, including Brushless DC motors, integrated motor drives, Stepper Motor, Hansen PMDC Brush Motors, and many more. The integrated motors are compact and have advanced technology to provide a new level of motion capability [21].

6.7   NOVEL USE OF UNMANNED AIRCRAFT SYSTEMS IN AGRICULTURE: AERIAL AUTONOMY IN THE TWENTY-FIRST CENTURY

6.7.1   INTRODUCTION

Unmanned aerial vehicles are gradually being used to perform a greater number of functions in a spectrum of applications, such as photography and agriculture. Earlier, they were only used by the military to gather intelligence but, nowadays, they are used in various sectors. Farmers benefit greatly from the usage of UAVs in the agricultural sector; they may cover an entire field with a UAV, and they can utilize UAVs for crop health monitoring, pest control, and a variety of other applications. The UAVs can be controlled by a person on the ground or they can conduct pre-programmed tasks. Farmers will not have to walk from one spot to another because the majority of the field is wide, which makes the farmers tired, and they will be able to see many aspects of the field from the air. The aerial perspective allows the farmer to compare the differences in soil between two locations and as well as whether or not the level of water is similar throughout each patch. After gathering and processing the information from the aerial view, the farmers can improve the efficiency of the crop and can find a better and more efficient solution to deal with the detected problem [22]. The UAVs are of various types, differently and specifically designed for each sector like the cinematography UAVs are specifically designed to focus on quality and its movements capture any particular moment.

6.7.2 UNMANNED AIRCRAFT SYSTEMS

Unmanned Aircraft Systems, often known as drones, were not very popular in the twentieth century. They were deployed by the military to conduct surveillance of areas where humans could not, or would be unsafe, to go. However, in the twenty-first century, UAVs are a necessity in the military, and the local public frequently uses these systems in several different ways. This technology does not carry humans; instead, it leverages aerodynamic forces to fly. The UAV is a single-board computer; its architecture consists of sensors, actuators, software, communications, and a loop principle. The position sensor gives an idea to a drone about its location in the air. The actuators manage the movements of the drone. The software takes the data from the sensors and controls the system to manage its speed and other things. The loop principle consists of an open and closed loop: the open loop positively provides signals without considering the feedback from the sensors, and the closed loop considers feedback from the sensors to adjust the motion of the device. The UAVs use radios to communicate, they transfer the data this way, be it a video or any other data [23]. The majority of drones used for agricultural purposes are MK Okto XL 2, EM6-800, Parrot AR/2.0, among others. The sensors commonly used in drones are RGB, Multispectral, Laser, Thermal, and Multiscanner. As these drones are being used for agricultural purposes, they consist of a nozzle to spray the pesticides from the air, a camera to capture the view from the air, and various other things that can be added to them for agricultural use [24].

6.7.3 AERIAL AUTONOMY IN THE TWENTY-FIRST CENTURY

The autonomy of unmanned aerial vehicles (UAVs) varies greatly. However, in recent years, a junction of identified needs and technological advancements have resulted in a significant shift in the utility of UAVs. UAVs are attracting considerable interest in some countries, whereas advancement is much slower in others. The market for agricultural unmanned aerial vehicles (UAVs) is quickly expanding, and several new businesses have developed. Agricultural UAVs are expected to rise to a market size in the billions of US dollars by 2050, contributing to around 25 percent of the worldwide UAV market, according to market research. Many drones may be controlled manually using a portable device, and some can even maintain a pre-programmed flying path. A few drones, such as the DJI Agras MG-1P, can configure flight paths for several drones from a single controller, which can even acquire complete control of several of the unmanned aerial vehicles if necessary. MAVLink is a standard drone communication protocol that broadcasts the UAV's coordinates, GPS position, and speeds [25].

6.7.4 CASE STUDIES

We will be discussing a few case studies based on Unmanned Aircraft Systems. According to one case study [26], UAVs offer a lot of scope in the agricultural sector since they reduce fertilizer waste, labor waste, and man hours wasted. It also gives credible information that can be used to determine water and fertilizer shortfalls. Weather conditions continue to impair newer drones, causing problems in monitoring large fields. The operational costs of UAVs are significant, and there are numerous improvements that may be made, such as battery life, camera quality, the number of nozzles and their types, and many other things. Farmers will soon be able to fly over their farmland with their drones, analyzing them from above. The second case study [27] used electronic traps and drones to identify pests in grapes, olives, and a variety of other crops. The electronic traps identify pests as targets and relay data to the UAV, which then uses its speed and efficiency to spray pesticides on the targeted crops before returning to the base. In the third case study [28], the usage of unmanned aerial vehicles (UAVs) in India is still debatable, but the government is gradually bringing drones to the public's attention; in 2018, the Ministry of Aviation enacted a law legalizing drones for public use. However, in the farming sector, Indians are still unsure, believing that drones will be unable to do tasks, such as spraying, in Indian farms. Drone-based agriculture will take time to gain traction in the Indian market, due to extreme weather, pest infestations that cause crop damage, and other reasons will hinder the adoption of smart farming in the country (see Table 6.1).

6.7.5 CHALLENGES AND FUTURE SCOPE

The price of a UAV is the most difficult factor to address throughout development since when more complex sensors are put into the UAV, the cost rises, making the machine unaffordable to farmers. In the fields, flight durations are quite limited, making it difficult to record the entire field in one shot and access the data. The UAV's functioning is still hampered by bad weather [34]. The development of a system that can control both the monitoring and spraying processes is another future project we looked into. The data is read by sensors on the ground and sent to the drone, which

TABLE 6.1
Comparison Table

Ref.	Year	Contribution	Future Work
[29]	2018	In this paper, they discussed about a modern method to farm the crops the whole time of the year without any interval. They introduced the Aeroponic system. The technology opens up great possibilities to improve efficiency, consistency, and sustainability for farmers and producers.	The only constraint that exists and has been discussed is the use of cloud and big data to collect real-time field data.
[30]	2018	In this paper, a drip system based on sensors is to be proposed which can assist the farmer and function to water their fields in order to manage the use of water in agriculture. Rainwater and groundwater levels are clearly decreasing day by day, necessitating the development of innovative techniques to properly utilize water resources for agriculture.	To optimize the proportion of water saved, this technology should be used on a broad scale in the future.
[31]	2021	In this study, a drone is used to monitor the field's environmental data as well as the smart irrigation system.	In the future, the drone may have a system for analyzing crop growth, as well as an autonomous drone that can be controlled with hand gestures.
[32]	2018	In this case, a system was installed in the field that was interconnected with multiple sensors. It assesses the farm's state based on the sensors and then provides data to the farmer, reducing manual labor. The microcontroller used in the system is ATMEGA16 & GSM	To store rainwater, a water tank can be built. To assess the field, more complicated sensors can be used.
[33]	2020	The relevance of smart agriculture and its ramifications was highlighted in the study, as well as how they affect a country's economy.	The advancement in technology should make it more affordable, allowing small farmers to implement it on their farms.

analyses the crop's health and can carry out spraying operations based on the results of the sensors and the drone. Later, the weather information can be fed into the system so that the UAV can react appropriately [35].

REFERENCES

[1] K. Kumar. (2019). A Review Paper on ZigBee-New Era in Agricultural Monitoring. www.researchgate.net/publication/337561906_A_Review_Paper_on_ZigBee-New_Era_in_Agricultural_Monitoring.

[2] DHT11. (2021). Temperature and Humidity Sensor 16 July. https://components101.com/sensors/dht11-temperature-sensor#:~:text=use%20DHT11%20Sensors-,The%20DHT11%20is%20a%20commonly%20used%20Temperature%20and%20humidity%20sensor,to%20interface%20with%20other%20microcontrollers.

[3] Winsen. (2023). MQ-4 Methane Gas Sensor/ Nature Gas Detection Gas Sensor. www.winsen-sensor.com/sensors/combustible-sensor/mq4.html

[4] MQ-4 Methane Gas Sensor. (2018). October. https://components101.com/sensors/mq-4-methane-gas-sensor-pinout-datasheet

[5] H. Singh, R. Abdulla, S.K. Selvaperumal (2021). "Carbon monoxide detection using IoT." *Journal of Applied Technology and Innovation* vol. 5, no. 3, 7.

[6] Learning about Electronics. (2020). MQ-7 Carbon Monoxide Sensor Circuit Built with an Arduino. www.learningaboutelectronics.com/Articles/MQ-7-carbon-monoxide-sensor-circuit-with-arduino.php

[7] EOS Data Analytics. (2023). Soil Moisture Sensors: Smart Tool For Precision Farming. June. https://eos.com/blog/soil-moisture-sensor/#:~:text=A%20soil%20moisture%20sensor%20is,irrigation%20for%20optimum%20plant%20growth.

[8] Components101. (2020) Soil Moisture Sensor Module, April. https://components101.com/modules/soil-moisture-sensor-module

[9] Dragino. (2023). LHT65 LoRaWAN Temperature & Humidity Sensor. June. www.dragino.com/products/temperature-humidity-sensor/item/151-lht65.html

[10] Intel Real Sense. (2023) Intel RealSense depth camera D435 www.intelrealsense.com/depth-camera-d435/

[11] Hort Americas. (2023) Airflow Sensor. https://hortamericas.com/catalog/controlled-environment-technology/sensors/30mhz-airflow-sensor-0-2-m-s-2/

[12] A. Senthil Kumar, A. Aravind Kumar, S. Bharathi Raja, P. Karthik, (2020). "Agriculture based on robot using Raspberry Pi." *International Journal of Engineering and Technology* (IJERT) ECLECTIC–2020, vol. 8, no. 7.

[13] Arduino (2018). What is Arduino? www.arduino.cc/en/Guide/Introduction/

[14] S. Bhat, R. Sharma, Kavya, A.S. Pavithra. (2020). "Smart agriculture using IoT powered by ARM microcontroller." *International Journal of Engineering and Technology* vol. 5, no. 7.

[15] Electrical Technology. (2023). What is ATMega Microcontrollers and How to Make an LED Project with it. www.electricaltechnology.org/2018/01/atmega-atmel-avr-microcontrollers.html#:~:text=ATMega%20Microcontrollers%20belong%20to%20the,(RISC)%20based%20Harvard%20Architecture.

[16] Robomart. (2023). Atmel/Atmega Microcontrollers. www.robomart.com/atmel-microcontrollers/atmega168pa-au-atmel-arduino-ic

[17] Venture Mfg. Co. (2017). How Actuators are Playing Vital Role in Agriculture. September. www.venturemfgco.com/blog/actuators-used-in-agriculture/

[18] Progressive Automations. (2023). Actuators as a Keystone of Motion. www.progressiveautomations.com/pages/actuators

[19] Q. Zhang, F.J. Pierece, (2013). Agricultural Automation: Fundamentals and Practices. CRC Press, 1–385. https://books.google.co.in/books?id=TlrNBQAAQBAJ&pg=PA10&lpg=PA10&dq=regulator+and+servo+in+agriculture+automation&source=bl&ots=WYuZMXNQw-&sig=ACfU3U0HJ45DuFlEqCgkNDZLQcGgSTv-aA&hl=en&sa=X&ved=2ahUKEwiNxf7A8JH4AhVD6zgGHe6TD54Q6AF6BAg9EAM#v=onepage&q&f=false

[20] ESI Motion. (2023). Servo Drive Modules.
www.esimotion.com/how-servo-drives-are-used-in-todays-farming/#:~:text=
The%20Power%20of%20Servo%20Drives%20to%20Help%20Farmers&text=
Servo%20drives%20are%20responsible%20for,farming%20to%20the%20n
ext%20level.

[21] Electrocraft. (2023) Agricultural Robots.
www.electrocraft.com/motors-for/agriculture/agricultural-robots/

[22] C. Yinka-Banjo, and O. Ajayi (2019). "Sky-Farmers: applications of Unmanned Aerial Vehicles (UAV) in Agriculture." In G. Dekoulis (Ed.), *Autonomous Vehicles.* IntechOpen. https://doi.org/10.5772/intechopen.89488

[23] Wikipedia. (2023) Unmanned aerial vehicle. https://en.wikipedia.org/wiki/Unmanned _aerial_vehicle.

[24] J. del Cerro, C. Cruz Ulloa, A. Barrientos, J. de León Rivas (2021). "Unmanned aerial vehicles in agriculture: A survey." *Agronomy* vol. 11, no. 2, 203.

[25] M. Mazur, A. Wisniewski, J. McMillan (2016). Clarity from Above: PwC Global Report on the Commercial Applications of Drone Technology. Drone Powered Solutions.

[26] M.F.F. Rahman, S. Fan, Y. Zhang, L. Chen (2021). "A comparative study on application of unmanned aerial vehicle systems in agriculture." *Agriculture* vol. 11, no. 1, 22.

[27] P. Psirofonia, V. Samaritakis, P. Eliopoulos, I. Potamitis (2017). "Use of unmanned aerial vehicles for agricultural applications with emphasis on crop protection: three novel case-studies." *International Journal of Agricultural Science and Technology* vol. 5, no.1, 30–39.

[28] *Ag News.* (2020) Drones and Indian farming: A case study. September. https://news. agropages.com/News/NewsDetail---36671.htm

[29] I.A. Lakhiar, G. Jianmin, T.N. Syed, F.A. Chandio, N.A. Buttar, W.A. Qureshi (2018). "Monitoring and control systems in agriculture using intelligent sensor techniques: A review of the aeroponic system." *Journal of Sensors* vol. 2018, no. 1, 18.

[30] S.R. Barkunan, V. Bhanumathi, J. Sethuram (2019). "Smart sensor for automatic drip irrigation system for paddy cultivation." *Computers & Electrical Engineering*, vol. 73, 180–193.

[31] M.E. Karar, F. Alotaibi, A.A. Rasheed, O. Reyad (2021). "A pilot study of smart agricultural irrigation using unmanned aerial vehicles and IoT-based cloud system." arXiv preprint arXiv:2101.01851.

[32] S.J.S. Imtinungla, H. Bordoloi, (2018). "Agricultural Field Monitoring System using ATMEGA16 and GSM." *International Journal of Research in Advent Technology* vol. 6, no. 5, 811–816.

[33] E.R. Guzueva, T.G. Vezirov, D.K. Beybalaeva, A.A. Batukaev, K.G. Chaplaev (2020). "The impact of automation of agriculture on the digital economy." In *IOP Conference Series: Earth and Environmental Science*, vol. 421, no. 2, p. 022047. IOP Publishing.

[34] P. Velusamy, S. Rajendran, R.K. Mahendran, S. Naseer, M. Shafiq, J.G. Choi (2021). Unmanned Aerial Vehicles (UAV) in precision agriculture: applications and challenges. *Energies* vol. 15, no. 1, 217.

[35] P. Radoglou-Grammatikis, P. Sarigiannidis, T. Lagkas, I. Moscholios (2020). "A compilation of UAV applications for precision agriculture." *Computer Networks* vol. 172, 107148.

7 Storage Units and Transportation

7.1 TRANSPORTATION

Every day, IoT technologies extend into new domains. These new technologies will have enormous advantages for the healthcare, agricultural, and transportation sectors in particular. Machine learning and Artificial Intelligence will become more important in the transportation industry in the future, allowing more automated analytics and improved decision-making [1, 2]. Predictive judgments enabled by AI and machine learning allow transportation to operate with fewer interruptions, save costs, and assure safer travel.

7.1.1 Autonomous Navigation Control

In recent years, mobile robots that operate in agricultural areas have occupied a lot of research time. Communication, sensing devices, and processing technology have developed at a fantastic rate in recent years, resulting in significant advancements in the area of autonomous agricultural robot guiding systems. When determining an appropriate trajectory, the navigation algorithm must consider sensory information and move accurately within its surroundings to avoid colliding with anything. The purpose of this study is to provide an understanding of navigation systems for autonomous agricultural vehicles.

7.1.1.1 Navigation and Obstacle Sensing

When managing an agricultural robot in a complicated agricultural operation environment, the most critical guarantee for accomplishing automated operation of the agricultural robot is a trustworthy navigation system Weikuan Jia et al. [3] addressed the use of GPS/microelectromechanical systems (MEMS) sensor outputs to accomplish mobile robot track planning and tracking performance.

Sage–Husa adaptive filtering has a divergence issue, and the Kalman filtering technique was enhanced to suppress the divergence and continue to improve the dynamic response. This was required to strengthen the Sage–Husa adaptive filtering method and increase its stability and filtering accuracy.

The Integrated Adaptive Variable Structure (VSPID) and Proportional-Integral-Derivative (PID) stabilize the control system and enable mobile robots to perform

DOI: 10.1201/9781003213550-7

autonomous navigation, route planning, and tracking. To validate the upgraded filtering approach, a simulation experiment is set up and 800 sets of GPS fixed-point data are continually collected. As a result, it is determined that the expanded adaptive filtering approach has the potential to significantly reduce system status inaccuracy and signal divergence. The technology is guaranteed to be real-time, dependable, and adaptive, while also improving filtering accuracy. By selecting appropriate parameters, the upgraded VSPID controller may significantly improve control efficiency and include a switching and saturation error feedback mechanism to retain good tracking performance.

Rapid advancements in communication, sensor, and computation technology have resulted in significant advancements in agricultural autonomous robot navigation systems. Agricultural robots that are automated decrease labor expenses, save workers from doing dangerous tasks, and offer farmers up-to-date and accurate information to help them make management choices. So Shalal et al. [4] organized the examined work into three sections:

- Mobile robot navigation sensors
- Methods of computation
- Control techniques for navigation.

They explain how sensing devices like vision, Global Positioning System (GPS), and laser range scanners are deployed as major sensing systems in autonomous navigation robot systems. Although less widespread, ultrasonic sensors and radio frequency identification (RFID) have been recognized as significant sensors in the literature. Numerous computational strategies are used to deal with sensor data fusion in order to offer the necessary information for autonomous farm vehicle navigation. The Hough transform, Kalman filter, and picture segmentation are the most often used computer techniques in research. Steering controllers must respond appropriately to changes in the state of the mobile robot, its travel speed, the site circumstances, and other aspects affecting steering dynamics during autonomous navigation [5]. Numerous control systems have been created in the literature employing machine-learning techniques such as Neural Network (NN), Proportional-Integral-Derivative (PID), Fuzzy Logic (FL), and Genetic Algorithm (GA). Hence, the main principle underlying sensor fusion is that mobile robots may acquire more precise navigation, mapping, and location predictions by merging multiple sensor data. Hough transform combined with an appropriate picture segmentation approach may be used to map the environment and find rows. The Neuro-fuzzy algorithm was the most resilient strategy because Neuro-fuzzy is a concept that describes the combination of neural network (NN) and fuzzy logic (FL). A neural network facilitates learning and adaptation, whereas a fuzzy logic facilitates rule creation and decision-making employed for autonomous navigation of the mobile robot among the adaptive FL techniques.

7.1.1.2 Localization and Mapping

The R&D of autonomous navigation robotic systems capable of performing various active agricultural jobs (pruning, harvesting, or mowing) has increased. Cultivating, collecting, environmental monitoring [6], irrigation and fertilizer delivery, and other chores are now performed by robots. Robots must be capable of performing online localization and, if needed, mapping. The most often used method of agricultural localization is via the use of standalone Global Navigation Satellite System (GNSS) equipment. However, satellite signals are often unavailable or unreliable in a wide variety of agricultural and forest environments, requiring the development of novel solutions that are not dependent on these signals. Simultaneous localization and mapping, as well as visual odometry, have emerged as the most promising ways for boosting the reliability and availability of localization, as highlighted by Aguiar et al. [7]. After an extensive search, 15 publications on localization and mapping in agriculture were identified, 9 in the field of forestry, and 5 that give datasets for testing and assessment of these methodologies. The works were classified according to their smart agriculture, their method of localization and mapping, and their correctness, availability, or scalability. The fundamental result is that this area of research is still in its infancy, and various research questions remain unexplored. 3D localisation, in particular, is rare under these circumstances. Additionally, agricultural development has yet to create advanced mapping approaches such as topological and semantic mapping, which are presently accessible in other industries. The study on robot navigation systems in farming activities focuses on developing appropriate sensing, mapping, localization, route planning, and obstacle avoidance systems.

The most often encountered difficulties with GPS navigation include obstructions to the satellites' line of sight, worries about multi-path, and interference from other radio frequency sources. GPS cannot be used effectively for localization or navigation in specific orchards due to the fact that agricultural robots often travel under the tree canopy, obscuring satellite signals to the GPS receiver. As a consequence of these concerns, some researchers are developing autonomous navigation systems for robotic systems working in agricultural environments that do not depend on GPS as their primary sensor.

Vision technologies are becoming increasingly prevalent in outdoor agriculture applications such as mapping and localization. On the other hand, stereo perception can give the amount of depth and precision required for the generation of 3D field maps, localization, and autonomous navigation. In the majority of situations, mobile robot systems exhibit nonlinear behavior. The extended Kalman filter (EKF) was developed to deal with nonlinear systems. Libby and Kantor [8] employed two laser scanners and encoders to localize a mobile robot in an orchard setting using the EKF method. Since a result, it is determined that EKF is one of the most promising strategies for sensor data fusion for localization. It gives a precise estimate of the mobile robot's location and orientation for sensor data fusion, providing a precise estimate of its location and orientation. Also, to enhance its effectiveness, EKF is often integrated with a variety of optimization approaches like fuzzy logic and control systems.

7.1.1.3 Locomotion

As populations continue to grow, urbanisation accelerates, and high-quality commodities become more competitive in the marketplace, and environmental preservation becomes more important, agricultural robots are always being improved to address these challenges. In this regard, Oliveira et al. [9] examined the major existing uses of agricultural robotic devices for land preparation prior to planting, seeding, farming, plant care, collecting, yield calculation, and phenotyping.

For the most part, all robots were evaluated based on the following criteria: their locomotion technique, end usage, sensor presence, robotic arms, and/or computer vision algorithms. They were also graded based on their development stage and the country or continent from which they originated. The study called "Different There" is a thorough examination of agricultural robotic systems used for land preparation before seeding and planting as well as plant care and harvesting. The average harvesting success rate increased by 22.98 percent, and the average harvesting robot cycle decreased by 42.78 percent, according to this study of 62 agricultural robotic systems.

There are 37 percent of agricultural robots with 4WD, 64.52 percent without a robotic arm, 22.06 percent used for weeding, 32.23 percent utilise RGB cameras, 35.48 percent do not include/report computer vision algorithms, and 80.65 percent in the field, according to a new research.

Global population growth projections need urgent improvements in agricultural efficiency, human safety, and environmental sustainability, which are mutually conflicting features [10]. The research examined the connections between robots and agriculture with the goal of improving agriculture and achieving the vision of "intelligent farms" (smart farms). As a result, this chapter explores various characteristics that agricultural robots must acquire from industrial robots in order to accomplish the paradigm of the intelligent farm.

According to them, intelligent factories are built on a firm foundation of five concepts: (1) artificial intelligence (2) cyber-physical systems (CPSs) (3) the Internet of Things (IoT) (4) big data, and (5) cloud computing.

They also highlighted how autonomous robots for agriculture necessitate the building of unique robot architectures. This design is accomplished by examining the several methodologies used in the manufacture of traditional ground robotic systems that utilise wheels, tracks, or legs for movement.

As a result, it has been demonstrated that several small robots working collaboratively and cooperatively can: (1) accomplish the same work as a large vehicle with a lower total weight, thereby reducing soil compaction; (2) increased maneuverability and safety due to the robots' lower rigidity; (3) increase reliability in terms of fault tolerance, as the framework can continue to operate with a few modules out of service; and (4) re-plan the mission based on the results of the mission.

These characteristics – which are not reliant on the kind or structure of the robot – position multi-robot systems as the preferred alternative for outdoor unmanned ground vehicles (UGVs) in intelligent farms.

7.1.1.4 Manipulators

Employees in organic agriculture, which is becoming more popular, handle large compost bins during the fertilisation season. These tasks are very time-consuming and need a lot of mental and physical effort from the personnel. Agricultural robots might benefit from heavy-material handling technologies [11]. Mobile platforms and manipulators are designed and built once a fresh perspective on agricultural robots is gained. Parametric perturbation or uncertainty have to be taken into account while designing the control systems. Using real-world field tests, the most important component of this study confirmed the validity of both methodologies. The time and success rate of harvesting watermelons were found to be comparable to that of experienced harvesters.

The availability of realistic simulation for dynamic analysis, controller design and validation perception algorithms evaluation or software validation is essential to the growth of interdisciplinary research. However, this is the first and preliminary validation phase; in any case, it cannot replace an actual experimental campaign. As a result, the existence of prototype off-road mobility manipulators is an essential step in advancing agricultural robotics research discussed by Bascetta et al. [12]. The design of ROBI, a prototypes mobile manipulator for agricultural purposes, is described by Bascetta. The mechanical design and selection of mobility control system devices are described, emphasizing low price, lightweight, flexibility, and adaptability. A robot model is also developed that is sufficient for the preliminary calculations necessary to validate the design, particularly in terms of motor power and battery pack capacity, as well as an experimental evaluation of the in-wheel motors. Hence, one simulation based on a genuine agricultural trajectory demonstrates the behavior of the most essential electrical and mechanical characteristics, verifying the robot design's validity.

7.1.2 AGRICULTURE ROBOT VEHICLES

Agriculture is quickly transforming into an appealing high-tech industry, drawing new expertise, firms, and investors. The technology is rapidly advancing, improving farmers' output capacity as well as robots and automation systems as we know them. Agricultural robots assist farmers in a number of ways to enhance output yields. Drones, self-driving tractors, and robotic arms are among the new and novel uses for the technology.

7.1.2.1 Wheel-Type

Increasing agricultural productivity is dependent on increased automobile traffic. Planting, managing, and harvesting crops nowadays necessitates the use of tractors. However, as automobiles have grown in size, their impact on the soil has grown. Bawden et al. [13] outlined the development of a Small Robotic Farm Vehicle (SRFV). The use of robots in agriculture is seen as a revolutionary shift away from the existing trend of increased production via higher accuracy on bigger and larger machinery.

Consequently, the vehicle is a modular four-wheeled differential steering vehicle, lightweight with proprietary dual in-hub electric motors and emergency brakes. The vehicle is designed to balance minimum soil impact, stability, energy economy, and traction. Hence it is concluded that the vehicle would have a modest disruptive effect on the field due to a low mass distributed over four wheels.

Robot tractors are a significant device for addressing the issue of declining farmer numbers, especially elderly farmers. Tractor changes must be carried out to convert a manual tractor into a robot tractor. Yang and Noguchi [14] spoke about developing a new robotic tractor built on a conventional wheel-type CAN-bus tractor. The CANbus was implemented using the ISOBUS (ISO 11783) protocol. The RTK-GPS was employed as a navigation sensor.

An omnidirectional security system and an emergency stopping system were also developed to improve the robot tractor's safety. This study included three trials to show the performance of the manufactured robot tractor. The RMS values for the lateral and heading errors in the three tests were 0.05 m and 0.6 degrees, 0.02 m and 0.77 degrees, and 0.04 m and 0.75 degrees, correspondingly. According to the results, the CAN bus-based robot tractor does have a high and consistent navigation accuracy. The accuracy was satisfactory for all tests.

Improvements in mechanical design abilities, sensing technologies, electronics, and planning and control algorithms have enabled operations to rely on autonomous robotic systems Bak and Jakobsen [15]. The demand for such systems is being driven by rising financial pressures on farmers and public awareness of environmental issues and labor conditions. So Thomas Bak discussed that the robotic platform to map weed populations in fields was utilized to illustrate intelligent ideas for autonomous vehicles in agriculture, ultimately resulting in a new sustainable business model for improved agriculture. The vehicle seen here is designed to work in 0.25 and 0.5 m row crops, but is integrated with a camera for row navigation and weed identification. The wheels are combined with a chassis, resulting in a versatile platform for experimentation and implementation. The platform's monitoring enables real-time localization and control. The platform's movement is controlled by platform software, built on an intentional hybrid design that permits interfacing with farm management and planning systems. A simple change to the wheel modules will enable the steering wheel range to be increased to 1808, giving greater freedom to situate the ICR. To improve the robustness of the localization, we are investigating methods to include a row guiding system into the sensor fusion solution. While the emphasis of this chapter has been on the reactive behavior of the route tracking method of control, research is also being conducted on the plan-execution framework and the deliberative computations in the planning/management interface.

7.1.2.2 Crawler Type

Due to its lengthy winter season and the amount of snow gathered, which routinely surpasses 1 metre, Hokkaido, Japan's northernmost island, does not have a long time for producing wet rice. Negative temperatures have no positive influence on wet rice production. Crawler tractors are generally implemented in Hokkaido due to their low ground pressure and great traction effectiveness, enabling them to operate smoothly over paddy fields and complete tasks more quickly than do wheeled tractors. This work aims to construct a crawler-type robot tractor employing algorithms and controllers developed in the laboratory. The crawler-type tractor was modified in this study using robotic technology to create a robot crawler-type tractor [16]. As navigation sensors, RTK-GPS (Real-time kinematic global positioning system) and IMU (Inertial measuring unit) were utilized. The lateral and heading errors were determined by fusing these two navigation sensors. The lateral and heading errors were utilized to determine the vehicle's steering angle required for autonomous navigation. A navigation map is generated that the robot tractor will follow. An automated running test was performed to verify accuracy. Hence, it is concluded that the measured lateral and heading prediction accuracy was around 1 cm and 0.2 degrees, respectively.

7.1.2.3   Robot Combine Harvester

A majority of the farmers in Japan are now physically declining at an alarming rate. In addition, the average age of farmers who are now available is increasing. Following this trajectory, it is very feasible that Japan's agricultural self-sufficiency rate could fall in two decades. To address this issue, one potential solution would be to utilize agricultural robots in real-world applications, such as robot tractors, robot combine harvesters, and so on [17]. This study proposed and built a robot combine harvester in recognition of the relevance and need of producing such agricultural robots. For positioning and posture data, this robot uses an AGI GPS receiver, and an IMU. CAN-BUS is used to control it. To evaluate the accuracy, a straight-running test was done. A lengthy route of more than 150 meters was employed to assess the accuracy of the combined harvester under controlled conditions. The first lateral error was around 20cm, and the initial heading error was roughly 1.8 deg. After starting up, the combine harvester proceeded at 1.0m/s toward the targeted path. Furthermore, lateral and heading abnormalities were measured throughout the test. A straight running test was carried out to evaluate the accuracy, and the findings suggested that this robot may be employed in real wheat and paddy harvesting in Japan.

To address the ageing society's growing labour shortfall, intelligent and autonomous additions to mechanical devices such as combination harvesters for monotonous daily work are necessary. The electrical alteration for its reaping unit is based on a particular combine harvester, and it includes the selection of motor and reducer, 3D design, and finite element analysis for two kinds of operating conditions. To evaluate the accuracy, a straight-running test was done [18]. Furthermore, an electrical driver approach is developed, automatically altering harvest speed depending on vehicle walking pace. Finally, various wheat harvesting field tests confirmed the accuracy of the electric refit. The remaining components will be electrified, and field testing will be conducted to further investigate the robotic process of the combination harvester.

7.2   STORAGE UNITS AND MAINTENANCE

In sub-Saharan Africa, annual post-harvest food losses might amount to up to 30 percent of total yield. Latin America and the Caribbean account for 6 percent of global food losses; the area loses roughly 15 percent of its agricultural yield. This loss is caused by 28 percent at the producer level and 22 percent during post-harvest processing and storage. Therefore, remedies to post-harvest losses are essential for agriculture's potential demand-supply gap to be reduced. Numerous researchers have addressed this problem globally by inventing post-harvest transport and storage solutions that have a positive environmental and social impact simultaneously.

7.2.1   Underground Storage Structures

Minimizing storage losses is essential for a nation like India. Currently, storage loss in India is 10 percent, which is very significant compared to other emerging nations.

60–70 percent of food grain produced in India is kept at the household level in indigenous storage systems. Low-cost grain storage is essential for minimizing storage losses. Indigenous grain storage buildings, with minor modifications, provide a more cost-effective alternative to contemporary storage structures. Several considerations such as moisture in stored grain, storage structure temperature, and types of storage bin and so forth, influence the choice of these grain storage systems [19]. Sandeep's paper shows ideal qualities of storage structure, as follows:

1. The structure must be raised and distant from areas of high humidity.
2. The structure must be completely airtight, including the loading and unloading areas.
3. The structure must be rodent-proof and sanitary.
4. The structure must be coated with an impermeable clay layer to protect it against termite or other insect attacks.

The following are a few examples of indigenous farmers' traditional storage structures.

(i) Underground pits
(ii) The Pusa bin
(iii) Domestic Hapur bin
(iv) Coal tar drum bin

Hence, if experienced staff is unavailable, the Pusa bin may give a more viable solution. If climatic circumstances are unfavorable, subterranean pits are a viable solution. When mobility and ease of construction of storage structures are necessary, Hapur bins are an excellent option for farmers. If the humidity and moisture levels in the environment are high for the majority of the year, we propose Coal Tar Drum bins to farmers.

7.2.2 SURFACE STORAGE STRUCTURES

7.2.2.1 Pussa Bin

It is estimated that around 25–40 percent of food grains produced in tropical nations are wasted due to insufficient storage facilities. Effective storage design is critical for restraint and proper holding of the material and for minimizing grain damage caused by moisture condensation or excessive temperatures. The storage container must be built to resist the pressure changes that occur during loading/unloading. The Indian government developed some improved storage structures like Pusa bins. To resist rodent attacks, the bin is designed on a firm surface. If the surface is not too hard, a burned brick platform is constructed. The dry construction is then covered with a 700 gauge black LDPE film in the shape of a mosquito net. All four sides and the top of the construction are coated with mud before it is ready for usage [20].

The manhole is blocked with mud after the structure has been filled with grain, and a diagonal cut in the film covering it has been sealed with adhesive tape. Hence it is concluded that after it has dried entirely and been filled, the Pusa bin is effective for efficient functioning.

To store something is to keep it safe. Surplus output is stored for later use in this procedure. It encompasses all forms of storage, including traditional/indigenous, scientific, and controlled/ambient ways and methods maintained by commercial or governmental institutions [21] Low-cost grain storage is essential for reducing storage losses. A less expensive alternative to contemporary grain storage buildings is to use indigenous grain storage structures that have been modified in some way. Thus, they discussed the Pusa bin storage construction, which is similar to other traditional mud storage structures. A plastic film is applied to all of the bin's interior surfaces to keep the storage structure dry. This is where the importance of enhanced storage buildings and scientific grain storage in the form of warehouses comes into play. Hence, it is concluded that it gives a secure and cost-effective method of storing grain for extended periods.

7.2.2.2 CAP Storage (Cover and Plinth)

In India, grain is now stored in cover and plinth (CAP) storage for short periods. When there were limited inside areas, these CAP storages also were utilized. Various studies and research have been undertaken all over the globe to enhance large-scale grain storage for on-farm, open, and short-term grain storage. As a result, Sandeep Bhardwaj [22] combines vital and useful studies on cover and plinth and storage. This study analyzes the efficacy of hermetic bags in cover and plinth and on-farm storage for successful insect species management for three to four months. The study monitors the grain storage system in CAP storage. In general, traditional structures are difficult to sanitize, and the infestation may have developed with grain kept from the previous season. Because of this, CAP storage is an appropriate storage option in India for shorter-term grain storage. With the emergence of significant developments in grain-storage bags, notably hermetic bags and triple storage bags, cover and plinth storage has great possibilities. The loss in grain quality during CAP storage was similarly minor. However, certain improvements are necessary to prevent various forms of infestation in the storage bags in light of future problems. Hence, hermetic bags have been shown in studies to be successful in managing insect pests for three to four months in cover and plinth storage and farm storage.

The government purchases food grains from farmers but lacks storage capacity. The Food Corporation of India (FCI) does not have enough grain silos (modern storage facilities) and covered godowns (warehouses) with enough storage capacity. As a result, throughout the nation grains are kept outdoors under CAP storage (cover and plinth). As a result, grains are vulnerable to rodents, dampness, birds, and pests. Private sector engagement in agriculture warehousing has recently expanded, making this area more competitive, although much more work is still needed. The present study aims to review the concerns and challenges confronting agricultural warehousing, particularly in the food grains storage facility sector, and to try to uncover potential solutions. Food grains in the central pool managed by SGAs in Punjab and Haryana have suffered extensive damage due to blatant disrespect for safe and scientific storage standards [23]. Furthermore, the inability to dispose of defective merchandise as soon as possible resulted in storage space becoming jammed. In the Punjab and Haryana regions, the loss due to damaged goods was 21.168 Cr INR and 13.09 Cr INR, respectively. During peak procurement seasons, open storage in the form of CAP is normally expected to be used. So to maintain the quality of the food grains, storage in the CAP should be limited to no more than a year, with at least one stock turn-over every six months. Furthermore, for optimal aeration, the cover should be removed at least twice a week. Thus CAP storages and silos to better manage stocks with enough responsibility and accountability awarded with adequate and qualified people allotted with high-level monitoring and speedy decision-making independence and delegation of responsibilities given to the nodal heads.

7.2.2.3   Silos

Grain is a critical source of nutrition for both animals and humans. The primary need in the food sector is to keep grain from deteriorating. The silo is the most often used grain storage device because of its ability to manage storage, drying, and ventilation. Grains in the silo were estimated using the K-next neighbours (KNN) method by using air radar. As of the writing by Duysak & Yiit [24], a model silo was used to gather the backscattering signal of varying grain quantities for different stack configurations using a built, stepped frequency continuous-wave radar (SFCWR). A k-fold cross-validation technique was used to assess the KNN's accuracy after 5,680 measurements were collected. For this study, SFCWR data was transformed into range profiles using the inverse Fourier transform, and the range profiles revealed eight features. To determine the optimal feature combination for classification, a total of 255 potential feature combinations were created and then trained and assessed. Hence the greatest accuracy of 96.71 percent was obtained by using five chosen characteristics. Using machine learning techniques, the amount of grain may be precisely predicted by extracting valuable properties from range profiles.

In the grain-storage business, moisture detection has been a major problem for many years, particularly in silos. Managing and selling rice and grain requires accurate moisture analysis in silos. Monitoring agricultural silo moisture distributions using nondestructive approaches and algorithms has been studied. Non-destructive volume tomography based on radio frequency (RF) was assessed by Almaleeh et al. [25]. In the next step, tomographic imaging or computational intelligence technologies like artificial neural networks were employed to assess the accuracy and efficiency of identifying moisture distribution in agricultural silos. To assess the moisture content in the silo, correlations between the attenuation values of numerous RF sensor networks may be produced and examined using tomography. Using these three methods, it is feasible to conclude that grain moisture content may be determined quickly, precisely, and non-destructively using grain samples.

7.2.3   Maintenance

Farmers are usually self-sufficient when it comes to maintenance. This raises the possibility of an accident, since the farmer would not be qualified to do some maintenance chores, and also because agricultural machinery and vehicles are becoming more complex, requiring the need for specialized training in repair and maintenance.

7.2.3.1 Moisture Monitoring

Water is a finite resource on a global scale, and farming is a major market. As a result, an efficient and affordable approach to farming practices and irrigation scheduling must be taken. To ensure adequate irrigation, it is important to check the soil moisture content in irrigation fields regularly. Researchers Garg et al. [26] discuss several ways for measuring soil moisture content, for both field and laboratory, including remote sensing, but the fastest and most accurate is through the utilization of soil moisture sensor electronic equipment. Several soil moisture sensor discussed in this article like tensiometers which is less expensive but have maintenance issues, Granular Matrix Sensor, which is also inexpensive but it is less accurate and sensitive to soil salinity and temperature; they also discuss Time-domain reflectometry which has accurate and quick response, but it is costly; next, they discuss frequency domain reflectometry which has the advantage of measuring different depths for the same location but for this soil calibration is required; lastly they discuss VH400 soil moisture sensor which is insensitive to salinity along with rapid response time, but data loggers used by it are expensive. Hence it is concluded that the VH400 soil moisture sensor, for example, is a small and portable device that provides real-time soil moisture measurements in a short period of time when connected to a data logger through SMS, GSM, Bluetooth, or even storage memory cards; these techniques are time efficient and labor demanding. The advancement of wireless sensor applications in agriculture enables farmers to boost their efficiency, production, and profitability and maximize crop yields with minimal irrigation water consumption.

An irrigation scheduling study necessitated the development, implementation, and evaluation of a wireless sensor network for gathering soil moisture and weather data. Soil moisture sensors and wireless data recorders measure soil moisture, while sensors and electrical equipment gather meteorological data, and finally, a wireless modem transmits the collected data to the internet through the WSN [27]. For usage in the WSN, an antenna mounting was developed and manufactured. When a data logger and spring-loaded mount were employed to measure soil moisture, the spring-loaded device was made of PVC pipe and a U-shaped base. The mount shielded the antenna from damage when it was struck by farm equipment, such as a fertiliser and chemical sprayer. The antenna may return to its upright position for signal transmission after going through the equipment. Detected radio signal intensity of the Em50R data recorder decreased with increasing distance between the data logger and receiver. As the logger's antenna grew higher, it became harder to see. The antenna of the Em50R data recorder must be placed slightly just above plant canopy in order to guarantee good data connection. Due to its antenna's placement inside the cotton, soybean, and corn plant canopy, the Em50G data recorder was able to send data.

For a period of two years, the WSN was installed and used in cotton, corn, and soybean fields. The WSN did a great job of gathering and transmitting data. With the exception of summer thunderstorm-induced data transmission delays, the WSN presented no substantial operating challenges. Hence it is concluded that throughout the agricultural growing seasons, data from the WSN, including soil moisture and weather information, were successfully accessed through the internet and utilized to schedule irrigation and conduct relevant research.

7.2.3.2 Quality Monitoring

Water is an essential resource for plant growth and plays a vital role in agriculture. This article discusses the necessity of water quality monitoring in indoor agriculture and how the Internet of Things (IoT) water sensors are key for crop yield enhancement. Wenshen, Jia et al. [28] discuss the IoT based water quality monitoring device because Internet-of-things-based technologies monitor remotely, gathering data regardless of whether a person is present physically in the premises, continuous monitoring is a feature of IoT water sensors; the screening process is ongoing and dynamic, providing near real-time feedback on your desired data, and IoT monitoring program is capable of sending text-based monitoring notifications, water quality monitoring is made simple and effective using IoT technologies, the cost of IoT near-real-time monitoring is low and IoT water sensors may be used to track a variety of characteristics

(i) pH level
(ii) Salinity
(iii) Oxidation Reduction Potential

Hence, it is proven that when it comes to water, real-time water quality monitoring systems with IoT sensors are an excellent kind of technology to address the difficulty of environmental management.

Water is utilized in various activities such as consumption, farming, and travel, all of which have a significant impact on water quality. A variety of businesses and resources contaminate today's water, and water analysis is the most important task for globalization to address this enormous issue. The use of sensors and an LCD to monitor water quality in sewage water for agricultural use is a clever way to ensure that the water is safe for agricultural use. Water-quality parameters like pH, salinity, temperature, and Biochemical Oxygen Demand (BOD) as well as Total Dissolved Solids (TDS) will be estimated in this chapter in order to identify deviations and provide warning messages if there is an unusual level, that is, the value is higher the predetermined level or standard set in Arduino Mega 2560 Controller. This chapter aims to do this [29]. Some chemical spills or treatment plant concerns may also create major crop cultivation and soil-quality challenges because of its extraordinary value. IoT sensors are used to gather data from the water and transmit it to the microcontroller, where it sends a warning message to farmers or customers and collects data on real-time consumption of variables in the waters by using a GSM foundation without any human purpose to assassinate. The parameters pH, Turbidity, Temperatures, TDS, and BOD must be monitored in the framework suggested. An LCD panel displays these values, which are stored in the cloud and communicated to the consumer by SMS, using a GSM Module. This sends an alarm message and provides corrective procedures for improving water quality. Hence it is concluded that this system of implementation offers a convenient method of analyzing and monitoring the pH value, Turbidity, TDS, BOD, as well as temperature values.

7.2.3.3 Improved Sorting

Demand for high-quality fruits is growing as the population grows. Numerous nations' GDPs are reliant on its export. The export of fruits and vegetables is a major contributor to Pakistan's GDP. The present quality detection, sorting, and dispensing systems have a number of drawbacks, including low yield, high time consumption, and higher expense. An image processing-based fruit sorting system is the goal of this project, which aims to increase fruit sorting, quality assurance and production while also lowering the amount of time spent by workers. As a result, Abbas et al. [30] explains a comprehensive hardware system that includes both a mechanical component and a camera-based image processing component. These two procedures work in conjunction to accomplish the final purpose of fruit sorting, which ensures that it is removed when a rotten apple arrives. The categorization of fruits is accomplished via the use of standard image processing methods in MATrix LABoratory (MATLAB). With the help of Arduino, the dispensing portion is finished on the conveyor belt setup. As a result, image processing-based fruit sorting provides a reliable and cost-effective alternative to the current inefficient and time-consuming human sorting technique. The method streamlines the procedure and benefits the fruit industry. However, this categorization will be more robust if other variables include circumference, form, or shape recognition.

Automated grading has been used because of the drawbacks of manual grading like inconsistency and tediousness. The use of ICT will be employed to improve the status of the agriculture industry [31]. An automation process for sorting and grading agricultural goods is driven by the idea of integrating ICT and agriculture. Instructors award grades based on their observations and experience. Before grading can begin, a photo of the fruit must first be taken, either with an ordinary digital camera or with a camera on a mobile phone. MATLAB then conducts extraction of features, classification, or grading on the image. When it comes to fruits, a variety of fruits are employed to categorise them. In the table (see Table 7.1), the five fruits are clearly shown, demonstrating the precision with which they were classified. Apples, bananas, and mangoes all have a very high degree of classification accuracy. It is common to confuse oranges and carrots with apples and bananas because both fruits are the same size and shape, which makes sense.

7.2.3.4 Suitable Environment for Food Safety Compliance

Annually, it is estimated that up to 10 percent of the population in industrialized nations will get a food-borne illness. To avoid or minimize the risk of food-borne disease, it is required to implement appropriate control measures across the food chain, including farm and primary sector stage – the implementation of a health and safety food management system built on Hazard Analysis and Critical Control Points (HACCP). HACCP is largely regarded as the most successful method of ensuring the safety and acceptability of food. However, the traditional HACCP technique is not entirely relevant to farm-level food safety regulation at the moment.

TABLE 7.1
Specimen Classification

S.No	Items	Accuracy
1.	Banana	81.2%
2.	Mango	98.75%
3.	Apple	96.25%
4.	Orange	6.52%
5.	Carrot	0%

Source: Mustafa et al., 2009.

Nonetheless, HACCP concepts are beneficial in revealing possible dangers and necessary remedial steps. Specific rules for ensuring food safety are presented, along with the rationale for their usage. The following topics are covered: (1) traceability of animals; (2) animal feed and fodder; (3) water; (4) maintain hygienic conditions for animals; (6) livestock medicine, and disease prevention; (7) agrochemicals, detergents, and disinfectants; (8) the quality of milk; (9) waste from animals; (10) biosecurity [32]; and (11) fumigation of eggs in poultry production. In the future, improved slurry treatments for pathogen control may be a possibility.

Hence, while the European Council Nitrates Directive is primarily concerned with environmental protection, it also has beneficial consequences for food safety. Farmers are compelled to keep animal manure throughout the winter months, which reduces pathogens applied to the ground.

7.2.3.5 Equipment Maintenance

When working with agricultural tools and machinery, it is essential to prevent stoppages and breakdowns. If sowing or harvesting is delayed, the effect may be reduced yield, worse quality, and so forth. So Noren [33] discussed several methods to avoid it:

(i) One critical approach for avoiding failures is having a system for routine maintenance. Interviews with mechanics at workshops and insurance company inspectors reveal that a significant portion of failures is preventable because it is due to insufficient maintenance and improper handling.

(ii) It is preferable to use smaller tools and drive more quickly. It is worth noting in this context that the life of a transmission in a tractor, for example, is more than doubled if the driving speed is raised from 4 to 7 kilometers per hour at constant power.

(iii) Farmers often do service and repairs on their farms. Numerous farmers are competent and perform excellent jobs. However, in many situations, repairs are performed incorrectly, which might result in further failures.

(a) Prior to filling the hydraulic system, it is required to clean it and replace the filters.

(b) Bearings should be inspected regularly. If a bearing's sound is suspicious or becomes too heated while operating, it is recommended to replace the bearing to prevent a breakdown.

Hence, utilizing agricultural equipment and machinery entails a risk of injury and health problems. As a result, precautions must be made to remove these hazards.

REFERENCES

[1] R. Ben Ayed, M. Hanana (2021). "Artificial intelligence to improve the food and agriculture sector." *Journal of Food Quality*, vol. 2021. https://doi.org/10.1155/2021/5584754

[2] P. Solanki, D. Baldaniya, D. Jogani, B. Chaudhary, M. Shah, A. Kshirsagar (2021). "Artificial intelligence: New age of transformation in petroleum upstream." *Petroleum Research* vol. 7, no. 1 https://doi.org/10.1016/j.ptlrs.2021.07.002

[3] W. Jia, Y. Tian, H. Duan, R. Luo, J. Lian, C. Ruan, D. Zhao, C. Li (2020). "Autonomous navigation control based on improved adaptive filtering for agricultural robot." *International Journal of Advanced Robotic Systems* vol. 17, no. 4. https://doi.org/10.1177/1729881420925357

[4] N. Shalal, T. Low, C. McCarthy, N. Hancock (2013). "A review of autonomous navigation systems in agricultural environments." In *SEAg 2013: Innovative Agricultural Technologies for a Sustainable Future. Barton: Australia 22–25 Sep 2013.*

[5] T. Talaviya, D. Shah, N. Patel, H. Yagnik, M. Shah (2020). "Implementation of artificial intelligence in agriculture for optimisation of irrigation and application of pesticides and herbicides." *Artificial Intelligence in Agriculture* vol. 4, 58–73. https://doi.org/10.1016/j.aiia.2020.04.002

[6] A. Kshirsagar (2018). Bio-remediation: Use of nature in a technical way to fight pollution for a long run. *ResearchGate.* https://doi.org/https://doi.org/10.13140/RG.2.2.26906.70088

[7] A.S. Aguiar, F.N. dos Santos, J.B. Cunha, H. Sobreira, A.J. Sousa (2020). "Localization and mapping for robots in agriculture and forestry: A survey." *Robotics* vol. 9, no. 4, 1–23. https://doi.org/10.3390/robotics9040097

[8] J. Libby, G. Kantor (2011). "Deployment of a point and line feature localization system for an outdoor agriculture vehicle." In *Proceedings–IEEE International Conference on Robotics and Automation*, 1565–1570. https://doi.org/10.1109/ICRA.2011.5980430

[9] L.F.P. Oliveira, A.P. Moreira, M.F Silva. (2021). "Advances in agriculture robotics: A state-of-the-art review and challenges ahead." *Robotics* vol. 10, no. 2, 52. https://doi.org/10.3390/robotics10020052

[10] P. Gonzalez-De-Santos, R. Fernández, D. Sepúlveda, E. Navas, L. Emmi, M. Armada (2020). "Field robots for intelligent farms—inhering features from industry." *Agronomy*, vol. 10, no. 11, 1638. https://doi.org/10.3390/agronomy10111638

[11] S. Sakai, M. Iida, K. Osuka, M. Umeda (2008). "Design and control of a heavy material handling manipulator for agricultural robots." *Autonomous Robots* vol. 25, no. 3, 189–204. https://doi.org/10.1007/s10514-008-9090-y

[12] L. Bascetta, M. Baur, G. Gruosso (2017). "ROBI': A prototype mobile manipulator for agricultural applications." *Electronics (Switzerland)* vol. 6, no.2, 39. https://doi.org/10.3390/electronics6020039

[13] O. Bawden, D. Ball, J. Kulk, T. Perez, R. Russell (2014). "A lightweight, modular robotic vehicle for the sustainable intensification of agriculture." *Australasian*

Conference on Robotics and Automation, ACRA, 02-04-Dece. www.araa.asn.au/acra/acra2014/papers/pap147.pdf.

[14] L. Yang, N. Noguchi (2014). "Development of a wheel-type robot tractor and its itilization." *IFAC Proceedings*, vol. 47, no. 3, 11571–11576. https://doi.org/10.3182/20140824-6-ZA-1003.00952

[15] T. Bak, H. Jakobsen (2004). "Agricultural robotic platform with four wheel steering for weed detection." *Biosystems Engineering*, vol. 87, no.2, 125–136. https://doi.org/10.1016/J.BIOSYSTEMSENG.2003.10.009

[16l R. Taka, O. Barawid, K. Ish, N. Noguch (2010). "Development of crawler-type robot tractor based on GPS and IMU." *IFAC Proceedings* vol. 43, no. 26, 151–156. https://doi.org/10.3182/20101206-3-JP-3009.00026

[17] Z. Zhang, N. Noguchi, K. Ishii, L. Yang, C. Zhang (2013). "Development of a robot combine harvester for wheat and paddy harvesting." *IFAC Proceedings* vol. 46, no.4, 45–48. https://doi.org/10.3182/20130327-3-JP-3017.00013

[18] P. Wang, M. Tian, H. Wang, W. Jiang, Q. Cao (2020). "Electrical modification and experimental study of combine harvester reaping unit." *IOP Conference Series: Materials Science and Engineering* vol. 790, no. 1, 012168. https://doi.org/10.1088/1757-899X/790/1/012168

[19] B. Sandeep. (2014). "Grain storage structures for farmers." *ResearchGate*. www.researchgate.net/publication/264348323_Grain_Storage_Structures_for_Farmers?channel=doi&linkId=53d9a7720cf2631430c7d961&showFulltext=true.

[20] S. Behera (2021). Agricultural Structures and Environmental Control. *SoABE OTHER FARM STRUCTURES*.

[21] TNAU. (2015). *Seed Storage: Structures*. Seed Science and Technology. https://agritech.tnau.ac.in/seed_certification/seed storage_Structures.html

[22] B. Sandeep. (2014). "Grain storage structures for farmers." *ResearchGate*. www.researchgate.net/publication/264348323_Grain_Storage_Structures_for_Farmers?channel=doi&linkId=53d9a7720cf2631430c7d961&showFulltext=true.

[23] C. Kumar, C.L. Ram, S.N. Jha, R.K. Vishwakarma (2021). "Warehouse storage management of wheat and their role in food security." *Frontiers in Sustainable Food Systems*, vol. 5, 270. https://doi.org/10.3389/FSUFS.2021.675626/BIBTEX

[24] H. Duysak, E. Yiğit, (2019, April 1). Level measurement in grain silos with extreme learning machine algorithm. *2019 Scientific Meeting on Electrical-Electronics and Biomedical Engineering and Computer Science, EBBT 2019*. https://doi.org/10.1109/EBBT.2019.8742047

[25] A.A. Almaleeh, A. Zakaria, S.M.M.S. Zakaria, L.M. Kamarudin, M.H.F. Rahiman, A.S.A. Sukor, Y.A. Rahim, A.H. Adom (2019). "A review on the efficiency and accuracy of localization of moisture distributions sensing in agricultural silos." *IOP Conference Series: Materials Science and Engineering* vol. 705, 012054. https://doi.org/10.1088/1757-899X/705/1/012054

[26] A. Garg, P. Munoth, R. Goyal, (2016). "Application of soil moisture sensors in agriculture: a review." *Proceedings of International Conference on Hydraulics, Water Resources and Coastal Engineering (Hydro2016), CWPRS Pune, India*, 1662–1672. www.researchgate.net/publication/311607215.

[27] R. Sui, J. Baggard (2015). "Wireless sensor network for monitoring soil moisture and weather conditions." *Applied Engineering in Agriculture*, 193–200. https://doi.org/10.13031/aea.31.10694

[28] W. Jia, L. Pan, Y. Qian, J. Wang, W. Wu (2011). "Agro-food farmland environmental monitoring techniques and equipment." *Procedia Environmental Sciences*, vol. 10(PART C), 2247–2255. https://doi.org/10.1016/j.proenv.2011.09.352

[29] S. Panigrahi (2020). "Smart farming: IOT-based smart sensor agriculture stick for live temperature and humidity monitoring." *SSRN Electronic Journal.* https://doi.org/10.2139/ssrn.3651933

[30] H.M.T. Abbas, U. Shakoor, M.J. Khan, M. Ahmed, K. Khurshid, (2019). "Automated sorting and grading of agricultural products based on image processing." *2019 8th International Conference on Information and Communication Technologies, ICICT 2019,* 78–81. https://doi.org/10.1109/ICICT47744.2019.9001971

[31] N.B.A. Mustafa, S.K. Ahmed, Z. Ali, W.B. Yit, A.A.Z. Abidin, Z.A. Md Sharrif (2009). "Agricultural produce sorting and grading using support vector machines and fuzzy logic." *ICSIPA09–2009 IEEE International Conference on Signal and Image Processing Applications, Conference Proceedings,* 391–396. https://doi.org/10.1109/ICSIPA.2009.5478684

[32] A. Kshirsagar, M. Shah (2021). "Anatomized study of security solutions for multimedia: deep learning-enabled authentication, cryptography and information hiding." In I.A. Ansari and V. Bajaj (Eds.), *Advanced Security Solutions for Multimedia.* IOP Publishing. https://doi.org/10.1088/978-0-7503-3735-9ch7

[33] O. Noren (2009). "Maintaining working conditions and operation of machinery." In P.B. McNuty and P.M. Grace (Eds.), *Agricultural Mechanization and Automation,* vol. 1, pp. 1–16. Paris: Encyclopedia of Life Support Systems, UNESCO. https://play.google.com/store/books/details/Agricultural_Mechanization_and_Automation_Volume_I?id=G-GvCwAAQBAJ&hl=en&gl=US.

8 How to Increase Production with Use of Robots?

8.1 SPATIAL VARIABLENESS MEASUREMENT

Agricultural fields are hardly uniform. Instead, Akış [1] shows geographic diversity in soil parameters, landscape features, agricultural stressors, and crop yield or quality. Precision agriculture tries to detect a spatial variability pattern that is economically important to crop performance and utilizes this knowledge to modify agricultural input applications by adjusting fertilizer, herbicide, and irrigation rates in response to these patterns. When maintaining farm areas using precision farming methods, spatial heterogeneity does not have to be disregarded. Variable-rate fertilizer, herbicide, irrigation, and seed application are examples of key applications in which precision agriculture is employed to handle geographical variability efficiently. Most irrigated fields have substantial spatial diversity in soil qualities that impact water penetration and availability to plants. A consistent rate of irrigation water application is inefficient, resulting in overwatered parts and under-watered areas. Hence the spatial variability applications in precision agriculture are meant to enhance the efficiency of agricultural input applications, resulting in increased profitability and environmental quality [2].

8.1.1 GPS

Under changing climatic circumstances, maintaining agricultural productivity and improving input-use efficiency are critical to ensuring food security in the future [3]. Because soil characteristics, including nutrient levels, soil organic carbon (SOC), salinity, pH, and soil moisture, among others, have a significant impact on crop productivity, their spatial variability; site-specific and highly efficient management must be assessed. So Fathi and Mirzanejad [4] discuss RS, GIS, and GPS, which may be used to measure spatial variations in these qualities pretty well.

Remote sensing methods, together with (geographic information systems) GIS and (global positioning systems) GPS, have recently captured the interest of agricultural experts all around the globe in order to cover such gaps in traditional methodology. With the introduction of very advanced hyperspectral sensors, it is now feasible to use satellite data to monitor numerous soil parameters such as pH, saline, alkalinity, humidity, or nutrient status, among others. GIS and GPS are also

DOI: 10.1201/9781003213550-8

essential components of geospatial technology. GIS is a framework that allows for the collection and examination of spatial and geographic data, while GPS (formerly NAVSTAR) is a satellite-based radio-navigating system. GIS is used to construct soil databases for evaluating any soil property. In GIS, attribute data are connected to geographical data. On the other hand, GPS is used to find various soil sample sites, assisting producers in developing maps of fertility changes across the fields, allowing crop inputs to be varied in the field relying on GIS maps and real-time crop conditions sensing. As a result, these methods may be used to successfully retrieve spatial interpolation of multiple soil characteristics, which can be highly valuable in site-specific control, leading to greater input utilization efficiency and sustained agricultural production for global food security.

The interpretation and analysis of soil spatial variability is a critical component of site-specific farming. According to this research, the soil chemical characteristics, texture, or variance structure of the area were examined. One of the 13 soil chemical variables Kaur evaluated was soil texture in a desolate area inside Iran's Fars region [5]. With coordinates being recorded for every 100 locations, soil samples were taken from 60 square meters of depth, scale from zero to 30 centimeters. Three steps of statistical analysis were performed. To begin, we studied the frequency distributions and used the Kolmogoroph-Smironoph test to determine their normality. Second, the data distribution was characterized using standard statistics like mean, highest, median, minimum, Standard Deviation (SD), skewness, coefficient of variation (CV), and kurtosis. STATISTICA was used to perform these analyses [6]. Thirdly, we employed the GS+ to evaluate the spatial dependency of soil characteristics using the geostatistical approach. As a consequence, it was observed that the extent of spatial dependency within soil properties varied. Although phosphorus had the smallest geographical dependency (49.50 m), the percentage of calcium carbonate equivalents seemed to have the longest (181.94 m). Each parameter demonstrated a high degree of geographical dependency. The findings reveal that spatial patterns among numerous soil characteristics may change within a single area. Farmers' management was discovered to affect soil nutrients. Kriging and Variography may be helpful approaches for creating effective soil sample processes and application of variable rate inputs for site-specific farming.

8.1.2 Crop Sensors

Numerous optical sensors are employed in agriculture, varying from sensors that check soil parameters to sensors embedded in combines that measure the protein concentration of wheat grains while harvesting. However, in this research, Trevisan et al. [7] explore optical sensors that can be used to assess the reflectance of crops from a short distance using certain wavelengths and how this information might be used.

When an optical sensor is linked to a GNSS receiver, it is simple to record reflectance values with latitude and longitude coordinates and then import the file into a GIS program to show the measurement results and also their dispersion in a field using maps.

Even in places where constant amounts of nitrogen were sprayed, NDVI (Normalized Difference Vegetation Index) spatial diversity exists, indicating that crops behave differently within the same field. The technology for applying nitrogen at a variable rate, utilizing the crop as an indication and optical sensors to detect, is very promising since it allows for nitrogen conservation in areas where the plants are not actively absorbing it. Hence the method of recommending nitrogen using optical sensors demonstrated significant nutrient savings, making agriculture more lucrative and reducing the danger of nitrate pollution of groundwater.

Farmers in Extremadura, Spain, must handle fertilizer more effectively in their crops. One of the primary issues is a lack of technical understanding regarding crop production, phenological stage, and geographical variability. In this regard, the purpose must be to develop techniques and sensors that may assist in establishing a more appropriate crop fertilization requirement in each location and throughout the crop cycle to increase agricultural efficiency. The purpose of this research by Pinheiro and Gusmo dos Anjos [8] was to examine the effect of geographical variability on the capacity of various sensors (massive or punctual) to assess the nitrogen status of a processed tomato crop through a dualex sensor in order to assist technicians in designing a more effective fertilization management plan. The findings indicated that regional heterogeneity had a significant impact on the sampling and assessment of nutritional status in tomato processing farms. The many measurements made with SPAD and Dualex sensors revealed great variability between points and even within the same plant, which increases significantly when the crop is completely matured. The leaf analysis results enabled the detection of excessive fertilization in all zones, but particularly in the first crop phase. Satellite photos enabled the identification of zones for the growth and production of various crops; this may be a useful tool for selecting sample places on the farm.

8.1.3 SOIL SENSOR

Water is an essential ingredient in the growth of plants. That is why irrigation must be considered carefully, as it should neither be excessive nor inadequate. Soil moisture sensors were incredibly beneficial for detecting water levels, significantly assisting farmers and lowering expenses. A soil sensor allows for more effectively arranging irrigation sessions by increasing or lowering their frequency and/or intensity without washing away important nutrients or dehydrating the plants. A remote soil moisture sensor enables agriculturalists to assess water levels in the field without physically being there. A soil moisture detector is a sensor that determines the present state of the soil's moisture content. Sensors incorporated into the irrigation purposes significantly improve the efficiency of the water supply chain and distribution schedule. These gauges aid in reducing or increasing irrigation to promote optimal plant development.

8.1.3.1 NIR and MIR Spectroscopy

Although soil organic matter (SOM) is a good indication of soil fertility and quality, it is also critical for regulating the soil dynamics of different agro–chemicals; as such, SOM is a critical component of agricultural soil. Gholizadeh et al. [9] explored the possibility of using Vis-NIR or mid-IR spectroscopy to quantify and assess SOM amount and quality. They investigate the effectiveness and generalizability of Vis-NIR and mid-IR calibration procedures, with a particular emphasis on the least-squares support vector machine (LS-SVM) method. Additionally, they explain the geographical scope of the tests as well as the calibration scales used (field, local, and global). Numerous soil properties may often be accurately estimated using Vis-NIR and mid-IR spectroscopy. The concentration of clay, the SOC and SOM content, as well as the soil moisture content are the most easily recognized factors. Thus, whether laboratory or field sampling of ground soils is performed, research has shown that mid-IR spectroscopy is typically more accurate and generates more stable calibrations for measuring SOM than Vis-NIR spectroscopy.

Rapid and cost-effective assessment of soil parameters is regarded as critical for monitoring and documenting agricultural soil conditions to execute site-specific management strategies. Due to the high costs and time commitment associated with standard laboratory measurements, they cannot be considered acceptable for large datasets. The article by Angelopoulou et al. [10] discusses any use of research labs or proximal detecting spectroscopy inside the visible as well as near-infrared (VNIR) – short wave infrared (SWIR) wavelength range like a substitute for computational chemistry studies in order to determine soil organic carbon as well as soil organic matter. Thus laboratory observations are a well-established approach for estimating soil parameters; there is currently no widely acknowledged universal model with widespread applicability. The increased interest in soil spectroscopy is seen in the international efforts to establish Soil Spectroscopy Laboratories (SSL), but without an agreed procedure. Additionally, research has been undertaken on using proximal soil sensors for in situ applications capable of determining SOC in real-time and across a broader geographic range. Overall, the findings are encouraging for estimating SOC, but further study is needed in terms of sensor selection, preprocessing approaches, and calibration methodologies.

8.1.3.2 Raman Spectroscopy

Raman technology, which encompasses Raman spectroscopy (RS) and its numerous derivative approaches, has been extensively employed in agriculture, food, and biosystems to identify a variety of compounds. The article by Weng et al. [11] discusses current advancements in two widely used Raman technologies, RS and Surface Enhanced Raman Spectroscopy (SERS), focusing on their technological progress, applicability, and problems, as well as spectrum processing approach. To begin, the genesis, principle, fault, and evolution of RS were discussed.

The present condition, existing challenges, and future development of RS and SERS in agricultural, food, and biosystems were then reviewed, including adulteration detection, plant disease identification, farm chemical detection, food additive determination, and toxicity analysis. Finally, the spectrum analysis techniques of noise reduction, extraction of features or variable selection, or modeling were discussed in-depth, demonstrating how they may be used to do automated and intelligent spectral analysis without depending on specialists. In conclusion, both RS and SERS have several drawbacks. Due to the limited sensitivity of RS, it cannot identify traces. However, SERS is prone to signal interference from other components in a sample and has poor stability and sensitivity. However, as optic, nanotechnology, and instruments advance, Raman technology has a broad range of potential applications in agriculture, foodstuff, or biosystems.

Agricultural goods and food are necessary for survival and also contribute significantly to the global economy. With the growing demand for a high-class existence, experts emphasize quality and safety management. Numerous approaches have been used to detect and identify agricultural goods and food. So Yang and Ying [12] discuss Raman spectroscopy due to advancements in Raman spectrometry as well as the capability of personal computers; Raman spectroscopy has gained prominence as an analytical tool.

With its narrow and highly resolved bands, Raman spectroscopy enables the non-destructive retrieval of physical and chemical information from materials. It enables quick online analysis without the need for sample preparation. Hence, due to several benefits like non-destructive detection, minimal sample preparation, and rapid measurement, Raman spectroscopy is a valuable instrument for assessing internal quality and safety. Raman spectroscopy's narrow and well-defined bands make it an excellent tool for subjective, structural, and quantitative research.

8.1.3.3   Nutrient Monitoring

In today's world, population growth is increasing. As a result, there is a need for increased food production. Fertilizers boost crop production; however, the soil's nutrient level and crop monitoring are optimal for producing more crops. As a result, Harshani et al. [13] address the use of the Internet of Things to detect soil factors such as pH, soil humidity, temp, or humidity. The soil moisture content and pH value of the soil are critical elements for crop development.

Numerous sensors are used to detect and monitor soil characteristics. Additionally, infrared sensors are utilized to detect illness in plants. For future usage, the detected values are kept and maintained in the cloud server. Additionally, an application is being created for farmers to determine the pH level of nutrients in the soil, the moisture content of the soil, and the temperature of the soil to maximize crop yield. Thus, the soil is analyzed for cultivation and crop efficiency by regularly measuring the soil's temperature, humidity, soil moisture, and pH range. Not only does the pH range dictate the sort of crop that may be grown, but it also helps to minimize fertilizer use.

Agriculture accounts for just 22 percent of the Indian economy's revenue. The primary reason for this decline is natural disasters and differences in the nutrients in the soil as a result of environmental changes. Overcoming obstacles caused by natural disasters is difficult. Technology may be used to understand differences in soil nutrient levels, therefore assisting the farming community in developing a helpful answer. Akhil et al. [14] suggest a new model that detects the nutrient level of soil using a variety of chemical sensors and recommend the addition of fertilizers to normalize the soil. NPK (Nitrogen, Phosphorus, and Potassium) levels are measured using fiber optic sensors in a specially constructed module that includes pH and moisture sensors as well as an NPK sensor. The Global System for Mobile Communications (GSM) module included into Arduino transmits these values to the web server. In order to come up with the appropriate recommendation, the acquired data is compared to those in the data set. This SMS message is sent to the farmers' mobile phone numbers through the recommendation system. It uses sensors and the Django Web framework, a Python-based web development tool. It has therefore been shown that the model described here has an accuracy rate of 90 percent.

8.1.3.4 Moisture Monitoring

It takes a long time to keep track of soil moisture levels in a vast crop. On-the-field moisture sensor circuits will be combined with a robotic kit to build an efficient and cost-effective humidity monitoring system in this project. Subdivision into smaller grids is used to cultivate a big tract of land. Moisture sensors are incorporated in each grid. Upon discovering that a sensor has detected that the ground is dry, the robot begins its investigation. Dijkstra's shortest path method is used to identify the most efficient route to the topic of interest. Using proper image processing techniques, the robot subsequently estimates and communicates the field's total moisture content. A small research area was formed above which a camera was put at an appropriate height to capture an aerial view of the region. The work by Das et al. [15] was designed and tested in this manner. So far, a prototype has been developed for an automated system to monitor agricultural fields' moisture content. That's why this technique produces smooth, continuous robotic movement. Productivity might rise even higher with more powerful robotic devices, allowing this procedure to be performed in agricultural fields in real time.

In recent years, environmental issues have come to the forefront because of rapid economic and social development. One such issue in agriculture is the use of pesticides via the application of pesticide sprays. Pests may be prevented, eliminated, or controlled with the use of pesticides. In greenhouses and agricultural areas, chemical pesticide spraying is the most efficient way to keep pests at bay. Using normal pesticide distribution procedures in agricultural fields and greenhouses may pose a number of health concerns to humans. An improved methodology for spreading pesticides in agricultural fields and greenhouses was devised by Divya Vani and Raghavendra Rao [16]. Using an Arduino and a Wi-Fi shield, a soil moisture sensor may be connected to an Android application. In order to keep track of the soil moisture, a sensor constantly checks the soil. A database is used to populate the output. Moisture readings will be shown using a look-up table that includes the date and moisture content after getting the data from a database. Anywhere between zero and one hundred represents a dry environment; between one hundred and three hundred represents a humid environment or an ideal; and anywhere between seven hundred and one thousand represents an excessive environment. As a result, farmers stand to gain greatly from this technology since there is no financial risk involved. Depending on the findings of the parameter measurements, the farmer may be able to develop crops, which would boost agricultural output.

8.2 YIELD MONITOR

One of the most critical data-collecting tools in Precision Agriculture (PA) is yield monitoring and mapping. An article by Keskin et al. [17] explains the on-the-go yield monitoring equipment that must be installed on combined harvesters to capture geo-referenced yield data and subsequently generate a yield map of the field. This article

discusses on-the-go yield monitoring equipment that must be put on a combined harvester to collect geo-referenced yield map data. Figure 8.1 depicts the architecture of
the system components.

As illustrated in both figures, a yield monitoring device for this type of combined
harvester consists of a moisture sensor, flow sensor, a header position switch, a
ground speed sensor, a Differential global positioning unit, a cutting width sensor, a
grain density sensor, a grain loss sensor, (if the flow sensor is truly volumetric), and
a desktop console.

8.2.1 PESTICIDES

Consumers are concerned about pesticides in agricultural products, both primary and
secondary. It was the purpose of this research by Jallow et al. [18] to determine the
amounts of pesticide residues in common fruits and veggies in Kuwait. The "Quick,
Easy, Cheap, Effective, Rugged, and Safe" (QuEChERS) multiple-residue extraction
technique was used to evaluate 150 fresh vegetables and fruits for the presence of 34
pesticides. LC-MS/MS and gas chromatography-mass spectrometry (GC-MS) were
then used to assess the samples. Of the samples tested, only 11 percent showed pesticide residues over the maximum residue limit (MRL) or included levels that were
lower than the MRL. Pesticide residues from two to four different pesticides were
found in 40 percent of the samples, whereas residues from four different pesticides
were found in 40 percent of the samples. More than a dozen pesticides, including
imidacloprid and cypermethrin, as well as acetamiprid, malathion and chlorpyrifos-
methyl, were found to have exceeded their maximum residual levels. One apple
sample tested positive for Aldrin, an organochlorine pesticide, at levels below the
MRL. In Kuwait, pesticide residues are found in a wide range of fruits and vegetables,
highlighting the need for extensive intervention measures to protect consumers from
any possible health risks. Regular pesticide monitoring and sensitization of producers to better pesticide safety procedures, notably adhering to permitted pre-harvest
intervals, are recommended.

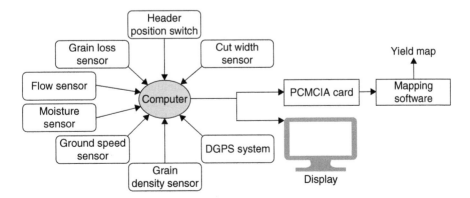

FIGURE 8.1 Schematic of component yield monitoring system for combined harvester.

8.2.2 FERTILIZERS

One of the primary goals of intelligent farming is to monitor agricultural fields efficiently and effectively while minimizing necessary resources such as fertilizer, pesticides, power, water supply, and labor costs. Fertilizer, in particular, is a significant resource. Arai et al. [19] proposed that an artificial intelligence-based fertilizer control system combined with an intelligent drone-based rice field observation system should improve the quality and quantity of harvested rice crops while reducing fertilizer needs. The proposed artificial intelligence-based fertilizer control strategy for enhancing the quantity and quality of cultivated rice crops is based on SPAD data, rice leaf spectral reflectance at 550 and 870 nm, stem count, plant height, culm length within a week of heading, panicle count (book/stock), ear length, air temperature, humidity levels, and atmospheric pressure. Then, artificial intelligence (AI) calculates when and how much fertilizer should be applied. Using rice paddy fields at the Saga Prefectural Research Institute of Agriculture in Japan, it was found that the suggested technique allows for precise management of rice crop quality and output by altering fertilizer type and supply quantity. Using 800 nm wavelengths in the near-infrared range, this test found that they successfully predicted protein content and yield. It's possible to control this via fertilization, but only if the outcome can be anticipated ahead of time. Yield prediction is essential in agriculture. Any farmer is curious about the product he is going to get. Historically, production prediction was based on farmer expertise with a specific field and crop. Yield prediction is a significant challenge that has yet to be resolved using existing data. Bondre and Mahagaonkar [20] propose and demonstrate a method for forecasting agricultural yields based on historical data. This is accomplished by training machine learning algorithms such as the Support Vector Machine and Random Forest on agricultural data and recommending the best fertilizer for each crop. The article focuses on developing a prediction model that may be used to forecast crop yields in the future. Hence, crop yield prediction depending on the location and practical application of algorithms have shown that increased crop yields are possible. As a result of the initial study, it is concluded that Random Forest is preferable to Support Vector Machine for soil classification, with an accuracy of 86.35 percent. Support Vector Machine is superior to Random Forest algorithm for agricultural production prediction, with only accuracy of 99.47 percent.

8.2.3 STERILE INSECT TECHNIQUE

With growing consumer demand for healthier, residue-free agricultural products, the hunt for more ecologically friendly pest control techniques has risen. The Sterile Insect Technique (SIT) is a very efficient, species-specific, and ecologically sound method for controlling insect pests on a large scale [21]. It has been successfully used against various species of fruit flies, including Ceratitis capitata. It includes releasing a vast number of carefully raised and sterilized male insects into the target region, where they mate with wild females of the same species, resulting in the inability to produce offspring and progressively reducing the pest population. Hence, the use of SIT led to a massive increase in the export of fresh fruits and vegetables to Mexico, Chile, South Africa, and the United States, among other countries.

Pre-harvest losses in impoverished nations are believed to be about 40 percent, whereas post-harvest losses add another 10 percent to 20 percent, the majority of which are caused by insect pests. There is scarcely a more inefficient use of resources than investing water, fertilizer, seeds, land, time, effort, and money in food production only to have it destroyed in part or whole by insects and other pests. As a result, an increasingly critical strategic component of improving productivity and ensuring global food security will be an investment in better insect pest control techniques, the Sterile Insect Technique (SIT). Currently, it takes an average of ten years to bring a new synthetic pesticide to market, at an average price of around US$120 million. Developing an SIT package for a particular major pest [22], which includes bulk rearing and aerial release and field monitoring and suppression, requires much less cost. The expense of insecticide development is likely to continue to climb due to more demanding regulatory criteria, which will be reflected in more costly newer insecticides, leading to increasingly competitive pricing for biologically-based approaches such as SIT.

In general, non-chemical pest control tools, such as biologically based techniques like SIT, will become more economically viable due to more realistic accounting for the adverse environmental impact of synthetic pesticide applications and increased investment in applied R&D.

8.3   AID OF AGRICULTURE

Crops offer information that can be converted into profitable choices only when they are handled effectively. Current developments in managing data are accelerating the growth of Smart Farming since data has become a fundamental component of contemporary agriculture, assisting farmers with essential decision-making. Valuable benefits emerge as a result of objective data collected by sensors to enhance production and sustainability. In this kind of data-driven managed farm, data is used to increase efficiency by reducing resource misuse and environmental damage. The future of sustainable agriculture is being laid by data-driven agriculture and robotic solutions using artificial intelligence technologies. Consequently, they look at the current state of creative farm business solutions by rethinking each critical step, from data capture in field crops to variable interest rate applications, in order to allow farmers the best choices while also saving the environment and transforming how food would be produced in the future so that it can sustainably feed the world's expanding populace.

Hence, this investigation demonstrates that having consistent information about farms enables farmers to make the best choices. Agricultural management systems may organize farm data so that the results are tailored to each farm. This digital assistance for farmers joins forces with automation and robotics to bring in the coming concept of Agriculture 5.0.

The relationship between foreign assistance and economic development has long been a source of disagreement, with no solid agreement emerging. This study divides foreign aid into four categories: agricultural support, social infrastructure support, financial assistance, or non-investment help. Kaya et al. [23] show that when aid is focused toward the agriculture industry of developing nations, it is favorably and substantially associated with the development and may have a short-term effect on economic growth.

Our research employs panel data from 66 countries, numerous estimators, and model parameters to examine the effect of agricultural assistance on per capita income. Almost all of the calculations in our investigation revealed a favorable and robust association between agricultural assistance and economic development. Results for non-aid control variables were also similar across models and theories and other empirical evidence. From the early 1980s to 2008, agricultural aid accounted for just around 4 percent of total government development assistance to poor countries, a remarkable drop. Correcting this decline in agricultural aid-giving may increase aid's overall effectiveness in promoting economic growth, according to research.

8.3.1 HARVESTING AND PICKING

Agriculture has several challenges, including a rise in unemployment and rising costs associated with fruit harvesting. Labor savings and agricultural scale-up are required to address these issues. Onishi et al. [24] suggest a technique for recognizing fruits and harvesting them automatically with the use of a robot arm. The location of the fruit is detected rapidly and precisely using a Single Shot MultiBox Detector, and the three-dimensional position is detected using a stereo camera. After inverse kinematics is used to calculate the angles of the joints just at the detected location, the robot arm is moved to the position of the target fruit. The fruit is subsequently harvested by rotating the robot's hand axis. Hence the experimental findings indicated that over 90 percent of the fruit was identified. Additionally, the robot can pick fruit in 16 seconds.

Agriculture, like industry, may benefit from the use of automation. Agriculture robots face a wide range of issues. On the one hand, unlike industrial facilities, agricultural surroundings are not organized and regulated. Modules, on the other hand, may construct industrial testing methods to adapt individual robots to specific occupations. However, complicated agricultural operations cannot always be broken down into basic actions. Agricultural applications need more adaptable and durable robots for the reasons stated above. Precision agriculture aims to use a variety of technologies to learn about crop spatial and temporal variability [25]. Among several other technologies, the use of airborne robots to map fields and detect weeds or irrigation deficiencies, as well as the use of ground robots to provide precise treatments to plants, should be emphasized. Moreover, greenhouses agriculture has used robots for a variety of tasks, including environmental element monitoring, which is critical for crop management, and also plant watering and spraying. Finally, although the use of robots for planting and harvesting is in its infancy, numerous sensing, position, or grasping systems have been developed.

8.3.2 WEED CONTROL

Weed control is often considered to be the most challenging task faced by organic farmers. Poor weed management is the primary cause of poorer plant productivity in organic farming. Weed losses surpassed losses generated by any other type of agricultural pests in the majority of cases [26]. In water-stressed situations, weeds may reduce crop yields by even more than half merely by competing for moisture. Due to the general environmental and toxicological hazards produced by herbicides, developing safe weed-control methods has become critical. Many cultures have successfully embraced mulching, biodegradable, soil solarization, mulch, hot water, natural herbicides, and such agronomic practices as safe weed control strategies in organic farming discussed by them.

Additionally, there are several intriguing novel and non-traditional ways of weed control in organic farming – for example, the Fresnel Lenses, Electric Weed Control, and Lasers. Agronomic practices such as cultivar selection or stale seedbeds have a large influence on weeds as well. Growers practicing organic agriculture must keep three things in mind: (1) start with a clean environment and preserve it; (2) prevention is always superior to treatment; and (3) one-year's seeds result in seven-year weed development. Methods of weed control that use many tactics rather than a single one are now more likely to be successful and long-lasting. Finally, one may argue that good and sustainable weed control strategies include a variety of measures rather than relying only on one. Additional study is needed to create novel weed control technologies and clean agricultural practices.

Weed is a rogue planet that obstructs the development of the primary crop. The weed flora composition varies according to the kind of agroecosystem. Rainfed systems have distinct weed flora from irrigated systems. Similarly, annual crops will have a distinct weed pattern compared to permanent crops. Weeds are the primary biological constraint on widespread adoption of low-intensity tillage or no-tillage connected with conservation agriculture and are regarded as one of the essential areas of crop production under conservation agriculture, as they necessarily prevent the use of traditional weed management methods such as plowing to begin preparing the field for sowing discussed in this chapter. Brajendra Parmar [27] also discusses conservation strategies important to maintain agricultural output and fulfill future local and global food demand. In this environment, effective weed management is important to the achievement of these systems. Herbicide usage is advantageous when implementing conservation principles. However, chemical weed management is essential to achieving conservation agriculture's aims of minimizing negative environmental effects and herbicide resistance development in weeds. Hence, integrated weed management approaches might be used to control weeds in conservation agriculture.

8.3.3 Autonomous Mowing, Pruning, Seeding, Spraying and Thinning

Agriculture is rapidly evolving into a high-tech sector, attracting new experts, businesses, and investors. Technologies are expanding fast, boosting farmers' output capacity and robots and automation technology. Agricultural robots help farmers increase their crop yields in a variety of ways. From drones to self-driving tractors to robotic arms, technologies are being used in new and unique ways. Agricultural robots automate repetitive and tedious activities for farmers, freeing them to concentrate on overall production yield improvement. Harvesting, weed management, autonomously mowing, pruning, planting, spraying, and thinning, and sorting and packaging are just a few agricultural applications for robots. So they discuss Robotic

Process Automation (RPA), a cutting-edge technology that utilizes artificial intelligence to automate massive amounts of repetitive operations (AI). RPA may be used to automate transaction processing, data manipulation, reaction triggering, and communication with other digital systems.

8.3.4 PHENOTYPING

Agriculture's biggest threat is a changing climate driven by rising greenhouse gas emissions, which results in severe temperatures and bad weather conditions. Global warming's effect varies by geographical location, necessitating tailored solutions for the world's many agro-ecological zones. Due to restricted resources and inefficient farming techniques, farmers in low-income nations are susceptible to climate change. Thus, increasing crop output while minimizing the agricultural effect on the environment would need sustainable intensification of agriculture via contemporary methods for plant breeding, cultivation, and crop management. So Chawade et al. [28] showed much interest in high-throughput field phenotyping, resulting in numerous innovative procedures for documenting different plant features of interest.

8.3.5 PRECISION BREEDING AND PHENOTYPING OF PLANTS

Agriculture has a variety of requirements due to the diverse sizes of plots and fields, the variety of objectives, and the need of the actions required after phenotyping. While phenotyping is performed on several thousand tiny plots in plant breeding to assess them for different qualities, it is done in broad areas in plant cultivation to identify the emergence of plant stressors and pests at an early stage. Hence, the main hurdles are the creation and reporting of correct phenotyping data for appropriate interpretation of the acquired findings and repeatability. Additional problems in precision agriculture include automated and quick, even real-time, analysis required for appropriate and timely interventions in fields and greenhouses.

Addressing the issues posed by a fast-growing population as well as a slowly accelerating rate of grain production, maximizing rice's production and quality potential, or developing new technologies and methodologies in crop breeding are all critical. So, environmentalists discuss phenotyping, which is a critical link between environmental impacts and gene function and is essential for crop development. However, because of the complexity of the unstructured environment, it is challenging to extract high-throughput rice phenotypic characteristics in the field. The goal of the chapter by Zhang et al. [29] was to propose a design strategy for a field robot that produces visual space to assess rice quality. The truss system, which is integrated with a manipulation module as well as a vision system, determines the item's location by evaluating position data acquired during the seedling growth stage. Three manipulators were built by replicating human activities such as pushing close rice, extending the panicle, and rubbing rice longer to eliminate overlap. To quantitatively quantify phenotypes, three image sensors were used: a CCD camera, a structural light sensor, and a laser sensor. The simulation was created to ascertain manipulator workspaces. The quantity of accessible space in between clapboards of the rice-separating manipulator has been determined to be 1.6 10-3 cubic meters, the effective range of movement of the height monitoring manipulator has been determined to be 1300mm, and the maximum workspace of the panicle-expanding manipulator was determined to be 32,500 square millimeters.

8.3.6 SORTING AND PACKING

Due to a lack of sufficient technology throughout harvesting, packing, storing, and shipping, the annual average loss has gone up to 40 percent of output. Two Brazilian tomato varieties were exposed to post-harvest handling techniques, including sorting, refrigeration storage, and varied carton packing, in order to reduce horticultural production losses [30]. These treatments were investigated for their influence on the shelf life of vegetables. At 7°C, 13°C, and ambient temperature (24°C), the color, hardness, taste, and weight loss of ripe green tomatoes were determined. Hence this research demonstrates that post-harvest storage temperature affects the ripening qualities of fresh tomatoes, including coloring, firmness, pH, sweetness, sourness, and weight loss. Reduced temperature extends the shelf life of tomatoes, based on comparable quality findings achieved for products stored at ambient temperature – 24°C for nine days or at 13°C for 22 days. While sorting and packaging affect certain individual features of tomatoes, this does not seem to affect their shelf life.

REFERENCES

[1] R. Akış (2015). "Spatial variability of soil solute and saturated hydraulic conductivity affected by undrained water table conditions." *Precision Agriculture*, vol. 16, no. 3, 330–359. https://doi.org/10.1007/s11119-014-9379-0

[2] A. Kshirsagar (2018). "Bio-remediation: Use of nature in a technical way to fight pollution for a long run." *ResearchGate*. https://doi.org/https://doi.org/10.13140/RG.2.2.26906.70088

[3] A. Kshirsagar, M. Shah (2021). "Anatomized study of security solutions for multimedia: deep learning-enabled authentication, cryptography and information hiding." In I. A. Ansari and V. Bajaj (Eds.), *Advanced Security Solutions for Multimedia*. IOP Publishing. https://doi.org/10.1088/978-0-7503-3735-9ch7

[4] H. Fathi, M. Mirzanejad (2015). "Spatial variability of agricultural characteristic to evaluate productivity potential in Iran." *Journal of Environmental Science and Technology* vol. 8, no. 1, 13–24. https://doi.org/10.3923/jest.2015.13.24

[5] H. Kaur, A. Kaur, B. Singh, R. Bhatt (2020). "Application of geospatial technology in assessment of spatial variability in soil properties: a review." *Current Journal of Applied Science and Technology*, vol. 39, no. 39, 57–71. https://doi.org/10.9734/cjast/2020/v39i3931104

[6] StatSoft, Inc. www.statistica.com/

[7] R.G. Trevisan, D.S. Bullock, N.F. Martin. (2021). "Spatial variability of crop responses to agronomic inputs in on-farm precision experimentation." *Precision Agriculture*, vol. 22, no. 2, 342–363. https://doi.org/10.1007/S11119-020-09720-8/TABLES/5

[8] F. Pinheiro, W. de P. Gusmo dos Anjos (2014). "Optical sensors applied in agricultural crops." In *Optical Sensors–New Developments and Practical Applications*. IntechOpen. https://doi.org/10.5772/57145

[9] A. Gholizadeh, B. Luboš, M. Saberioon, R. Vašát (2013). "Visible, near-infrared, and mid-infrared spectroscopy applications for soil assessment with emphasis on soil organic matter content and quality: State-of-the-art and key issues". *Applied Spectroscopy* vol. 67, no. 12, 1349–1362. SAGE Publications. https://doi.org/10.1366/13-07288

[10] T. Angelopoulou, A. Balafoutis, G. Zalidis, D. Bochtis (2020). "From laboratory to proximal sensing spectroscopy for soil organic carbon estimation-A review." In *Sustainability* (Switzerland), vol. 12, no. 2. https://doi.org/10.3390/su12020443

[11] S. Weng, W. Zhu, X. Zhang, H. Yuan, L. Zheng, J. Zhao, L. Huang, P. Han (2019). "Recent advances in Raman technology with applications in agriculture, food and biosystems: A review." *Artificial Intelligence in Agriculture* vol. 3, 1–10. https://doi.org/10.1016/j.aiia.2019.11.001

[12] D. Yang, Y. Ying (2011). "Applications of raman spectroscopy in agricultural products and food analysis: A review". *Applied Spectroscopy Reviews* vol. 46, no. 7, pp. 539–560. Taylor & Francis Group. https://doi.org/10.1080/05704928.2011.593216

[13] P. R. Harshani, M. Newlin Rajkumar, T. Umamaheswari, R. Tharani (2017). "Monitoring the nutrient level for efficient crop productivity using IOT." *SJ Impact Factor* vol. 6, 887. https://doi.org/10.22214/ijraset.2017.11044

[14] R. Akhil, M. S. Gokul, S. Menon, L. S. Nair (2018). "Automated soil nutrient monitoring for improved agriculture." *Proceedings of the 2018 IEEE International Conference on Communication and Signal Processing, ICCSP 2018*, 688–692. https://doi.org/10.1109/ICCSP.2018.8524512

[15] S. Das, B. Pal, P. Das, M. Sasmal, P. Ghosh, (2017). "Design and development of Arduino based automatic soil moisture monitoring system for optimum use of water in agricultural fields." *International Journal of Engineering Research & Science (IJOER)* vol. 3, no. 5, 15–19.

[16] P. Divya Vani, K. Raghavendra Rao (2016). "Measurement and monitoring of soil moisture using cloud IoT and Android system." *Indian Journal of Science and Technology* vol. 9, no. 311–8. https://doi.org/10.17485/IJST/2016/V9I31/95340

[17] M. Keskin, Y.J. Han, R. B. Dodd. (1999). "A review of yield monitoring instrumentation applied to the combine harvesters for precision agriculture purposes." 7th International Congress on Agricultural Mechanization and Energy. www.researchgate.net/publication/310625141. A_Review_of_Yield_Monitoring_Instrumentation_Applied_to_the_Combine_Harvesters_for_Precision_Agriculture_Purposes_Hassas_Uygulamali_Tarim_Icin_Bicerdoverlere_Uygulanan_Verim_Goruntuleme_Algilayicilari.

[18] M.F.A. Jallow, D.G. Awadh, M.S. Albaho, V.Y. Devi, N. Ahmad (2017). "Monitoring of pesticide residues in commonly used fruits and vegetables in Kuwait." *International Journal of Environmental Research and Public Health* vol. 14, no. 8, 833. https://doi.org/10.3390/ijerph14080833

[19] K. Arai, O. Shigetomi, Y. Miura (2018). "Artificial intelligence based fertilizer control for improvement of rice quality and harvest amount." *International Journal of Advanced Computer Science and Applications* vol. 9, no. 10, 61–67. https://doi.org/10.14569/IJACSA.2018.091008

[20] D.A. Bondre, S. Mahagaonkar, (2019). "Prediction of crop yield and fertilizer recommendation using machine learning algorithms." *International Journal of Engineering Applied Sciences and Technology* vol. 4, no. 5, 371–376. https://doi.org/10.33564/ijeast.2019.v04i05.055

[21] S. Tapsuwan, T. Capon, M. Tam, J. Kandulu, P. Measham, S.Whitten (2020). "Willingness to pay for area-wide management and sterile insect technique to control

fruit flies in Australia." *International Journal of Pest Management* vol. 66, no. 4, 351–367. https://doi.org/10.1080/09670874.2019.1652369

[22] United Nations Information Service. (1973). "Some insect pests close to eradication thanks to 'sterile male technique.'" *Biological Conservation* vol. 5, no. 2, 86. https://doi.org/10.1016/0006-3207(73)90083-9

[23] O. Kaya, I. Kaya, L.Gunter (2012). "Development aid to agriculture and economic growth." *Review of Development Economics* vol. 16, no. 2, 230–242. https://doi.org/10.1111/j.1467-9361.2012.00658.x

[24] Y. Onishi, T. Yoshida, H. Kurita, T. Fukao, H. Arihara, A. Iwai (2019). "An automated fruit harvesting robot by using deep learning." *ROBOMECH Journal*, vol. 6, no. 1, 1–8. https://doi.org/10.1186/s40648-019-0141-2

[25] J. Roldán, J. del Cerro, D. Garzón-Ramos, G.-A. Pablo, M. Garzón, J. de León, A. Barrientos (2017). "Robots in agriculture: state of art and practical experiences." *Service Robots*. https://doi.org/10.5772/INTECHOPEN.69874

[26] H.F. Abouziena, W.M. Haggag (2016). "Weed control in clean agriculture: a review 1. *Planta Daninha* vol. 34, no. 2, 377–392. https://doi.org/10.1590/S0100-83582016340200019

[27] P. Brajendra (2018). "Weed management in conservation agriculture: A brief review". In *ResearchGate*. www.researchgate.net/publication/336125179_Weed_management_in_conservation_agriculture_A_brief_review.

[28] A. Chawade, J. Van Ham, H. Blomquist, O. Bagge, E. Alexandersson, R. Ortiz (2019). "High-throughput field-phenotyping tools for plant breeding and precision agriculture." *Agronomy* vol. 9, no. 5, p. 258. https://doi.org/10.3390/agronomy9050258

[29] J. Zhang, L. Gong, C. Liu, Y. Huang, D. Zhang, Z. Yuan (2016). "Field phenotyping robot design and validation for the crop breeding." *IFAC-PapersOnLine* vol. 49, no. 16, 281–286. https://doi.org/10.1016/j.ifacol.2016.10.052

[30] L. De Castro, L.A.B. Cortez, C. Vigneault (2006). "Effect of sorting, refrigeration and packaging on tomato shelf life." *Journal of Food, Agriculture and Environment* vol. 4, no. 1, 70–74. www.researchgate.net/publication/266370688_Effect_of_sorting_refrigeration_and_packaging_on_tomato_shelf_life.

9 Quality Assurance and Control (End Product Monitoring)

9.1 AI ENABLED GRADING ROBOTS

9.1.1 WHAT IS GRADING IN AGRICULTURE

Grading is different for various fruits and vegetables, and it highly depends on the form of products, such as commercial-grade versus fancy grade. So, grading is defined as dividing the products into lots with characteristics such as shape, size, weight, performance, and quality. Products are separated into different groups and lots based on their quality. The quality of fruits and vegetables is divided based on the grades, with the letter grade 'A' being given the highest quality level for the processed food. In contrast, the grades 'B', 'C' and 'D' contain an increasing number of products with less desirable characteristics based on eligibility. Grading categorizes the products into dissimilar groups based on some of their significant features, which helps fix the prices for different products. The importance of grading includes easy sales, reasonable price, information of product, cost of transportation being less, less or no risk, and many more. Standards and growth help lower the costs in the supply chain by creating uniform products flowing through the system [1]. So, the primary purpose of grading is as follows:

  i. Post-harvest damage reduction
  ii. Avoiding unfairness in the transaction
  iii. Segregation based on quality
  iv. Increase marketing efficiency through different marketing methods
  v. Improvement of trading systems to make sure that quality goods are sold to the customers
  vi. Cost-saving
  vii. Fulfilling market demand

Grading is mainly divided into three grades, namely

  a. Premium Grade
  b. Grade 1
  c. Grade 2

DOI: 10.1201/9781003213550-9

Premium Grade: This includes all those fruits and vegetables that are free from damage and defects.

Grade 1 and Grade 2: This includes those that have an acceptable level of damage and defect. The main difference between the two lies in maximum flexibility.

Let's talk about the traditional grading. Traditional grading was human-dependent. In the later stages, mechanical devices were employed to differentiate agricultural products based on their dimensions and weight. These devices are still being used for grading and sorting. Grading was carried out manually using simple to complex tools that depend on the commodity type and the resource availability. Later, the image processing algorithms emerged, and visual techniques were added to make the process smooth. These algorithms were tuned so that they were able to detect minor defects that humans were not able to detect. With automatic detection, these algorithms ensure a detection performance far beyond the speed and accuracy of any trained operator.

Grading Criteria: The division of fruits and vegetables into separate lots follows a certain criterion. So, there are mainly five criteria upon which the grading is carried out.

1. Freshness: Agricultural produce highly depends on the level of freshness, and the tolerance level should be between 3–0 percent for a good agricultural product. Those that lack this quality are strictly prohibited from sale. Some examples of the level of freshness are smooth skin of the agricultural produce, no signs of wrinkling, and soft texture, and the product is not mature enough if it is wilted.
2. Damage: Agricultural products that show any signs of damage are strictly prohibited from sale as it will affect the products' taste, presentation, and texture. Some signs of injury are those that can or cannot be detected on skin surfaces due to pests and infectious diseases. Damage can be detected based on three aspects:
   a. Mechanical injuries such as breaks, bruises, and cuts
   b. Holes or the bite marks done by pests
   c. Micro-organism effects, such as bad odor, molds, and rot
3. Size Uniformity: Some agricultural products have a uniform size with a tolerance level between 3–10 percent. A packaging unit is generally considered uniform if the weight of the product is within the specified size.
4. Maturity: Maturity is considered uniform and must be that only one or a combination of maturity index is almost in a single lot. Color ripeness that is used for trading are indexed from number 1 to 6.

9.1.2 How Artificial Intelligence Techniques are Shaping the Grading Procedures

The task of vegetable and fruit grading is in high demand in the markets, which require quality from both of them. Robots employed with algorithmic software help speed up the time processing and help in error reduction. So, let us discuss some of the research related to computer vision and image recognition that has helped grade fruits and vegetables.

Megha and Lakshmana [2] proposed an automatic and effective tomato-grading system based on computer vision and image recognition. The software was developed based on image-processing techniques to analyze tomatoes captured from hardware for defects and ripeness. Initially, the image of the tomato is captured by a camera but consists of specular reflections and *noise*, which degrades the quality of the image. So, filtering is applied to the image in order to reduce the noise. Segmentation is then carried out to extract tomato regions from the image. The image is then converted to binary one using the Otsu method, which partitions the image into background and tomato. To detect whether the tomato is defective or not, features extraction and selection are carried out. The statistical features for red, blue, and green colors are carried out. The ripeness of the fruit is closely related to its color, so the average of these three colors is estimated, which means is compared with a threshold, so if the threshold is greater than the mean, then the tomato is ripened, otherwise not. In the second phase, Sequential Forward selection is carried out, which extracts 13 features. Those features are fed into the neural network, giving an overall accuracy of 96.47 percent in evaluating the quality of tomatoes.

Sivaranjani et al. [3] worked on the grading system for cashews using the deep convolutional neural network, and various parameters are considered for optimization. The traditional image classification features were extracted before the classification process. The CNN algorithm was improved through deep CNN. Multiple steps were involved using deep CNN, such as feeding the input image, initializing the sequential neural network, performing a convolutional operation on training images and extracting features, whereby the feature maps were passed to the activation function. Max pooling was carried out to select the largest element from ROI. The next step is to convert all resultant data into a 1D continuous linear vector before the last fully connected layer. The Softmax operator is used to improve the classification accuracy. So, deep CNN helps set a trademark in the image-classification challenges.

Alturki et al. [4] proposed computer vision-based algorithms for date grading and sorting in order to reduce human interference. This paper talked about computer-based vision algorithms' accuracy based on pre-selected date fruit samples from Saudi Arabia. This consists of an electro-mechanical system that places date fruits on a strap to carry through the classification process. After processing a date's fruit data, the system presents it to the shape recognizer box through a computer-based classifier. The classifier then performs quality assessments, classifies date fruits into different classes, and directs the sorter to the appropriate box for future manufacturing. There are mainly four stages: date fruits segmentation, disconnecting the labels from regions of date fruits, density extraction, and classification of date fruits. The result was making the histogram verify the difference between each date fruit.

Momin et al. [5], implements geometry-based mass grading of mango fruits using image processing. The authors developed an image acquisition and processing system to extract the perimeter, roundness features, and projected area. The images were acquired using an XGA format 8-bit gray-level camera using fluorescent lighting. Image segmentation was carried out and categorized into three categories namely pattern recognition, thresholding, and deformable models. The RGB values were converted to HSI with the help of color space conversion relationships. Various steps were involved in carrying out this conversion such as reading the RGB image, representing the image in the range [0,1], calculating the HIS components and representing the saturation in the ranges of [0,100] and [0,255] for convenience. Statistical significance and analysis were evaluated using paired t-test. The image recognition system achieved an accuracy of 97 percent for the projected area, 36 percent for roundness and 79 percent for the perimeter. This grading system is efficient and straightforward and can be considered a suitable first stage for mechanizing mangoes' commercial grading.

These were the works carried out by some famous authors surrounded by different artificial intelligence techniques, such as image processing and computer vision. The automation task became very smooth with these methods, and a higher accuracy was obtained for different fruits, respectively. With these techniques, the agricultural robots' grading and sorting of fruits and vegetables achieved a much higher precision compared to previous times, which showed the dominance of artificial intelligence in the agriculture industry.

9.2   DEFECT DETECTION

Image-processing packages are extended with the aid of giving a pc imagination and prescience in numerous fields. In photo processing, extraordinary facts are extracted from the photograph, additionally offering vital concepts and algorithms inside multimedia, clinical, and agriculture. Here, a mixture of hardware and software programs is used for the motive of processing photographs. Nowadays, pc imaginative and prescient generation are adopted within the agriculture subject to discover defects in products. In India, agriculture is the most crucial subject because; the majority of Indians depend on farming. So, there may be need to locate defects and enhance product, and it will automatically increase the market price. In food industries, before sending products to the marketplace, there's a need for grading. Grading is generally completed on the premise of outside defects on the skin of fruits or vegetables. Traditionally, food merchandise is inspected via guide inspection, which consumes more time and is less efficient for massive industries. The computer vision techniques are more useful, as they offer a dependable end result. Image processing using advanced generation makes it feasible to carry out automated grading of fruits and vegetables with image processing.

This reduces the price, improves satisfaction, increases the marketplace return and user-acceptance ratio. Some automatic grading structures are to be had that use classic techniques on the basis of shade, texture, length, and shape. But capturing some of this information is a challenging undertaking. In an automated grading system, characteristic extraction and class are primary and tough obligations. But before that, to enhance the visible outcomes of the enter photographs, preprocessing picture enhancement is carried out using median filtering, which enables doing away with noise and enhances the end result. Also, to enhance assessment and brightness consequences, the photograph is transformed from rgb2gray. Image segmentation is one of the important steps used to segment faulty components through iterative tri-class thresholding, Otsu's approach to greater focus on the precise defective parts. Then, defect feature extraction is finished using GLCM and classifies pictures by using the usage of the nearest neighbor (kNN), compared with educational photos that can be saved in the database [6]. Next, discovering the sample similarities and classifying them into four classes: Category 1, Category 2, Category 3, and Category 4 [7]. This will enhance the efficiency of grading gadget and additionally offers better outcomes. This device could be very beneficial for apple grading.

Many researchers have labored on image-processing programs inside the agriculture field to discover culmination or leaf diseases, finding defects in the end result. This is done using size, color, and texture for grading apples. Human inspection requiring visible reorganization isn't always accurate, and it requires more enjoy. The coloration and texture are critical features for culmination and vegetable evaluation. The texture is useful to establish the basic parameters. Classification of the input photos is likewise a crucial undertaking because accuracy varies according to class, and efficiency relies on several categories. The authors of [6] evolved the Fuzzy C way (FCM) clustering approach that's used for illness segmentation, and capabilities from defects are extracted using the Histogram of Oriented Gradients (HOG) technique, and apple types are determined by the use of the Multi-Class Support Vector Machine (MSVM) with an accuracy of 97.5 percent for 2 class grading. that is, wholesome or defective and 94.66 percent for Multi-Category Grading, that is,. healthy apple, slightly defected apple, and severely defected apple. In [8], the authors proposed a comparative look at approximately the overall performance of various thresholding techniques along with Otsu, Isodata and Entropy and distinct Artificial Neural Network (ANN) strategies, including Linear Discriminant Classifier (LDC), Fuzzy Nearest Neighbor Classifier (fuzzy okay- NN), Nearest Neighbor Classifier (okay-NN), Adaptive Boosting (Adaboost) and Support Vector Machine (SVM) with bandwidths RE and IR.

The disorder segmentation was accomplished using the thresholding technique. Statistical capabilities were extracted from the defect phase, and results were labeled using a supervised classifier. The classification accuracy became highest with the SVM classifier with the Isodata threshold approach in the RE band with an accuracy of 89.2 percent. In [7], the authors proposed a method to grade 'Jonagold' apples based on their outer quality. Ground color grading category and the Gaussian version of fruit color has been used for disease detection. Geometric, shade, and texture features had been taken into consideration to categorize the fruit. The apples were divided into four grades (Extra, Class I, Category II, and Reject). The usage of Linear Discriminant Analysis (LDA) gave an accuracy of 72 percent turned into carried out. In this method, the fruit in class 'Extra' was graded better than those belonging to different groups, and because of bruises had been poorly graded. In [9] authors have developed a system for grading apples using fuzzy logic (FL) as a decision-making aid. They have used color, length, and the defects of apples; excellent qualities were measured via a different system. By using equal sets of apples, grading was done via both a human expert and an FL machine, designed for this purpose. Grading outcomes acquired from FL showed 89 percent agreement with the consequences from the human expert, supplying correct flexibility in reflecting the professional's expectations and grading requirements in the results [9]. K-Nearest Neighbor's set of rules is likewise used to examine information. It uses Euclidean distance measures to determine the space among factors within the input statistics and educated facts.

In [10], authors proposed new culmination popularity strategies with a combination of 4 features analysis techniques i.e., shape, length, and color, texture-based totally method to grow recognition accuracy. For feature extraction, they calculated to suggest a value for RGB factor and shape via threshold segmentation and also calculate place, perimeter, roundness, and entropy values. The reputational result of accuracy was up to 90 percent, using the KNN set of rules [10]. But the hindrance of this method is that the most effective two instructions have been considered for grading. The authors of [8] proposed a comparative look at the performance of various ANN to grate the apples. The fruit photo became separated from the historical past through the threshold method. The intensity values of every pixel were used as local capabilities, in addition to nearby features: Average, Standard Deviation and Median, decided on as global capabilities. In comparison performance of LDC, the creator, fuzzy k-NN, k-NN, SVM, and AdaBoost classified apples into wholesome and defected categories. The highest accuracy of 90.3 percent was achieved with the aid of an SVM classifier. The principal difficulty in this was that only two instructions have been considered for grading.

Further, the authors of [8] proposed the apple grading system with the cascade SVM approach. The defective vicinity is segmented utilizing the use of MLP-based approach with a clever pixel class. The Sequential Floating Forward Selection (SFSS) method is used for function extraction. The multi-class apple classification was executed with cascade SVM type with 85.6 percent accuracy. The textural features are taken into consideration; however, this technique is computationally highly priced.

The authors of [11] evolved a gadget for grading apple ailments by using multi grading classification. The color, morphological and texture capabilities are extracted from the shape preprocessed image. And, based on the percent of affected locations, apple is classified into one in all classes as normal, partially affected, fairly affected, and bad. In [12], the author developed a gadget for apple fruit photographic defect identification using multivariate analysis techniques for defect segmentation. The gadget makes use of visual and close to infrared regions for the examination. This technique groups all of the pixels having equal spectral property into the available cluster, regardless of the spatial function of the pixel, so the external defects may without difficulty be diagnosed with the use of this technique. But this requires the right setup to choose for the apple method , which is pretty high priced. We can see that from the proposed techniques, some of the methods have the best two or three-class grading, and in some of the work, the dataset size used for the experiment became very small, because of which, the performance of the method could not be evaluated correctly. Those authors, who have worked on multispectral classification, could not get extra accuracy.

9.3 MONITORING SENSORS

9.3.1 GRAIN ELEVATOR QUALITY INSPECTION

The utilization of quality management systems (QMS) has become a transcendent pattern in numerous businesses, including manufacturing, medical care, and administration. A QMS is a collection of facilitated exercises that guides organizational strategy to meet or surpass client assumptions (ISO,2008). Authorization or affirmation by independent auditing bodies might be achieved if the QMS meets published guidelines.

Well defined for farming and livestock handling are QMS, like the American Institute of Baking's (AIB) Quality System Evaluation (QSE). Comparable yet less extensive than ISO, the AIB standard has typical components with ISO 9001, for example, documentation, self-reviews, the board obligations, item control, and estimation confirmation [13]. In this review, with ideas also, going with language more natural to the grain, taking care of industry, executing a quality administration, the framework was a decent middle-of-the-road venture toward ISO affirmation [14, 15]. The American Institute of Baking [14] mission is to safeguard the well-being of the food production network. AIB has made the quality framework assessment (QSE) quality administration framework with food handling the real target of the certificate [13].

In the agricultural area, past QMS sway evaluations, for the most part, have incorporated the whole food supply chain [16, 17]. These associations have objectives comparative objectives to those of non-horticultural organizations shifting focus over to QMS to work on inward functional furthermore, satisfy client needs [18, 19].

Estimating the effect of QMS requires information that not all organizations will share. Distributed research reflects this using hierarchical information [19]. Results from the food store network viewpoint fluctuates contingent on the item and interaction type, however most spotlight on microbial food handling [20, 21].

There have been restricted investigations of the food inventory network post-collect and before handling [18]. Due to the low edge of ware items, while assessing a QMS, organization information stay the most esteemed presentation metric in deciding viability. Even though associations inside the agricultural and food production network have generally been hesitant to share inner information, setting explicit functional knowledge and technique are expected to work with continuous improvement in current cycles.

9.3.1.1 Measurement of Quality Indicators

The administration of grain quality envelops a few processes and is significant to business execution. Grain lifts should get, estimate, store, and ship grain at a quality level that helps and meets client demands, which is very essential for Grain Quality Measurement. One essential part of this the process is stock administration, which starts with the examination of approaching grain. In-bound grain is examined, mixed, and put away as per quality grades set by the Grain Inspection, Packers, and Stockyards Administration (GIPSA), an office of the United States Department of Agribusiness (USDA). Also, grain is a natural item, susceptible to decay. Bad quality grain implies a danger to purchasers and end clients, since it disintegrates at a higher rate than grain at a better grade [22]. Indeed, grain quality estimations are challenging to normalize since some evaluating measures are randomly characterized [23].

Major aspects of assessments in the United States are based on reference principles of the National Institute of Standards and Technology (NIST) for weight, volume, and length. In any case, there is no "outright" proportion of grain grades and official grades hold subjectivity coming about in estimation blunder [23]. The consistency of reviewing (accuracy) and closeness to the genuine worth (exactness, as characterized by an authority reviewer) are significant estimation qualities in grain evaluating. It is estimated on each following qualities grain test mentioned by authors [23]:

1. Test weight – Weight of estimated volume of grain in grams per quart cup and struck off as indicated by systems illustrated by the Federal Grain Inspection Administration (FGIS); estimations were switched over entirely to kilograms per hectoliter (kg/hL).
2. Dampness content – The part (percent) of water on a all-out weight premise in grain test estimated by a adjusted Montomco dampness meter aligned by GIPSA.
3. Damage – The portion (percent) of bits with shape, or then again bugs, infection, heat, or generally really harmed by an outwardly arranged work test

9.3.2 NEAR-INFRARED SPECTROSCOPY (NIR)

9.3.2.1 What is Near-Infrared Spectroscopy in Agriculture?

NIR spectroscopy is used for functional, intermediate, compositional, sensory analysis of ingredients and final products. It is deployed mostly in food and feed, dairy, agricultural and chemical industries which are under constant pressure for manufacturing the products to meet customer requirements while increasing profitability and plant production. NIR is used in qualitative, quantitative analysis as well as process control. It can provide information on fat, protein, moisture, and starch content. NIR applications vary in each industry and even vary from one company to another along with their specific products and needs. NIR wavelength must start with a spectrometer that converts infrared light to a usable signal. The wavelength range is generally measured in nanometers. The wavelength that is required to measure protein content in grain is different from that required to measure amino acids in feed ingredients. As NIR is a quality assurance and control method, it can measure organic and pure substances and inorganic minerals and salts. These substances include vitamins and nutrients, carbohydrates, fats, emulsifiers, preservatives, binders and thickeners, sweeteners, and sugar replacements. These substances in food give out unique infrared emissions. So, NIR senses these emissions and informs about the proportions of these substances in a specific food compound. The amount or concentration of these substances is shown with the help of various levels of intensity of specific infrared colors.

The NIR analysis method is well suited for the quantitative determination of major constituents in all the food and agricultural products. The main benefit of NIR is that it provides rapid analysis data for better decision-making in the agricultural production processes. The traditional analysis methods required a lot of sample preparation which, on the other hand, in NIR, no chemicals or consumables are needed to that extent. Certain parameters need to be known first for calibration by the NIR measurement device. The calibration is stored in the NIR device memory. It has pre-set factory calibrations but can use other calibration techniques as well as can produce other algorithms for a specific calibration using certain techniques such as multi-linear regression and advanced partial least squares method termed as PLS. NIR depends on certain principles which define its working.

- Initially, near-infrared light is directed onto a sample
- The light is then modified according to the sample's composition, and detection of this modified light happens.
- The spectral adjustments are changed over to data concerning the piece of the sample
- These algorithms are termed calibrations

9.3.2.2 Workings of Near Infrared Spectroscopy

In this method, an unknown substance is illuminated with a broad spectrum of infrared light, which can be absorbed, reflected, transmitted, or scattered by the sample. The illumination is mostly in the wavelength range of 800 to 2500nm. The light intensity is measured before and after interacting with the sample and a combination of scattering and absorbance caused by the sample gets calculated. Light gets absorbed at certain frequencies in varying amounts by the sample. Specifically, the bond vibrations result in NIR bonds. The bands that are observed in NIR are typically very broad, which leads to spectra that are more complex to interpret than FTIR spectra. It becomes somewhat difficult to assign specific features to chemical components. Cautious advancement of many alignment tests and utilization of multivariate adjustment strategies are fundamental for insightful close infrared techniques. NIR can penetrate much further into a sample compared to FTIR and is not affected by fluorescence. So, even if NIR is not as chemically specific as FTIR, it is very useful in probing the bulk material with little or no sample preparation.

9.3.2.3 Applications of NIR Spectroscopy in Agricultural and Food Production

The demand for agricultural production and sustainable farming is continuously increasing day by day. Near-Infrared spectroscopy is being used in various agricultural product areas, such as fruits and vegetables, beverages, dairy, cereals and grain stocks, olives, grapes, and fish. This method can deliver accurate, cost-effective, and rapid results in the lab and the field with little sample preparations, and multiple parameters can be measured with the same scan. Let us dive deep into these applications and understand what role NIR methods play in agricultural production.

  i. Fruits and Vegetables
      NIR spectroscopy is being used by Avantes instruments that are utilized in numerous grading and sorting of fruits and vegetables such as apples, avocadoes, cherries, mangoes, and peaches. These are not limited to these fruits. Different parameters such as the acidity, water content, Ph, and soluble sugar content are being allowed by Near-Infrared Spectroscopy and give its rapid and non-destructive measurement. One application under development in Spain helps determine mango ripeness where it seeks to develop a mechanical arm that combines NIR spectroscopy and tactile sensors.
  ii. Beverages and Dairy

Dairy products are being analyzed using NIR spectroscopy to measure fat, proteins, carbohydrates, water, minerals in milk, and other dairy products. If we talk about powdered milk, the residual moisture affects shell-life and, on a larger scale, can inversely affect transportation costs and profit margins, too.

iii. Meat, Eggs, and Fish

The NIR method in meat enables the discrimination of proteins to fat content, moisture content measurements, pH, and color. It also can detect the presence of common contaminants such as volatile nitrogen. For meat production, these factors play a great role in determining the quality of meat and grading. These factors, in the end, determine the price of meat. Also, the non-chemical nature of spectroscopic sampling can strengthen the yields by monitoring egg quality through the shell.

iv. Forestry and Conservation

Certain species such as emerald ash borer, found throughout the western United States, are destroying forests and raising wildlife dangers as many trees can be killed across large areas. The mountain pine beetle also kills trees and destroys forests. If the beetle gets detected early, parks and forestry personnel can mitigate the damage by detecting an infestation before it can spread.

v. Soils, Manures, and Other Growing Constituents

Soil characterization plays an important role in determining what treatments are required and which crops should be grown in a particular area. Therefore, there are certain things towards soil management to the future of sustainable farming. Near-Infrared Spectroscopy permits rapid data collection of moisture content, soil density, and compaction.

vi. Applications in the Orchard

In the fruit sector, NIR techniques are becoming more widely adopted to detect non-destructive techniques to rapidly and cost-effectively identify the quality of fruit [24]. During the production, harvesting, storage, processing, and consumption of fruit, it is necessary to determine several quality parameters and criteria [1, 25]. Several reviews were summarized for determining the requirements and parameters of fruit using NIR. Pissard et al. show that the NIR technique can determine sugar, Vitamin C, and polyphenols content [26]. The recent developments in NIR spectrometers have enabled a significant reduction in the size and cost of these instruments. Still, at the same time, robustness was reduced to a certain extent.

9.3.3   MACHINE VISION ENABLED INSPECTION

9.3.3.1   What is Machine Vision, and How Is It Shaping the Food Industry?

With the advancement of cultivation technology, there has been tremendous growth in the total cultivation areas. The yields for agricultural products have also increased, which has increased the market value. The use of Machine Vision in the agricultural industry is one of the most robust, consistent, and economic techniques in the food industry. This technique includes image analysis and processing that has found different applications in the food industry. Machine Vision is the application of computer vision in real-world interfaces such as image processing and so forth. Machine Vision can be termed a technology that combines electromagnetic sensing, mechanics, optimal instrumentation, and image processing technology. It has been widely used for monitoring and controlling a wide range of applications. Deep research in machine vision has shown tremendous potential for the inspection and grading of fruits and vegetables. It is also used in performing quality analysis of different products such as meat, pizza, cheese, fish, and bread. Machine vision technology has many applications such as land-based and aerial-based remote sensing for precision farming, safety detection, classification, sorting, and process automation. This also provided numerical attributes of the objects or scenes being imaged.

Some of the machine vision systems can inspect the imaging objects in light invisible to humans, such as near-infrared (NIR), infrared (IR) and, ultraviolet (UV). This information is very helpful in determining pre-harvest plant maturity and diseases in them. Also, this technology is helpful in determining vegetable variety, maturity quality and, ripeness. Protection of plants is another important role that machine vision plays: detecting defects, diseases, functional properties, composition of plants, vegetables, and fruits. The main benefit of using machine vision is that it is fairly accurate, quite robust, and often yields consistent results. This technology improves the industry's productivity, reducing cost and making agricultural operations fast and processing safer for farmers and workers. It was found that the results of computer vision inspection were more consistent, cost-effective, and quite effective with higher speed and accuracy.

Machine vision can be used as a low-cost alternative to devices such as spectrometers. In a machine vision system, image capturing devices or sensors are used to generate the image of the samples. Some devices such as charged coupled devices, ultrasound, and near infrared spectroscopy create images. Even if X-ray and MRI imaging are used widely in medical applications as they have potential for detecting diseases and defects in agricultural products, their applications in agricultural sector are limited because of their high cost in investment, high maintenance and low operational speed. With the ever-increasing population and increased expectation of high-quality food products, there is a need to grow accurate and fast quality determination of food and agricultural products. Ensuring product quality is one of the challenging tasks before its export from the industries. With machine vision/computer vision being involved in the agricultural industry, it has been recognized as a potential technique for agriculture guidance and food processing.

9.3.3.2 Machine Vision Components

Machine Vision is the construction of meaningful descriptions of physical objects from images. Two-dimensional images are captured, processed, and analysis is carried out on them. This system is commonly used in agricultural applications that acquire reflectance or fluorescence images of agricultural materials under Ultraviolet or NIR illumination. These machine vision systems are being set up in a mechanical design that is uniquely structured to suit the application of a particular product. For instance, there are flat conveyor belts in poultry bone detection systems with no texture [27]. At the same time, the most conveyor belts for apple packing are roller conveyors. The machine vision components mainly consist of image illumination, frame grabber, image processing, and analysis.

1. Image Illumination: As discussed previously, the light range can be in UV, NIR, or VIS. There are applications in thermal imaging for agricultural products. This illumination system is a light source that focuses on materials. Many factors such as lighting type, location, and quality of color play an important role in bringing out the clear image of an object. When radiation from the lightning system illuminates an object, it is transmitted through, reflected, or absorbed. Several compounds emit fluorescence in the VIS region when excited with UV radiation. Proper illumination plays an essential role in a machine vision system. For a well-chosen lighting system, this incident light will present objects optimally, reducing many tedious image processing procedures. At present, lightning hardware is readily available for some of the common machine vision applications in agriculture.

2. Frame Grabber: There are various features involved in this step, such as image acquisition, image data preprocessing, and camera control [28]. Analog or digital images are being acquired by frame grabbers depending on the cameras. Many monochrome frame grabbers can take RS-170 video inputs while the color frame grabbers receive PAL or S-VHS input signals. There is a need for camera control here. The minimum requirement is minimum A/D circuitry and precision camera training. Some grabbers are capable of preprocessing images using functions such as First-In-First-Out and Look-Up table. These modern frame grabbing boards have a speed of 80–130 Mbytes/s, which is appropriate to meet the needs of many real-time operations in the food industry.

3. Image Analysis: Processing and analysis of the image is done using a computer to manipulate information inside an image which can be made useful. This generally consists of three steps: image enhancement, feature extraction of images, and image feature classification. Image enhancement is applied to images to correct poor contrast problems, resolve pixel-to-pixel operations to correct inconsistencies in acquired images, or noise reduction. Identifying image features is the next step where, after placing them, classification of features is done. Image analysis is further divided into three parts, namely

   a. Low-level processing: This step includes image acquisition and preprocessing. It is the transfer of an electronic signal from a sensing device to a numerical form. Removal of noise, correction of geometric distortions of images, blurring correction is all image processing arts [29]. Gaussian filters and averaging is used for noise reduction, causing a smoothness in the image.

   b. Intermediate level processing: This level of Processing involves image segmentation, representation, and description. Image segmentation is one of the most important steps in image processing techniques as the extracted data is highly dependent on the accuracy of this operation. Image segmentation involves dividing an image into regions that have a strong correlation with the objects.

c. High-level processing: Statistical classifiers or multilayer neural networks are used in high-level image grading processing, which involves interpretation and recognition. This step requires machine control for quality and sorting. Some methods such as principal component analysis, standard deviation, mean, and median can extract features from digital images. After identifying features, feature classification is performed using numerical techniques such as fuzzy inference and neural networks.

d. CCD Cameras: Machine vision systems use a wide range of cameras, ranging from monochrome cameras that perform simple size and shape image recognition tasks to common aperture multispectral cameras to detect surface defects and disease detection on fruits and vegetables. These imaging cameras receive light from the object's surface and convert it into electrical signals using silicon-based devices. Light-sensitive CCD devices convert optical images into an array of electrical signals. The more the intensity of light, the more electrical signals are generated, so they are directly proportional. An A/D device converts electrical signals to 8 or 16-bit data, then stored in the computer.

REFERENCES

[1] B.M. Nicolaï, K. Beullens, E. Bobelyn, A. Peirs, W. Saeys, K.I. Theron, J. Lammertyn (2007). "Nondestructive measurement of fruit and vegetable quality by means of NIR spectroscopy: a review." *Postharvest Biology and Technology of Tropical and Subtropical Fruits* vol. 46, no. 2, 99–118 https://doi.org/10.1016/j.postharv bio.2007.06.024

[2] M.P. Arakeri, Lakshama. (2016). "Computer vision based fruit grading system for quality evaluation of tomato in agriculture industry." *Procedia Computer Science* vol. 79, 426–433. www.sciencedirect.com/science/article/pii/S1877050916001861

[3] A. Sivaranjani, S. Senthilrani, B. Ashokumar, A.S. Murugan. (2018). "An Improvised Algorithm for Computer Vision Based Cashew Grading System Using Deep CNN." 2018 IEEE International Conference on System, Computation, Automation and Networking (ICSCAN). https://doi.org/10.1109/ICSCAN.2018.8541176

[4] A.S. Alturki, M. Islam, M.F. Alsharekh, M.S. Almanee, A.H. Ibrahim (2020). "Date fruits grading and sorting classification algorithm using colors and shape features." *International Journal of Engineering Research and Technology* vol. 13 https://dx.doi.org/10.37624/IJERT/13.8.2020.1917-1920

[5] M.A. Momin, M.T. Rahman, M.S. Sultana, C. Igathinathane, A.T.M Ziauddin, T. E. Grift (2017). "Geometry-based mass grading of mango fruits using image processing." *Information Processing in Agriculture* vol. 4, no. 2 https://doi.org/10.1016/j.inpa.2017.03.003

[6] S. Raj, D.S. Vinod (2016). "Automatic Defect Identification and Grading System for 'Jonagold' Apples." In 2016 Second International Conference on Cognitive Computing and Information Processing (CCIP). https://doi.org/10.1109/CCIP.2016.7802851

[7] V. Leemans, H. Magein, M.F. Destain (Dec 2002). "On-line fruit grading according to their external quality using machine vision." *Biosystems Engineering* vol. 83, no. 4, 397–404.

[8] D. Unay, B. Gosselin (Sept 2005). *Thresholding-based segmentation and apple grading by machine vision.* 13th European Conference on Signal Processing, 1–4.

[9] I. Kavdir, D.E. Guyer (2003). "Apple grading using fuzzy logic." *Turkish Journal for Agriculture* vol. 27, 375–382.

[10] P. Ninawe, S. Pandey (July 2014). "A completion on fruit recognition system using K-nearest neighbors algorithm." *International Journal of Advanced Research in Computer Engineering and Technology* (IJARCET), vol. 3, no 7, 691–697.

[11] K.A. Manik, S. R. Chaugule (2019). "Grading of apple fruit disease." *International Journal of Engineering Sciences and Research Technology* vol. 4, no. 9.

[12] K. Vijayrekhaa (2008). "Multivariate image analysis for defect identification of apple fruit images." IEEE 2008. Computer Science Technology.

[13] *Using a Systems Evaluation Approach to Managing Quality Grains.* (2015) International Quality Grains Conference. Indianapolis, IN: National Corn Growers Association and Corn Refiners Association.

[14] *The AIB International Consolidated Standards for Inspection: Grain Handling Facilities.* Manhattan, KS: AIB International.

[15] A Quality Management System for Grain Facilities. *An ongoing case study.* (n.d.) International Conference Technology Expo, Grain Elevator and Processing Society. Vancouver, BC: GEAPS.

[16] Caswell, J., Bredahl, M.E., Hooker, N.H. (1998). "How quality management metasystems are affecting the food industry." *Review of Agricultural Economics* vol. 20, no.2, 547–557.

[17] Manning, L., Baines, R.N., Chadd, S.A. (2006). "Quality assurance models in the food supply chain." *British Food Journal* vol. 108,.no. 2, 91–104. http://dx.doi.org/10.1108/00070700610644915

[18] G. Mumma, J. Albert, C. Warren, C. Mugalla, A. Abdulkadri. (2002). *Analyzing the Perceived Impact of ISO 9000 Standards on U.S. Agribusinesses.* Annual Meeting Paper. Long Beach, CA. American Agricultural Economics Assn.

[19] M.T. Rubio, V.R. Arias. (2005). "Study of the main motivations and discouraging factors for the implementation of ISO 9000 standards in Spanish agribusiness sector." *Journal of International Food and Agribusiness Marketing* vol. 17, no. 2, 229–243. http://dx.doi.org/10.1300/J047v17n02_12

[20] A.G. Da Cruz, S.A. Cenci, M. Maia (2006). "Quality Assurance Requirements in Produce Processing." *Trends in Food Science and Technology, 17*(8), 406–411. http://dx.doi.org/10.1016/j.tifs.2006.03.003

[21] Schroder, M.J., and McEachern, M.G. (2002). ISO 9001 as an audit frame for integrated quality management in meat supply chains: the example of Scottish beef." *Managerial Auditing Journal* vol. 17, no. 1/2, 79–85. http://dx.doi.org/10.1108/02686900210412289

[22] C.J. Bern, C.R. Hurburgh, T.J. Brumm (2008). *Managing Grain after Harvest.* Internal Textbook. Ames, IA: Department of Agricultural and Biosystems Engineering, Iowa State University.

[23] C.M. Laux, G.A. Mosher, C.R. Hurburgh (2015). "Application of quality management systems to grain handling. An inventory management case study." *Applied Engineering in Agriculture* vol. 31, no. 2, 312–321. www.researchgate.net/publication/276087483

[24] Y. Ozaki, C. Huck, S. Tsuchikawa, S. Balling Engelsen, Eds. (2020). *Near-Infrared Spectroscopy: Theory, Spectral Analysis, Instrumentation, and Applications.* Springer. https://link.springer.com/chapter/10.1007/978-981-15-8648-4_14.

[25] W. Saeys, N.N. Do Trong, R. Van Beers, B.M. Nicolaï (2019). "Multivariate calibration of spectroscopic sensors for postharvest quality evaluation: a review." *Postharvest Biology and Technology of Tropical and Subtropical Fruits* vol. 158, 2019–110981.

[26] A. Pissard, H. Bastiaanse, V. Baeten, G. Sinnaeve, J.-M. Romnee, P. Dupont, A. Mouteau, M. Lateur (2013). "Use of NIR spectroscopy in an apple breeding program for quality and nutritional parameters." *Acta Horticulturae* vol. 976, 409–414.

[27] K.K. Patel, A. Kar, S.N. Jha, M.A. Khan (2012). "Machine vision system: a tool for quality inspection of food and agricultural products." *Journal of Food Science Technology* vol. 49, no. 2, 123–141.

[28] Y.-R. Chen, K. Chao, M.S. Kim (2002). "Machine vision technology for agricultural applications." *Computer and Electronics in Agriculture* vol. 36, no. 2-3, 173–191.

[29] A. Judal, A.G. Bhadania (2015). "Role of machine vision system in food quality and safety evaluation." *International Journal of Advance Research and Innovation* vol. 3, no. 4, 611–615.

Index

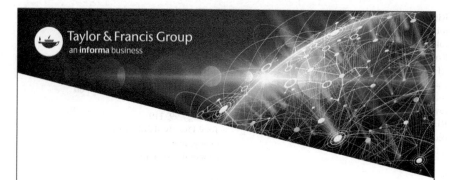